SEXUALITY
& GENDER

FOR MENTAL HEALTH PROFESSIONALS

SAGE has been part of the global academic community since 1965, supporting high quality research and learning that transforms society and our understanding of individuals, groups, and cultures. SAGE is the independent, innovative, natural home for authors, editors and societies who share our commitment and passion for the social sciences.

Find out more at: **www.sagepublications.com**

SEXUALITY
& GENDER

FOR MENTAL HEALTH PROFESSIONALS

A PRACTICAL GUIDE

CHRISTINA RICHARDS & MEG BARKER

Los Angeles | London | New Delhi
Singapore | Washington DC

Los Angeles | London | New Delhi
Singapore | Washington DC

SAGE Publications Ltd
1 Oliver's Yard
55 City Road
London EC1Y 1SP

SAGE Publications Inc.
2455 Teller Road
Thousand Oaks, California 91320

SAGE Publications India Pvt Ltd
B 1/I 1 Mohan Cooperative Industrial Area
Mathura Road
New Delhi 110 044

SAGE Publications Asia-Pacific Pte Ltd
3 Church Street
#10-04 Samsung Hub
Singapore 049483

Editor: Kate Wharton
Editorial assistant: Laura Walmsley
Production editor: Rachel Burrows
Copyeditor: Christine Bitten
Proofreader: Sharika Sharma
Marketing manager: Tamara Navaratnam
Cover design: Lisa Harper
Typeset by: C&M Digitals (P) Ltd, Chennai, India
Printed in India at Replika Press Pvt Ltd

Library of Congress Control Number: 2012955051

British Library Cataloguing in Publication data

A catalogue record for this book is available from
the British Library

ISBN 978-0-85702-842-6
ISBN 978-0-85702-843-3 (pbk)

CONTENTS

Additional case studies and further reading for each chapter are available at
www.sagepub.co.uk/sexuality

ABOUT THE AUTHORS

Christina Richards is Senior Specialist Psychology Associate at the West London Mental Health NHS Trust (Charing Cross) Gender Identity Clinic. She works in this capacity as an individual and group psychotherapist and psychologist. She lectures and publishes on gender, sexualities and critical mental health, both within academia and to statutory bodies such as police forces and the UK National Health Service.

Meg Barker is a senior lecturer in psychology at the Open University and a sex and relationship therapist. Meg has researched and written extensively on relationships, gender and sexuality – particularly on bisexuality, BDSM and polyamory – and co-edits the journal *Psychology & Sexuality* and co-organises the Critical Sexology seminar series.

ACKNOWLEDGEMENTS

CHRISTINA'S ACKNOWLEDGEMENTS

For Meg

And For Phil

Words can't say enough.

This being my first book the reader will hopefully indulge me and forgive the length of the following list. In many ways a book is the culmination of a life so far, with thinking and morality being derived from events quite aside from the matter under consideration. Consequently I have a great many people to thank, many of whom space precludes including. Errors throughout the book are, of course, entirely my own.

Many thanks to: Penny for being such a wonderful friend and mentor; Rob and Simon for more years of friendship than I care to remember; Richard for tea and wisdom; Erich and Karen for caring in different ways; Stef for not letting me give up (I hope I've done you proud); Richard and Mike for those memorable lunches; Helen for family; Andy for friendship in the wild; Alex for wise advice; Darren for expecting nothing but the best; James for giving me my life; my colleagues at the GIC for both friendship and seas of knowledge; my patients for the wisdom and knowledge that books can't hold; all of the activists and academics who move the fields forward – Riki, Kate, Jamison, Stephen and so many more. And to those clinicians who find a way with grace – Maddie, Randall, Nick – a high cost we pay, but one worth paying.

MEG'S ACKNOWLEDGEMENTS

I would like to thank all of the community members and activists who have been involved in my work over the past decade as participants, co-researchers, co-authors, readers, critics and supporters. I do hope that this book does you justice. Your courage and creativity continues to inspire, sustain and challenge me, and I am more grateful to you than I could possibly express.

I am also extremely grateful to Darren Langdridge. I simply wouldn't be where I am now, writing books like this, if it wasn't for your belief in me. Thank you for everything.

INTRODUCTION 1

Gender and sexuality are complex, and contested, to the point at which no definition can adequately encompass them. They have excited debate in academia, medicine, psychology and the personal, legal and political domains, as well as elsewhere, and no doubt will continue to do so for the foreseeable future. Of course, this creates a quandary for the busy professional who needs quick, accessible information on these important topics in order to go about the business of their day-to-day work. Should one reach for academic theoretical texts, which may be lengthy and not grounded in the reality of clients' lives, or for a concise clinical text which risks compromising complexity through brevity? Or should one look to community literatures which give a grounded view, but may miss aspects relevant to clinical decision making? To some extent the answer is "Yes". Given time, professionals should engage with all of these literatures, and indeed in order to become a specialist one would certainly need to. In this book, however, we have included something of each so that professionals can be confident of having a basic understanding, in a reasonable period of time, and a direction for future education as time and necessity dictate.

THE CONTENT

Most books for professionals in this area that we have come across have approached the topics in one of two ways. Some describe 'normal' human sexuality and/or gender and include much briefer mention of those who fall outside of this in some way (quite often in a tokenistic and/or pathologising manner). Others focus specifically on genders and sexualities which fall outside of *normativity*, for example concentrating on sexual and gender minorities. In this book we have adopted a third way, giving equal consideration to the diversity of sexualities, genders and relationship structures, including those which are more and less normative in wider society, and considering how such norms shift across time and within different groups. Of course no book could give complete coverage to all possible identities and practices, and we have been forced, of practical necessity, to include some generalisation where in fact there is complexity, and to avoid some repetition (where practices and identities have similar issues) in service of readability. We hope, however, that we have included in an accessible manner most of the identities and practices that a professional is likely to come across during the course of their career, and have also provided the necessary information to find out more on each item.

Gender, sexuality and relationships are of relevance for everyone, whether we see ourselves as located within the 'norms' of remaining a masculine man or a feminine woman throughout our life, of being heterosexual, and of aiming for a monogamous committed relationship; or whether we are located outside of this in some way, for example in the case of lesbian, gay, bisexual and transgender (*LGBT*) people, or those who challenge conventional ideals of sexuality, gender and relationships in other ways, such as asexual people (who don't experience sexual attraction), those who operate outside the *dichotomy* of men and women, or who question the divisions between romantic and other kinds of relationships. In all of these situations people engage with sexuality, gender and relationships.

Wider views of all these areas have also shifted markedly in the last few decades, for example in: changes in gender equality; societal acceptance and recognition of diverse genders, sexualities and relationship forms; and the increased prominence that sex and romantic relationships have been afforded (the *sexualisation of culture* and the idea that it is imperative to be in a couple). This means that people are more aware of the various identities and practices that are possible in all these areas, and also that they may experience more anxiety about them.

Those who fit within the 'norms' may worry about how well they fit, attempt to fit too rigidly, and experience difficulties when they don't adapt to wider cultural shifts. Those who are 'outside the norm' in some way may experience tensions with others (including experiences of discrimination and alienation), pressures to conform in other ways, and questions about how to live their identities and practices without much of a rulebook.

Consequently gender, sexuality and relationships can relate to the kinds of problems that people present with in a variety of ways, and it can also be difficult to determine when they are of relevance, and how. For example, one person may not find being something other than heterosexual and cisgender (see Glossary) remotely difficult; another might struggle due to concrete experiences of prejudice and discrimination from those around them; and another's difficulties might be related more to their own anxieties about how others *might* treat them. Some people have rigid assumptions about what it means to be a man or a woman and become very distressed trying to match up to these, while others might flexibly engage with *masculinity* or *femininity*, and others find different ways of conceptualising gender which are more congruent.

For readability we have kept references to a minimum and focus on providing further reading for those who wish to engage in further education.

However, all the chapters are grounded thoroughly in the relevant research literatures and in existing guidance from national psychological, psychiatric and therapeutic bodies. We have also drawn upon community literatures in order to consider the group norms and diversities of experience in each area, and – of course – brought in our own clinical experience.

TERMINOLOGY

The book focuses on the overlapping areas of gender, sexuality and relationships in its three main sections, and we expand upon the ways that these link together throughout. By *gender* we mean a person's sense of their own identity in relation to being a man or a woman, or identities beyond this conventional *gender dichotomy* (see Chapter 5). We cover the relationship between gender and biological sex in more depth throughout the first section of the book, and particularly in Chapter 3. The term *sexuality* refers to types of sexual attraction, identity and practice as well as to people who do not experience attraction. By *relationships*, we mean primarily romantic relationships which are either monogamous or non-monogamous in structure (see Chapters 13 and 14).

PRACTICES AND IDENTITIES

We differentiate between *practices* and *identities* throughout the book. People may practise something (and indeed be very good at it), but do not have it as an identity. For an (non-sexual[1]) example; the first author likes to *toast*, that is she likes to heat bread and then cover it in butter and marmalade for breakfast. She clearly *toasts* (practice), but does not define as *a toaster* (identity). Similarly, many people have played computer games, maybe on a console at a party, or minesweeper or solitaire on the office computer or a mobile phone app. Such people do not define as *gamers* (identity), even though they do *game* (practice). In contrast some people buy magazines and attend large gaming conventions as well as having advanced computers. They may queue up at midnight for the latest game release. They are *gamers* (identity), usually for the things that they do in addition to their actual gaming. Indeed when queuing up at midnight for the latest game (and so not at their computer) they would state that they are still gamers – it is who they *are*, not what they happen to be *doing*. This is exactly analogous with sexuality. A man may have sex with another man (practice) and define as something other than

---

[1] We rather enjoy the fact that this book requires this caveat.

gay or bisexual (identity). For this reason sexual health professionals have terms such as *MSM* (men who have sex with men) and *MSMW* (men who have sex with men and women) as these terms do not denote identity, but simply practice.

SAFER AND LESS SAFE TERMS

We have ensured throughout the text that safe, or perhaps we should say *safer*[2], terms are included in *italics* in the first instance. Thus we have *gay* as a safe term and gay thereafter. In contrast, unsafe terms, or terms which relate to a problematic concept (either generally or in that specific instance), are usually in 'scare quotes'. For example, 'homosexual' is in scare quotes because *gay* or *lesbian* are the preferred terms. (For this reason translators rather than interpreters are often preferred in professional practice as if you say 'gay' to a client it would be unfortunate if it was communicated as 'homosexual'). Italics have also occasionally been used for emphasis – as above with *safer,* but are never used with an unsafe term.

We do recognise that some compassionate professionals may disagree with aspects of the material, perhaps particularly the terminology. In all cases the specific instance with a particular client is paramount. For example, you may come across a client who expresses a preference for an identity term which we have included in scare quotes. Of course we cannot comment on what you do within the intricacy of the situation in front of you. Nonetheless some general guide is needed, and we have gone with language which is currently most prevalent among the groups and communities concerned. To avoid confusion we have included direct quotes, that is those things that people have actually said, or might say, are in "double quotation marks".

One possible point of confusion is around our use of scare quotes for 'same gender' and 'other gender'. This is done because gender is such a complex matter that even if both parties identify as men, for example, they will not necessarily be the 'same'. Similarly, as there are people who identify outside of the man/woman *gender dichotomy,* and as there are many overlaps between men and women, the phrase 'other gender' becomes problematic. This is covered in more depth in the first section of the book.

---

[2] In the complex world of gender, sexuality and relationships, if one thing is assured it is that you will inadvertently offend someone, not uncommonly a group of people you were previously unaware of. Kindness and continued education are key. This involves both having good intentions and being mindful of the impact even well-intended words and behaviours actually have.

While we generally aim to use accessible and familiar language where possible, we have used some terms which may be unfamiliar to the reader. Therefore there is both a standard glossary and a shadow glossary at the end of the book to aid the reader. The shadow glossary is for terms which are generally not safe. They may be reclaimed and used by clients in which case you may feel free to use them with that client, but not to use them for other clients. This remains the case even if you yourself identify with them.

It is worth becoming comfortable with sexual terms in general. Indeed one should be able to use them with a client without feeling embarrassed simply for using a word. Try saying "fuck" or "cunt" out loud now (we're assuming you're not reading this on a train or waiting for a PTA meeting). How do you feel? Could you do it at all?

One of the best ways to establish rapport with a client is to be genuinely matter-of-fact about any aspect of their gender, sexuality or relationship. This does not mean being 'tolerant' or 'accepting' – only people in positions of power are able to be these things and a sense of this can therefore reinforce a problematic power hierarchy. Similarly, it is important not to use inappropriate words or to mispronounce words. Some people seem to consistently mispronounce words, perhaps because they are unfamiliar, or perhaps to distance themselves from a threatening concept. For example, people might speak of a person's 'sec-*sue*-ality' (rather than sexuality) or mispronounce 'poly-*aim*-ory' (rather than polyamory), or hyphenate 'bi-sexual' (rather than bisexual). Such practices should be avoided. Similarly, it is not acceptable to turn an adjective or a verb into a noun – a person is a *gay man*, or a *trans woman* (when their sexuality or gender is pertinent respectively – otherwise they are a simply a man or a woman). They are not 'a gay' or 'a transsexual': they will doubtless have a raft of other qualities beyond their sexuality or gender.

We have used the words *professional* and *practitioner* throughout the book to be as inclusive as possible of all people working in the field, be they counsellors, psychologists, physicians, psychiatrists, therapists, primary care workers, nurses, social workers, etc. We have used *client* throughout rather than *patient*, as it is hopefully the most inclusive word for people who may present to any of the above listed professionals.

PATHOLOGY

Gender, sexuality and relationships have long been associated with law and medicine, and each chapter makes reference to how each group has been viewed by these professions. However, it is important to recognise that none of the sexualities, genders or relationship structures that we cover are problematic (or pathological) per se. Consequently, professionals should generally assume that any of the identities and practices covered in this book are irrelevant to the issue before them unless presented otherwise (and should make notes accordingly, leaving out mention of the identity/practice unless directly relevant).

For the non-normative identities and practices that we cover, as mentioned previously, it is possible that clients will experience problems because of the tension between what they're doing and societal pressures (sometimes called *minority stress*[3]), while for the normative ones it is possible that clients will experience problems because of trying to follow a rigid version (in order to remain regarded as 'normal'). This is a most important point.

In this book we cover some identities/practices which are widely regarded as 'normal' and some that are widely seen as 'not normal'. For people within the norm, problems are generally assumed *not* to be related to their identities and/ or practices, when in fact they might well be – whereas for people outside the norm, problems are often viewed as being *inevitably* related to their identities and/or practices when many times they are not.

'NORMALITY' AND MORALITY

We are not really concerned with mapping what is 'normal' here – indeed that is why we have chosen to scare quote the word. So much of human behaviour is statistically not normal, indeed is many standard deviations away from the mean. Much of this we celebrate, for example an exceptionally beautiful poem, walking on the moon, running 100m in under 10 seconds: none of these are 'normal' but none are 'bad' either. We are also not concerned with what is 'natural'. Most of what people do is not natural (riding bicycles, cooking food, reading and writing books) and much that is found in the natural world (fighting over resources, mates and territory) is not pleasant.

We similarly do not concern ourselves with morality as such because much of it is socially derived and specific to time and place. What we do concern ourselves with, morally, is the distinction between transgression

---

[3] While the widely accepted phrase *minority stress* can be useful, it is worth remembering that some 'non-normative' sexualities, genders and relationships could be viewed as majority rather than minority, for example some statistics on bondage fantasies, attraction to more than one gender, and having some form of (open or secret) non-monogamy, put these above 50% of the population. The phrase *marginalisation stress* might be more appropriate than *minority stress*.

and coercion (Denman, 2004). Everything within this book is either non-transgressive, or transgressive of some social norm (but bear in mind that many of the practices in the latter category often have low, or no risk of STIs or unwanted pregnancy). None of it, however, is *necessarily* coercive: all are possible to practise consensually. Of course, all sexuality has the possibility of coercion: heterosexual sexual encounters can potentially be rape, just as BDSM can potentially be abuse, but neither of them, or anything else in this book, is *necessarily* so. For those professionals who do have moral concerns we suggest that they refer to the policy codes of the organisations they belong to and work for and to the relevant anti-discrimination laws. If professionals still feel that items contained within this book are morally questionable it is worth considering the manner in which the book is being approached (Richards, 2011). Professionals may even find it valuable to dip their toe into an unfamiliar practice or two: you never know what you might discover ...

DIFFICULTIES WITH PRACTICES AND IDENTITIES

Similarly, we avoid pathologising terms such as 'sex addiction' within this book, although any practice, including the normative ones, *could* be experienced as problematic or compulsive under certain circumstances. In each chapter we instead focus on exploring whether any discomfort may be derived – as it very often is – from social opprobrium rather than from the practice or identity itself. It is useful for professionals in such cases to determine where any distress is coming from.

> Is the problem the client's problem, or is it a problem that somebody else (or wider society) has with what the client is doing?

If you are having some difficulty considering an issue with a group you feel uncomfortable about, it can be useful to transpose the group under consideration for another. While, of course, different groups have different experiences and needs, in practice it can help to clarify one's thinking. For example, if patients on your ward are complaining that a trans woman (well dressed, sitting quietly watching the television) is "really a man, and shouldn't be on the ward" some professionals may be worried that these views should be taken into account. Transposing culture, or religion, allows one to see that if the person was thought to be of a different cultural background from the patients, or of a different religion, and so should be moved, their request would be denied and instead education would be provided.

LEVELS OF KNOWLEDGE

If you have bought this book the following text box will most likely not apply to you. However, it is a key point and so we felt it is important to include for people you may lend the book to.[4]

It is unacceptable for professionals not to have a basic level of knowledge about the gender, sexuality and relationship structures of their clients.

Some professionals appear to believe that their mere presence has some quality of healing, regardless of who they are working with, and that consequently actual knowledge acquisition is rather beneath them. Our view is that professionals are paid (whether by the taxpayer, their employer, or their clients or through the time of others) to have knowledge and skills, and that this includes a basic knowledge of such fundamental matters as sexuality, gender and relationships. Also, it is appropriate that professionals should try to develop their knowledge about the sexualities, genders and relationships that they are unfamiliar with such that clients from those groups will have an equivalent experience to those from more familiar groups. Research suggests that lack of knowledge on the part of the practitioner can severely damage rapport, and that expression of stereotypical views, in particular, can put clients off seeking professional help again in the future.

A good rule of thumb is to at least match the level of knowledge available in the general culture in which you find yourself. For example, if you know what a *condom* is, you should know what a *dental dam* is as they are pretty analogous in terms of STI prevention. You don't have to have watched every episode of *The 'L' Word* or read the works of Sappho in the original Greek,[5] you simply need enough common knowledge not to exhaust, exploit and/or alienate your client. If you do need training, a client in distress is not the person to give it; there are plenty of community groups and professionals happy to offer just that. Of course, your client's experience will differ from other people's, but having a starting point, a sense of possible directions, as you have with someone from your own sexuality or gender, for example, is useful.

---

[4] Of course we're sure you'll pay all relevant fees …
[5] Of course dental dams are used by groups other than lesbians – see comment on generalisations above.

AFFIRMATIVE THERAPY

Once professionals have a basic knowledge of sexuality, gender and relationships they are well on their way to practising affirmatively. Affirmative practice is important because it can be especially difficult for many people to consider more marginalised genders, sexualities and relationships as valid. This means that negative societal messages may have been internalised by clients such that even when an identity or practice is recognised as personally authentic it may still be regarded as 'wrong' or 'not normal'. Professional power can be affirmatively leveraged here to explain that the client is not 'wrong' or 'not normal' per se (perhaps using this book). A practice or identity of course may or may not be right for that client at that time; however the de facto assumption should be that it is an acceptable possibility. Of course for clients who have had their identity or practice for any period of time, it should generally simply be accepted and attended to only as necessary. It is most important that professionals do not question marginalised identities and practices on the grounds that they are non-normative (see above).

In addition, professionals should be wary of assuming that non-normative practices and identities are reasonable possibilities only for people who are normative in all other respects (and perhaps who do not have children) and are not acceptable for others (younger or older people, or people with physical or learning disabilities, for example). Instead, usual standards will need to be employed. Children of parents with non-normative identities and practices will need to be told things that are appropriate for their age and understanding as necessary, just as with *heterosexuality* and *cisgender*. People with disabilities will need to have their specific needs accommodated, and so on.

ATTRACTION TO THE PROFESSIONAL

In affirming a person's nascent or established identity it may be that a client becomes attracted to you as a professional who is both safe and who seems to understand. In such cases, one should proceed with caution and the feelings should be explored with other professionals, and sometimes the client, as appropriate to the setting and your practice. It may be that you need to refer on to another affirmative professional, however it should be carefully explained to the client that this is not a rejection of them, and is certainly not because of their identity or practice.

An additional difficulty which may arise with professionals who are open to diverse sexualities is with clients who use the opportunity for open discussion as a means of arousal. Language (body and verbal) of clients, as well as a great deal of detail when it is unwarranted, can be signifiers of this occurring. In these cases simple questioning as to whether it is occurring in a matter-of-fact manner and then exploration if it is appropriate to your role, or referral/asking them to desist, are useful courses of action.

COMING OUT

Additionally, if you are affirmative it may be that the client feels secure enough (perhaps having tested the waters with a hypothetical example) to come out to you about their practices or identity. This is a great honour and should be treated as such. It is important not to overdo positive regard for the identity or practice as the client may only be testing it out, or may feel that such a response is disingenuous. It is an excellent opportunity, however, for the client to be able to safely talk about, or possibly explore, emerging feelings and meanings.

OTHER PROFESSIONALS

For those professionals who are not in the talking professions, perhaps general practitioners, nurses or other medics (who will nonetheless do a good deal of talking), affirmative practice can be realised through considering the implications of the client's practice or identity within your decisions. For example, this might include an understanding of the possibility of consensually received abrasions during a medical check-up (see Chapter 6. This is not to say all abrasions should be ignored if people say that they are fine – just a recognition of the possibility and then a decision of what action, if any, to take). Similarly, when considering prescriptions, medics may wish to consider the impact of a lowered sexual desire, or the inability to have a sexual encounter, on a person for whom sex is a large part of their identity.

THE CLINICIAN ILLUSION

Lastly, professionals who practise affirmatively may find that they get a great many referrals of clients of a specific group, as clients ask to see someone who understands and colleagues are happy to refer on people whom they have difficulty with or do not understand. This should be addressed with colleagues who may consider some groups (such as trans people, for example – see Chapter 2) to be a specialist case in circumstances where any competent professional could see them.

Additionally, professional burnout may occur when every person one sees of a particular group has a problem. This can result in some professionals thinking, especially if they have no other contact with that group, that those people from this group necessarily have a problem. This is called the *clinician illusion* – of course if one only sees a certain group as a clinician every one of them will have a problem: that is what people come to clinicians for. Professionals do well to vary their workload a little and also to meet members of these groups outside of a clinical or work context.

DIVERSITY

We recognise that, for reasons of space, we are primarily writing from the minority standpoint of contemporary Western culture. While we have mentioned some of the variety in cultural understandings of gender, sexuality and relationships, these are exceedingly diverse and often do not reflect contemporary Western norms and understandings. Professionals outside of contemporary Western contexts, or with clients from outside them, would do well to educate themselves to the specifics of those cultural understandings.

This is important as, even within Western contemporary understandings, there are a great many intersections between gender, sexuality and relationships, and race, religion, age and class to name but a few. A common example is the difference between people who live in small rural communities and those who live in large urban centres. A good rule of thumb is to assume that there is as much diversity within another culture, age group, religion or community as there is in your own. Again we have attempted to make some references to such intersections throughout the text, but additional reading on intersections is invaluable (see the further reading at the end of this chapter).

'COMMUNITY'

Because people come from diverse backgrounds it is important to recognise that not everyone from a group will necessarily be a member of a 'community'. Community support for people who are otherwise marginalised can be invaluable, but sometimes intersections can make it difficult for people to access a community which represents them specifically. For example, a person may feel marginalised if the vast majority of people in a gay community are white and they are not, even if they too are gay. For this reason also, it is important not to assume that things that were true of one client will be the same for the next one you see with the same identity or practice. Experiences of the 'same thing' can differ greatly depending on where it is viewed from.

It can also seem dismissive to some clients to assume that they are a member of a 'community' simply because they happen to have a particular identity or practice. People seldom talk about the 'heterosexual community' for example. Additionally, some people may be quite happy with their identities and practices and so not feel the need to engage with any form of community – either for support or contact with others. Many trans people, for example, simply go about their daily business as teachers, nurses, lawyers, professors, taking their kids to school, buying jam, watching TV, etc. without engaging with any trans community.

Finally, we mostly refer to communities (plural) rather than community (singular) throughout the book to acknowledge that there is rarely one community for an identity or practice, but several (for example, under 'lesbian community' we could include rural lesbian communities, communities of young anarchist queer women, specific lesbian club scenes, groups of BDSM and leather dykes, and many, many more).

QUEER PROFESSIONALS

Professionals will, of course, all have some sort of gender, sexuality and relationship structure themselves. We are aware of professionals with most of the identities and practices detailed within this book, so it is important for both professionals and clients alike not to assume that all professionals will be cisgender and heteronormative, for example.

Similarly, some clients may feel that when they find a queer professional that the professional will be a 'wonderful magical unicorn' who will understand them perfectly and connect with them deeply. Some professionals may be drawn in by this and very much enjoy the hero narrative. It is most important to resist this. Professional practice involves the professional identity first, most often with an appropriate degree of dispassion, rather than simply being a community member. A surgeon who can't cut when needed, or a psychologist who can't ask the hard questions, or any professional who doesn't know their limitations or professional boundaries because they want to be a hero, needs to find a different group to work with.

Professionals who *are* community members must be prepared to give up a good deal of support as they will effectively always be on duty within their communities due to the standards of most professional organisations. Community members could do well to recognise that professionals themselves often need support and may not be able to access it through the same channels as people who do not serve the communities in such roles.

SELF-DISCLOSURE

Self-disclosure for queer professionals is a tricky topic related to coming out. As cisgender heterosexual monogamy is often a norm, professionals who wish to make their sexuality, gender or relationship status outside of this known will often need to do so explicitly, rather than having it assumed. It is sometimes necessary to disclose one's identity (whether sexual, gender, or something else) but this should always be in the client's interest.[6] If in doubt, discussion with an affirmative colleague or supervisor is useful. Dual relationships and self-disclosure are dealt with more fully in Chapter 9.

It is important, of course, that one does not *out* colleagues, or make them do so if they are uncomfortable with it. There are many good reasons not to come out (for example, taking up too much of the client's session unnecessarily if the topic is not one of sexuality or gender) and the person dealing with the client must have final say. If the person dealing with the client wants to out another colleague there should be an absolutely valid reason for doing so – "the client suspects" is really not good enough – and again it must only be done with the permission of the person being outed.

Related to this we should be careful about bringing up a colleague's gender, sexuality or relationship status within a professional setting, for example asking their opinion as a person from a particular marginalised community, or asking questions about how it plays out in their personal life just before they are going to see a client. It can be difficult to have such aspects foregrounded when one is expecting to be treated as a fellow professional rather than an LGBT person, for example.

INCLUSION IN THE BOOK

BASIC SEXUAL PRACTICES

For reasons of simplicity and length we have not included a great deal in this book on anatomy or on the specifics of commonly portrayed sexual positions. There are a number of books which provide more information on this (e.g. Godson & Agace, 2002). When reading this book it is important to be aware that many of the practices may be carried out in a variety

---

[6] This may not be in their direct interest at that moment, but should be done at least with reference to their general interest – as with all interventions.

of ways, including partnered sex (with two or more people involved), solo sex, etc. For this reason we do not use terms such as 'couple counselling' or 'marriage counselling' as they exclude large numbers of people. *Sexual and relationship counselling* is preferred (see cosrt.org.uk). There are also a great many types of sexual expression, as the content of this book will show, including penetrative sex (vaginal, oral, anal, etc.), voyeurism, BDSM, etc. Professionals benefit from keeping open many possibilities when discussing sexuality, gender and relationships with clients as many present in a socially normative manner, when the reality of their identities, practices and desires are quite different.

PLURALISTIC APPROACH

We have taken a broadly pluralistic approach with regards to professional practice. It is common for people to work in multidisciplinary teams, but all too often these end up being multidisciplinary only in name with people mostly working independently and sometimes not even meeting to collaborate. Good practice with sexuality and gender often involves people from different specialities, perhaps a primary care medic, a sexual health worker, a specialist counsellor, etc. True collaborative working involves close contact and knowledge exchange, not merely about client details, but general education as well.

   We also take a pluralistic approach to psychotherapy as many different modalities can usefully be integrated with different clients at different times. The only exceptions are those that hold as axiomatic a heterosexual two-parent family as the ideal healthy model. These outdated theories have been thoroughly discredited (e.g. Golombok, Spencer & Rutter, 1983). A good rule of thumb when considering a theory about any group of people is to see if it is kind as history has shown that unkind theories (about non-white people, gay people, women, etc.) are usually plain wrong. It is a shame that so much work often has to be done to disprove them.

THE STRUCTURE OF THE BOOK

We have endeavoured to structure the book in a specific manner in order to assist busy professionals with navigating it in the short time between clients. To that end each chapter can be read independently, although where there are links between chapters these will be signposted. Some chapters are longer than others to include the variety of aspects involved with them – for example Chapter 2 on trans includes items relating to surgery which are obviously not needed in most of the other chapters. Each chapter has the same broad structure:

INTRODUCTION

Introduces the client group, provides any essential information required to read the chapter, and overviews the main issues.

COMMON CONCERNS

Outlines the most frequent issues people in this group present with to professionals.

KEY PRACTICES

Details the common types of sex, relationships and social interactions undertaken by people in this group.

WIDER SOCIETY

Considers how this group is seen in contemporary Western societies and cultures (e.g. how it is portrayed in the mass media, common assumptions), and how it is treated legally and medically.

GROUP NORMS

Details some rules and ideals that are commonly found within the group and considers how these impact upon individuals within it.

SUMMARY AND CONCLUSIONS

Lists key aspects that practitioners should be aware of and their main implications for good professional practice.

FURTHER READING

Lists some resources as a starting point for further investigation. Expanded further reading lists, including web materials, are available on the website which accompanies this book at: sexandgender.org.

Also available on the website at sexandgender.org are a number of case studies. We have not included these within the book for reasons of space and because it is so easy for them to be read as exemplars, and we are keen to emphasise diversity in all groups. A good rule of thumb is to assume the same level of variation and complexity in the identities and practices that are less familiar to you as there are in the ones which are very familiar (perhaps those that you fit into yourself). Any examples that we do mention in this book are fictitious and based on amalgams of different common experiences.

FURTHER READING

American Psychological Association (2012). Guidelines for psychotherapy with lesbian, gay, and bisexual clients. *American Psychologist, 67* (1), 10–42.

Butler, C., O'Donovan, A. & Shaw, E. (Eds.) (2009). *Sex, sexuality and therapeutic practice: A manual for therapists and trainers*. London: Routledge.

das Nair, R. & Butler, C. (2012). *Intersectionality, sexuality and psychological therapies: Working with lesbian, gay and bisexual diversity*. Oxford: Wiley-Blackwell.

Denman, C. (2004). *Sexuality*. Basingstoke: Palgrave Macmillan.

Shaw, L., Butler, C., Langdridge, D., Gibson, S., Barker, M., Lenihan, P., Nair, R., Monson, J. & Richards, C. (2012). *Guidelines for psychologists working therapeutically with sexual and gender minority clients*. London: British Psychological Society.

ADDITIONAL REFERENCES

Godson, S. & Agace, M. (2002). *The sex book*. London: Cassell Illustrated.

Golombok, S., Spencer, A. & Rutter, M. (1983). Children in lesbian and single parent households: Psychosexual and psychiatric appraisal. *Journal of Child Psychology & Psychiatry, 24* (4), 551–572.

Richards, C. (2011). Are you sitting comfortably? Reader injunctions: An addition to the methodologies of the human and natural sciences. *The Psychologist, 24* (12), 904–906.

1

GENDER PRACTICES AND IDENTITIES

TRANSGENDER (TRANS) – LIVING A DIFFERENT GENDER FROM THAT ASSIGNED AT BIRTH

2

This chapter aims to:

- Examine the ways in which trans people who live in a gender not assigned at birth differ from those trans people who do so on a temporary basis.
- Consider the various ways in which being trans sometimes relates to discrimination, reproductive capacity and emotional experience.
- Briefly outline the various physiological interventions available to trans people.
- Consider when referral onwards is necessary and when trans is irrelevant.

INTRODUCTION

Some *trans* people *transition* into a role they were not assigned at birth on a temporary basis. This may be for reasons of personal comfort and congruence, for sexuality, or for some other reason. Some people who do so are called 'dual role transvestites' if there is no sexual component, or 'fetishistic transvestites' if there is, although these are medical terms which are often regarded as pejorative and so cross-dressing is preferred, although still problematic. These groups where transition is transient, and/or related to sexuality, are covered, in detail, in Chapter 11. People who transition into genders other than 'man' or 'woman' are covered in Chapter 5.

This chapter covers those people who wish to live full time in a male or female gender role other than the one they were assigned at birth. Individually, they are known, when it is pertinent, as a *trans man* or *man with a trans history* (people assigned female at birth who transition into a male role); and a *trans woman* or *woman with a trans history* (people assigned male at birth who transition into a female role). Collectively this group is often known as 'transsexual' people, although again this is a medical term with which some people feel uncomfortable. It should be noted that the people covered in this chapter are (perhaps somewhat arbitrarily given recent brain studies) not considered to be intersex or to have a DSD (see Chapter 3).

Trans is generally the safe term for the people considered in this chapter, although again only when it is pertinent that the person is trans. When a person's trans status is not pertinent, trans men are simply men and trans women are simply women. Thus, if a trans woman is having her hormonal regimen adjusted she is a trans woman; whereas if she is in counselling for a recent bereavement she is simply a woman. For this reason the terms 'Male to Female' ('MtF') or 'Female to Male' ('FtM') should generally not be used (although they are occasionally used by trans people themselves) as the person may not be identifying with their past at the time, and indeed may never have identified as male or female respectively.

Trans people who have not transitioned have a sense of themselves as a man or a woman (their *gender identity*) which is at odds with both their birth-assigned gender and the way they present to society (their *gender role*). This may cause low mood, anxiety, and other difficulties which are known as *gender dysphoria* and has been linked with markedly increased rates of suicide and self-harm. Trans people who receive appropriate treatment and are able to live in a way which is comfortable to them, with a *gender presentation* (clothing, mannerisms, etc.) and gender role that are congruent with their gender identity, often do very well and have no higher rates of psychopathology than the general population (e.g. Hoshiai et al., 2010).

Trans people, both before and after transition, may feel an especial dislike, or even hatred, towards their bodies and may regard their DNA or endogenous hormones as poison. This hatred (as opposed to discomfort) can sometimes be addressed by a skilled practitioner through education regarding the wide variety of bodies in the general population and the effects of hormones and psychology – the former sometimes less powerful than many people think and the latter sometimes more powerful. In this way trans people may come to a place where their body is metaphorically like living in someone else's house – they are able to see it as reasonable – just not *theirs*. From this place physiological and psychological interventions effect far greater comfort in trans clients.[1]

Trans people often, but by no means always, undergo treatments in order to physically alter their bodies such that their gender presentation more easily matches their gender identity (see Barratt, 2007, and Ettner, Monstrey & Eyler, 2007, for a full overview of physiological interventions available to trans people). Interventions are generally carried out after the trans person has made a full transition into their preferred gender role, including a formal change of name and identification documents (ID), telling friends and

---

[1] Those who are particularly body (but not necessarily role) dysphoric (sometimes referred to as dysmorphophobia) sometimes suffer poorer outcomes from interventions and often wish for further surgeries as their sense of unease shifts from one body part to the next. Trans people who are particularly *gender dysphoric*, however, seem to do very well if properly evaluated and supported.

family (covered below), and often gaining some form of occupation in that role appropriate to their ability level – for example, paid or voluntary work or study for those able to do these (people with learning disabilities, etc. will have commensurate requirements to their abilities). Hormones are often the first physiological intervention after transition, as they are, to some very small extent, reversible, although many changes, for example voice deepening, will be permanent. These may then be followed by surgeries which are quite irreversible (outlined below).

COMMON CONCERNS

There are several different reasons why a trans person may approach a counsellor, psychologist or other health professional. Broadly speaking they fall into four groups.

- Those for whom this is completely incidental to the reason that they are seeking help or support.
- Those who would like some assistance to transition gender role.
- Those who are experiencing problems related to other people's perceptions of their trans status or transition.
- Those who have some personal concern about being trans.

Those clients in the first group should be dealt with just as you would a cisgender person (see Chapter 4), although with due regard for differing body morphology and trans-specific needs. In this way trans people are treated just as others are.

As the last three groups of people approaching a professional are so often intertwined we shall consider them together with much of the technical material concerning transition being included in the section on Key Practices below. Of note, however, is that some people can maintain concerns about being trans after transition, and of course other people's concerns about a person being trans may crop up at any time in a person's life. In these instances, and indeed when a person is transitioning, it is well to consider whether the matter is indeed trans-related, or a mask for some other difficulty. Is a relationship break-up due to the person being trans, or because one partner wanted to travel and the other to pursue their career? Is the weight gain hormonal or through lack of exercise? Are people commenting because the person is wearing female clothes, or because they are particularly erotic clothes? When seeing trans people professionally, not having a metaphorical neon sign saying 'TRANS', but rather a whispered hint behind one's shoulder that there may be a trans theme, is usually the best course of action.

AETIOLOGY AND BLAME

One common concern of trans people is "Why am I like this?". This can stem from a feeling of guilt about being trans and a wish to avoid blame. It is important for practitioners to reinforce that there is no blame to be apportioned. Trans people seldom choose to be trans and, given that it is an innocuous identity and practice, there would be no need for blame if they did. Of course people do sometimes feel hurt when someone close to them transitions, but that does not mean that the trans person *made* them hurt as it is not inevitable that they will be so. It can be profitable to explore how all parties involved can take responsibility for their decisions and feelings.

One of the key ways of avoiding blame is to consider the ways in which a person became trans – however this should be avoided where possible as we seldom devote time to considering why people are heterosexual or cisgender, for example. Nonetheless the empirical evidence suggests that being trans has nothing to do with rearing, as some psychodynamic theorists have suggested. Instead there is a suggestion that, at least for those who transition when young (sometimes called 'primary' trans people), there is a neurological difference – that their brains are literally hardwired to think like a gender different from the one they were assigned at birth (see Kruijver, 2004 – of note is the fact that all studies are post-mortem and so cannot be undertaken while the trans person is alive as a diagnostic test). In contrast those people who transition later (sometimes called 'secondary' trans people) – some of whom have often gone through a sexualised phase before wishing to transition – most likely have a multifactorial aetiology. Not all trans people will worry that being trans is problematic, and many younger people are becoming quite comfortable with their identities from an early age. This can be usefully accomplished by good social support including friends, family, community, etc.

TELLING OTHERS

If, after a period of time living in a male or a female role privately, a trans person determines to live full time in a gender role, then they will need to tell people about their decision to transition. In the first instance the person told is often a close friend or partner, or a professional, and it can be the most nerve-wracking event of the person's life (if you are the first it is a great honour and should be treated as such). Support and acceptance are vital. The opening of conversational space, as well as provision of calm reassurance, can have implications which will stay with a person throughout their life. Some people, when told of a person's intent to transition, may act in a negative manner, refusing to discuss it, being abusive, or even violent. Often this will settle of its own accord once any shock has abated. It is not uncommon, however, for close friends, family, etc. to have an inkling, or even to know, and to have been waiting for the trans person to tell them in their own time.

For those trans people who do not receive an accepting response, extra support can be gained through the internet, support groups, face-to-face support, reading, etc., and this may also be helpful for the family, friends, etc. of trans people who do struggle to accept and respect it. It is vitally important that professionals do not suggest that there is an issue where there is none. Well-meaning professionals may think that 'of course' a partner, parent or child will be shocked and outraged, but in fact many are not and are very supportive. Suggesting to such people that there must be a problem may cause difficulties unduly. For some people, especially couples, the status quo provided by a partner not being happy with the transition can be comfortable for both parties. The trans person's partner (whether or not they themselves are trans) keeps their partner as they've always been, and the person who nominally seeks transition is prevented from the difficulties of doing so without having to bear the responsibility for this. In such cases it can be useful to unpack the motivations of all involved.

Similarly, people may say that they themselves are unconcerned, but their neighbours, children, elderly parents, etc. have a problem and so their partner, or they themselves, cannot transition. It is useful to enquire how they know this (have they had a conversation?) and how much say do they have over those people's lives given that they give them so much power over their own life? Why do others get to decide? Often such fears are predicated upon the notion that trans is not acceptable. Of course relationships will need to be negotiated and some people close to the transitioning person (and again not everyone by any means) may need to seek further support. Very often, however, people are unconcerned provided that the trans person fulfils their other roles adequately – be that darts captain, parent, drummer, foreperson on the factory floor or whatever else.

Employers, particularly, seem to most often be unconcerned when people have had a good working history and large companies and organisations especially seem well able to assist employees to transition with the minimum of fuss (although see below for situations where transphobia does occur). Trans people are protected by law against discrimination within the UK and several other countries (e.g. HMSO, 2010). Again, fears of discrimination should be attended to (and indeed some accommodation may unfortunately have to be made), and may be usefully explored in relation to their validity and to any purpose they may serve.

A further example of trans people being inappropriately influenced is that of children. Children should be cared for and informed at an appropriate level, but should have no greater say than in any other matter.

A parallel example might be moving house where a child would have their concerns listened to and reassurance given, but would nonetheless not be allowed to stop a necessary house move on the grounds that they didn't like it. Similarly, a partner or parent of an adult trans person should not expect to be able to put limits on the trans person's behaviours simply because they don't like it. A trans person should not automatically be expected to leave their home due to transition, and should not lose it, or children, in any separation simply because they are trans. Looking out for the terms 'of course ...' and 'should' can be useful in identifying and questioning assumptions here.

Some people continually put off their transition until after some future life event (for example, their children passing their exams, graduating college, getting married, having grandchildren; their grandchildren passing their exams, etc.). In such cases additional reasons for this will always be found, for such is the nature of life. Similarly, some clients delay transition as they feel that, were they to transition now it would demonstrate that they could have done in the past – a thought that is unconscionable – and so they delay (Richards, 2010). Consequently, some clients end up transitioning just before death in order to be buried in the gender they feel is correct for them. Making these processes explicit with clients, and discussing the pros and cons of choices, and the choice implicit in not choosing, are useful avenues of exploration.

PRESENTATION AND SECOND ADOLESCENCE

If accepting of the transition, friends and relatives, as well as some professionals, may very occasionally cautiously offer presentation tips early in transition, such as how a person might dress, speak or move. This can sometimes be helpful *if appropriate and accepted* (if the person has a learning disability, for example), as people will not have been socialised in their preferred gender and may have concerns about how others relate to them. However, it is important that people are able to portray themselves through their presentation and trans people will, of course, become offended if given unwanted or unwarranted advice. It is also worth noting that there will always be a tension between authentic personal expression of one's gender and the fact that gender presentation is socially constructed – consider the different modes of dress globally.

Cisgender people are taught how to do their gender from childhood and so it often appears 'natural' (although it would appear 'unnatural' in different cultural contexts and at different times). Trans people who transition after childhood must learn how to do their gender, often from stereotyped images from the media. This means that during a second adolescence period trans people may need to take some time before their gender identity and gender presentation match. It is not uncommon for trans people who are transitioning to identify with a gender role which is much younger than their chronological age – perhaps teens or twenties. Again this can be a part of finding who their female or male identity is. A useful intervention may be to ask who their heroes are and why. This identity formation can also be complicated by the introduction of hormones and allowances should be made, while still expecting the client to remain the adult that they are. Blaming unacceptable behaviours on hormones does not render them acceptable. Once people have transitioned for any length of time all this will have settled down and they should not be advised on presentation as this is, of course, as offensive as with any cisgender person.

Professionals should advise clients to act in a considered manner as far as possible, as many trans people will wish to rush ahead as fast as possible having taken the plunge to transition. This can destroy relationships and others in the trans person's life may need independent support. However, there is nothing wrong with being trans – a point worth reiterating freely and often (as we have here) – and so trans people should not be unduly stymied by other people's opinions, or accept behaviours that would otherwise be unacceptable. It is not uncommon for professionals to unnecessarily ask of trans people "Have you had the operation yet?", for example. Do not do this! It is unnecessarily invasive and is very likely to cause offence. Unless it is your common practice to ask about genitalia you should treat your trans clients just as any other client – genitalia is generally irrelevant in day-to-day life after all.

SEX AND RELATIONSHIPS

Trans people are often worried that existing relationships may fail if and when they transition. In some cases they do fail almost because it is thought inevitable that they will, but in others things may change, or may remain much as they were before. Sometimes romantic relationships of long standing become more that of companions, not uncommonly sexuality has faded during the relationship as in many relationships between cisgender people. Trans people may have any of the sexualities included in this book and beyond, with the proportions being somewhat similar to the general population. Some trans people's sexualities change after transition, whereas some remain the same, but the name changes. For example, a trans woman who is attracted to women may be heterosexual ('male') before transition and lesbian afterwards. A trans man who is attracted to men may be heterosexual ('female') before transition and gay afterwards. In contrast a trans man may be attracted to women before transition and men afterwards. Bisexual trans people may or may not remain bisexual, and so on.

SEX WORK

Some trans people are sex workers, and some are very successful at it. In the UK there are fewer trans sex workers than in other countries as the large amounts of money needed for surgery are paid for through taxation (and interestingly are most often recouped by the exchequer through increased taxation of the trans person as they become settled and therefore frequently earn more). A few trans people (especially some young trans women), however, feel that as a trans person they have to be a sex worker – of course they do not – and employment advice for a job which is comfortable (if sex work is not) for them can be useful. Similarly, some trans people feel a sense of validation of their identity through sex work (or indeed unpaid sex), and work on self-esteem and considering other ways of expression can be useful here. Unfortunately there is often increased risk of homelessness, especially among the young, when trans people leave, or are forced to leave, home as they transition. This can lead to unwanted sex work and support should be given, both in terms of finding other employment and also STI (sexually transmitted infection) prevention, etc.

One difficulty of sex work peculiar to trans people is that physiological body alterations can materially affect their work – with trans people trading on their trans status having to compete in a much larger (cisgender) market, and so sometimes less successfully, after hormones and surgeries.

DRUG USE

Some trans people misuse substances either as a means of avoiding transition or as a means of dealing with the stresses of transition. With the UK National Health Service drug and alcohol problems must be well managed before hormones and surgeries are considered. Elsewhere in the world rates of infections from shared needle use are strikingly high – again often because trans people cannot gain the emotional and financial support they need to transition and so endeavour to find other means of ameliorating their distress.

The usual procedures regarding drug and alcohol abuse can be employed, and should be considered for middle class clients drinking a great deal of wine, for example, as much as they are for groups who are more conventionally regarded as substance abusers. Care should be taken that trans-specific needs – such as being allocated the right facilities – are attended to.

KEY PRACTICES

This section covers coming out, interventions including hormones and surgeries, and issues around referral, names and trans youth.

COMING OUT

Trans people are often concerned when they first realise that they are trans due to the stigma associated with this. Things are somewhat easier now that the internet allows people to gain information and support easily and discretely and indeed this is often the appropriate first port of call for people considering transition (although some may need support gaining internet access in a safe location). However, clients and practitioners alike should utilise internet resources with a critical eye and due caution.

Trans people can be told that there is a 'right way' of being trans which may be at odds with their own identities and feelings (see Group Norms below). In addition, young and vulnerable people may be scared by negativity and horror stories on the internet and so not seek the help they need – with disastrous consequences. There can also often be a heavy emphasis of hormones and surgeries as well as the necessity of 'passing' as the gender one identifies with – see below. In addition, some unscrupulous people can play on some trans people's low self-esteem to make them have surgery they don't need, or that they are too early in their transition for, or that is of a poor quality. Similarly, trans people can be targeted for sex or unequal relationships to which they feel unable to say no.

Professionals should also be wary of supposed 'professional' information both online and in the research literature. Some people purporting to be expert in trans care have actually seen few trans people, seldom more than a couple of hundred and almost never more than a thousand. Of course this skews their notion of what trans people are like. In addition, some professionals, especially some academics, co-opt trans experiences by theorising them when they themselves are not trans, or, again, have seen few trans people and none clinically. One current debate is that of autogynephilia or autoandrophilia – the idea that trans women and men are erotically aroused at the thought of themselves as women and men respectively; and that this is the reason for their transition. Except in extraordinarily rare cases this is incorrect and in the UK is treated as such. However, professionals new to the literature could be forgiven for thinking otherwise due to the proportion of papers on this topic.

Early in the process most people experiment with wearing clothing not normally attributed to their birth-assigned gender (cross-dressing). This is usually much easier for trans men than for trans women as in many cultures, especially those in the West there is little opprobrium attached to women wearing male attire, but much opprobrium, even violence, towards people perceived as male in female attire. Consequently, trans women often start to wear female clothes in secret and out of necessity have to borrow clothes, often from their mother or sister if they start when young. If this is the case they generally buy their own female attire when they gain sufficient money to do so, which may be kept hidden in a *stash* and worn in suitably private locations. This stash may occasionally be *purged* through throwing out all the female clothes accompanied by a feeling of disgust, only to be bought again when the wish to transition reasserts itself.

There may also be a period of hypermasculine protest for those assigned male at birth and, less commonly, hyperfeminine protest for those assigned female. This is a period of time when a person attempts to throw themselves into their birth-assigned gender, for example by joining the army and getting married if assigned male, as an attempted 'cure' for the cross-gender feelings. Unfortunately, it seldom works and may delay transition causing further difficulties in moving job and renegotiating family roles, etc. This buying and purging and/or hypermasculine/hyperfeminine protest can continue for many years, even into old age, until some event, not uncommonly the death of a parent, leaves the trans person feeling able to commit to a fuller transition. After this time some trans people may endeavour to erase their history in order to become a 'proper' trans person (see comments on hierarchies below). Professionals can profitably work with clients to examine the positive outcomes of their past lives – children, careers, etc. – while accepting that the client may have had an internal sense of gender identity which was incongruent with their gender role throughout that time.

Especially in adolescence, trans women's cross-dressing is often accompanied by masturbation, although this usually abates during adulthood and is not necessarily evidence of a fetishistic attraction to female clothes as a great many things acquire an erotic charge during adolescence (for that which continues into adulthood, see Chapter 11). This can then evolve into a determination to have physiological changes and to live full time in a female role with associated implications for social, work and family structures – see below. It is, of course, important that those people who remain aroused when cross-dressing, and who do not wish to transition gender role permanently, do not have physiological interventions which they will inevitably regret when the erotic charge diminishes, possibly simply through familiarity (see Chapter 11).

Some trans women, especially those who are younger or a little more fluid or genderqueer in their presentation (see Chapter 5), do not go through this lengthy period of dual role, but rather present in a more feminine manner from childhood or adolescence. This may be partly to do with their having a biological aetiology for their being trans – but may also be due to the greater latitude, especially in some Western urban areas in recent times, afforded to people who are assigned male at birth to present in a more feminine manner.

PHYSIOLOGICAL INTERVENTIONS

Being trans is simply another way of being and as such requires no 'cure'. Nonetheless some people have sought one in the past and some have had one thrust upon them. All have been unsuccessful. Trans people, even those who have suffered through a significant period of living in their birth-assigned gender role, generally remain gender dysphoric until their body is adjusted to fit with their experience of themselves. Endeavours to change people's minds through psychotherapy, behaviour therapy and even shock therapy have failed.

Consequently, the treatment of choice is now careful screening of trans people; supportive assessment and supportive psychotherapy where needed; and such physiological interventions as they may request and is thought appropriate by the expert professionals they are working with. Mandatory psychotherapy is damaging (Seikowski, 2007) most likely because it questions and troubles a comfortable, if nascent, identity.

TRANS MALE HORMONES

For a trans man, hormonal manipulation usually involves androgens alone, often via intra-muscular injection or topical gel. Independent suppression of oestrogens is not usually necessary as this is accomplished by androgens alone. Changes will induce beard growth, increasing musculature, stopping menses, increased body hair (and if genetically predisposed loss of head hair), deepening the voice, enlarging of the clitoris, and altering mood – including, all things being equal, somewhat increased aggression and sex drive. Masculinising hormones do not remove the breasts and so many trans men bind their breasts with a special elastic undershirt called a *binder* or through the use of bandages, and many opt to have them removed via a bilateral mastectomy and associated male chest recontouring.

TRANS FEMALE HORMONES

For trans women hormonal manipulation usually involves oestrogens and possibly an androgen suppressant. These will soften the skin, stop erections, possibly lead to a little less body hair – although electrolysis is usually necessary to remove body, and especially facial hair. Trans women on hormones will grow breasts, usually to about a cup size less than their mothers. If they are older, or have self-medicated with hormones bought from the internet, there is an increased likelihood of them requiring an augmentation mammoplasty surgery to increase breast size. Those trans women who have not taken hormones, or who have only recently started to do so, often use padding in their bras to approximate breasts. These can include ingenious homemade devices such as tights filled with peas, or specially made silicone forms that approximate the size, feel and weight of a natural breast. Once the male voice has broken feminising hormones have no effect upon it and so speech therapy and possibly pitch surgery may be needed to effect a feminine voice; although it should be noted that voices differ between male and female not only in terms of pitch, but also choice of words, tempo, intonation and a number of other factors which a skilled speech and language therapist should be able to assist with. All things being equal, trans women also experience a change in mood becoming somewhat more 'emotional' and crying more easily. While feminising hormones can decrease sex drive, trans women are often comfortable with their bodies for the first time in their lives after the commencement of hormones and so sex drive can actually increase, with the modest pharmacological decrease more than offset by the psychological boost.

INFERTILITY

Both trans men and trans women will become infertile after taking cross-sex hormones and so should be counselled regarding this, with gamete storage offered prior to their commencement. It may be possible for people to stop hormones for some months in order to store gametes once started on hormones, but this is by no means assured. This is particularly an issue for younger trans people who at 18 may see having children as very incidental to their wish to transition, in a way they then regret at 30. A useful intervention can be to ask them to consider how much they have changed since they were very much younger and ask them if they might not change over that time period again. Some trans people feel that their gametes are in some way gendered, or that if they cannot have children in a way consistent with their gender (i.e. a trans woman carry a child to term) then they do not wish to have children at all. Trans clients should be reassured that many cisgender people cannot have children in such a way and so use other means (for example, cisgender women use surrogate mothers also). The DNA each parent contributes is, after all, simply a strand of nucleic acid and so reproductive education may be useful.

TRANS PARENTS

Some trans people think that, because they are trans they will be harmful to their children and so they should not have them; or if they already have them they should leave them. This is incorrect, despite some erroneous theorising by people who see few, if any, trans clients. The empirical literature is quite clear that having a trans parent in no way harms a child, or indeed appears to affect their sexuality. Harm to children seems to be caused by acrimonious break-ups (as it is for other reasons) and so separations should be handled with as much grace as possible (Freedman, Tasker & Di Ceglie, 2002).

Some trans parents retain a sense of self-blame with an extraordinary degree of vigour. The reason for this seems to be the feeling that they have hurt their children (although as mentioned children are not always hurt in these cases) and so, were they to give up their sense of blame, they would therefore be callous towards their children. Living a life while torturing themselves allows them to feel that, in some way, they are still a good parent; being happy themselves would mean that they are a bad parent and that is untenable. It can be useful to explore whether there was any choice involved, who has responsibility for their emotions, whether the 'children' are now independent adults (it's always useful to ask the age of any children), etc.

TRANS FEMALE SURGERIES

Trans women may also opt to have surgeries to alter their bodies such that they are in line with their gender identities. These are usually carried out after hormones have fully suppressed androgen production and oestrogens have had a chance to take effect, as this gives a better feel for where the person will be after surgeries and is a good indicator of whether a person will be happy to remain in their new gender role for the rest of their life. A key point with surgeries is that they are irreversible – once surgery has been done even the best reconstructive surgeries are inadequate. This is especially the case with genital surgeries sometimes called sex reassignment surgery (SRS) or gender reassignment surgery (GRS) or gender confirmation surgery; but perhaps most appropriately genital reconstruction surgery (GRS) (as that is what actually happens). Trans people should be counselled about the realities of their new bodies and may require assistance from professionals as they may not have had socialisation to them. For example, some trans women believe that breasts consist of fat – in fact they consist primarily of mammary glands – they are identical to female breasts and can be induced to lactate. Basic sex education can also be useful as trans people are just as much at risk of STIs as their cisgender counterparts, but may feel that this is not so, or that they are not able to ask for protection, or even to refuse sex they do not want, on the basis that they are trans.

Trans women will only have an augmentation mammoplasty about 30% of the time if properly hormonally managed by a specialist endocrinologist. When they do have an augmentation mammoplasty it usually involves the insertion of a prosthetic breast either next to the developed breast or partially under the muscle also. Often trans women require a larger implant than their cisgender peers due to the proportionally larger size of the phenotypic male chest.

Trans women may also have a vagina formed from tissue that used to be their penis (with hair removal beforehand), with labia formed from scrotal tissue. The testicles are removed and the part of the tip of the penis, the glans, is used to create a clitoris, in the usual place, for erogenous sensation. The urethra is shortened and re-sited to allow the trans woman to urinate – for which she will likely sit down (as most cisgender women do). The neo-vagina will require regular dilation for the rest of the patient's life with an acrylic stent which she must place in her vagina periodically to stop it closing up. The cowpers glands are not removed and so there may be some lubrication when the trans woman is very sexually excited, but it is usual for her to need some form of other lubricant to be vaginally penetrated. Her prostate will also be left intact and should be medically treated accordingly. There is also another method of creating a neo-vagina using part of the colon (a colovaginoplasty) which is sometimes used if the patient has a very small penis, has been circumcised, or had puberty suppressed. However this is seldom used as it carries with it significantly higher risks. Some trans women who do not wish for vaginally penetrative sex, or who would be unable, or are unwilling, to care for a neo-vagina opt instead for a cosmesis in which the penis is removed, the clitoris is created and the labia formed, but no vagina is created.

TRANS MALE SURGERIES

Trans men may have a bilateral mastectomy and associated chest recontouring to effect a male chest. This can vary in outcome as larger breasts can mean less successful results and more scarring (scars may, of course, be tattooed over). In addition, if the breasts have been bound for long periods of time a poorer result may occur. Trans men may also have their clitoris released so it sits further forward and is more prominent – a procedure called a metoidioplasty. This is simpler and carries less risk than the creation of a neo-phallus by a phalloplasty. The phalloplasty uses tissue from the arm, abdomen or back to form a penis using microsurgical techniques which aim to include protective, but not erogenous, sensation and blood supply. Erogenous sensation is retained as the clitoris remains intact and is sited underneath. This is usually a multi-stage procedure which all too often has complications such as urinary incontinence and the man's penis being abraded by his underpants due to lack of protective sensation. Nonetheless, some trans men are pleased to have phalloplasties which allow them to stand to urinate and/or to penetrate their partners through use of a hidden prostheses and a pump in place of one of his testicles – the other being an appropriately shaped implant. The scrotum is often shaped from labial tissue and the vagina, womb and ovaries are often removed. It should be noted that some trans men may have their womb and ovaries removed independent from the creation of a penis of any kind in order to stop any chance of menses and to remove the risk of various problems which may be associated with other treatments.

For all surgeries having appropriate support, such as people to do the shopping etc. after surgeries, as well as emotional support, is invaluable.

NON-SURGICAL OPTIONS

Literature and clinical experience suggest that the standardised mortality ratio of hormonal treatment for both trans men and trans women is one (with gender-specific risk reversed) – provided it is safely administered and that the correct associated tests and monitoring are carried out. However, some trans people opt not to have hormones due to understandable health concerns or because they are concerned about physiological changes. Some trans people do take hormones when they have full information, but others, quite reasonably, opt not to as they are more or less happy with their bodies as they are, but nonetheless wish to live as another gender. Similarly, some trans people opt not to have surgeries, and this is not at all uncommon with trans men opting not to have genital surgeries as they are concerned with the risks and potentially poor aesthetic outcome. Instead some trans people may reconstrue the gendered meanings of their body parts. For example, a trans woman may determine that she has a very large clitoris where others may read it as a penis; or a trans man may determine that he has a *manhole* where others would read a vagina. Of course, these are reasonable positions given how society marks bodies in different ways which may not always accord with perceived reality – for example long hair is not always feminine (consider the WWF wrestler), and muscles are not always masculine (consider the female sportsperson). Within the UK, legal recognition of one's gender *for all purposes* including marriage, gender-specific jobs, prison, etc. requires no physiological change of any sort (HMSO, 2004), although this is by no means the case globally.

It should be noted that while hormones and surgeries are often important things for trans people, they are not a panacea. Some trans people can have rather magical thinking about surgery especially and can become somewhat depressed after the magic has worn off when they find themselves in the same or similar job, home relationship, etc. with the same set of joys and difficulties – with just a few swapped for others that are different in kind but not in degree. Similarly, trans people can often think that any change in their psychology or physiology is down to their hormonal regimen and, while it is important that practitioners are aware of this as a possibility, hormones should not automatically be considered as being the first port of call when a difficulty arises. It does trans people a disservice if they are referred for a hormonal check-up when they are depressed if they have recently suffered a relationship breakdown, for example. Time, friends, self-care and perhaps psychotherapy would be far more immediately pertinent.

REFERRAL

Very few issues for trans people will require the services of a specialist in trans care. Trans people are just the same as others in terms of jobs, children, parents, bereavements, illnesses, etc. Of course there are occasionally matters wherein the services of a specialist are required – an endocrinological illness for example – however these will be rare. Notwithstanding this if the matter is trans related and a professional does feel they are inadequately equipped to deal with the matter it is professionally negligent not to refer on to a professional who has the necessary expertise. This is the case whether it is a matter of medicine, psychology or psychotherapy, social work or any other matter.

Within the United Kingdom people who wish to have physiological interventions may have these at no cost (other than through taxation) via the National Health Service. This includes hormones and genital surgeries, although other interventions such as facial feminisation surgeries and chest surgeries are often dependent upon the area the patient lives in for funding. People will usually be seen by their general practitioner or primary care physician who may then send them to be screened by a psychologist or psychiatrist for a mental health issue presenting as gender dysphoria. If a person does not have a mental health issue, or if their mental health issue (including schizophrenia, bipolar, etc.) is being managed and is not the cause of their gender dysphoria, they will be referred to a gender specialist multidisciplinary team of psychologists, psychiatrists, surgeons, speech therapists, endocrinologists, etc. with whom they will work towards an agreed outcome (it is worth noting that the members of this team may themselves be LGBTQ etc.) If the person wishes to have physiological interventions these will usually come after a formal change of gender role, which will involve telling friends, family, work, etc. and making a change of name and identification documents (ID). At this point hormones may be initiated and then, when established, followed by any necessary chest surgeries; with genital surgeries following, usually after a period of two years from the change of gender role.

NAMES

Some clients may wish for assistance with changing their name – this is an important stage and should not be unduly influenced by clinicians. Having said that, some clients opt to choose a gender neutral name such as Sam in the hope that it will ease transition. Unfortunately, in some cases, this allows friends and family of the trans person not to make a cognitive shift (as they would with a change from Susan to Jeffrey say) leaving them thinking of the trans person in their old gender role. This can become particularly wearing for the trans person as their transition progresses, sometimes resulting in a further change to a gender unambiguous name.

It can also be useful to gently question clients who use the third person to refer to their gendered self. People who live in a dual role, being male at some times and female at others, may usefully employ this tactic to make syntactic sense, but for those who state that they have only one gendered identity referring to their other gender as "she" or using a name for "her" (or "he" and "him" for trans men) may demonstrate a degree of ambivalence, or at least non integration (as yet) of the identities (see Chapter 5 for the separate issue of those who explicitly identify as bigender).

Similarly some clients do not explicitly tell others, hoping that they will "just know". However, if they do know there is no reason not to discuss it, and if they don't and the client wishes to be thought of in their preferred gender, they will need to be clear. A period of adjustment may be necessary during which time more ambiguous clothing may be used, accessible toilets and such; but this should not be indefinitely as becoming established in the preferred gender role, and living just as a cisgender man or woman would is an important part of transition. Living in an ambiguous role, if not chosen, can be a major psychological stressor.

TRANS YOUTH

Trans youth are people who are under perhaps the age of 25; although the term usually refers to those who have not completed puberty yet. Most of this chapter refers to adult trans people, however trans youth is increasingly an issue, so is included briefly here. Most gender 'non-conforming' children (i.e. those who do not conform to conventional norms for their gender) will not transition gender when they grow up. The more they continue to be gender non-confirming as they grow up, the more likely it is that they will transition when they are adults. This is not to say that stopping the expression of gender non-conformity or offering psychological 'treatments' will stop the person being trans – rather they will be a miserable trans person, possibly with psychological problems. The best outcome seems to be assisting young trans people with their gender identities and expression as well as educating their social and educational networks such as schools, youth clubs, etc. Rather confusingly this is not to say that immediate transition is always the best thing either, as some young trans people who have transitioned have felt that they would like to transition back to their birth-assigned gender but have felt that they have not been able to due to all the interventions and change. Cautious, supportive interventions seem to be best.

For those young people who are extremely gender dysphoric, or cross-gendered in their identity and presentation, and who have been so for a long time, puberty-suppressing drugs called gonadotropin releasing hormone agonists (GnRHa) are sometimes administered when they reach Tanner stage 2 in puberty (just after the start). In this way the child can see a little of what puberty is like and, if they don't like it, it is stopped leaving them effectively pre-pubertal for sufficient time for them to fully consider if they would like to transition. If they would like to transition, cross-sex hormones are given and they develop accordingly; if they would not like to transition the puberty-suppressing drugs are stopped and they develop without the aid of drugs into their birth-assigned gender as an adult. Needless to say all this is done extremely carefully under the oversight of a large multidisciplinary team.

WIDER SOCIETY

Fear of abuse and violence is a very real concern held by many trans people. This may manifest in many ways, from physical attacks and abuse in public, to discrimination at work or at social events in which trans people may be subject to treatment which would be unthinkable for non-trans people (pulling at hairpieces, asking about genitalia, being told to use incorrect facilities, etc.). In addition, professionals and academics have sometimes co-opted trans voices, or been indiscreet with information about trans people in ways which have been damaging to trans people themselves. While it is important for professionals not to overplay these threats, as fear can be extremely disabling, it is important to recognise their potential and to treat fears accordingly – perhaps with gentle experimentation to see if they are being realised. Professionals may also leverage professional power to assist trans people who are subject to such abuse – perhaps with letters to employers, etc. if asked by trans people themselves. Professionals may also usefully engage with political activism in order to assist trans people in these regards, whether or not they themselves identify as trans.

CONFIDENTIALITY

Within wider society trans is often seen as an object of fascination and as such should have especial confidentiality associated with it. Within the UK, the law (The Gender Recognition Act 2004) states that if a professional finds out that someone (client or colleague) is trans in their professional capacity, and then tells someone else – perhaps a secretary or a supervisor in the course of their work – then they have committed a criminal offence and will receive a criminal record, and a category five fine. They will most likely also be sued by the client or colleague afterwards. There are no 'reasonableness' criteria within this law as it is an absolute offence – saying that 'of course my secretary must type my letters', for example, is no defence. However, if the client or colleague consents to their details being given, under necessary circumstances the law allows this. There are also exceptions for the detection of crime, terrorism, and if the client or colleague is unconscious and needs medical assistance and you are a medic. Whether UK law applies to you or not, this gaining of consent to communicate details is rather easily done and should already be standard practice for most professionals – it just needs making explicit.

TOILETS

With regard to toilets and single-sex facilities, there are sometimes concerns about trans people using the appropriate toilets. It is, however, not acceptable for able-bodied trans people to have to use accessible toilets for any significant length of time as they may be needed in a hurry by people with physical needs. Instead trans people should use facilities appropriate to their presenting gender. Most trans people will be especially discreet in such facilities as they do not wish to draw attention to themselves. If a trans person were to cause a disturbance, the situation should be handled in just the same manner as if a cisgender person had done so as their trans status is not relevant. Within the UK and various other countries many trans people are protected by law in their use of single-sex facilities appropriate to their gender. It can be useful in these cases to consider the matter transposed into another arena. If some people were complaining that a person of a certain class or religion had come into a toilet, gone into a stall, urinated and then washed their hands and left, they would be given short shrift.

SOCIAL GROUPS

It is worth noting that trans people can be made unwelcome in certain social groups. The mainstream of some religions (with notable exceptions) expressly forbids transition and are at best 'tolerant' in a way in which it is made clear that those in a position of power (i.e. non-trans people) are exercising that power over the trans members. This can also be the case in some lesbian, gay and, less commonly, bisexual spaces. Some radical feminist groups especially, may have a 'women-born-women' policy for membership which is problematic, exclusionary and rather counter-intuitive as it appears to be the only time that it is argued by this group that biology *is* destiny (cf. Serano, 2007). There are also class and cultural differences in the degree of acceptance of trans people, with some cultural groups having a history of recognition of some kind of gender transition.

Another group of people who have vilified trans people in the past, but who have shifted in positive directions of late, are medical professionals. It should not be forgotten that it was doctors who initially put their livelihood and profession on the line to fight for trans services, and continue to do so (often behind closed doors) with their multidisciplinary colleagues. It is also important to remember that medical professionals, like all other groups, are diverse and will have different levels of awareness and education around trans. Despite changes in this area, 'transsexualism' and 'gender identity disorder' are still classified as mental disorders in the main psychiatric taxonomies – the *International Classification of Diseases*, 10th edition (*ICD-10*) and *Diagnostic and Statistical Manual of Mental Disorders*, 4th edition, text revision (*DSM-IV-TR*) respectively. This allowed NHS funding in the UK and insurance funding elsewhere. However, many trans people and others argue that, given that being trans is not necessarily debilitating, it makes no sense to retain the diagnoses, especially after any surgeries, change of role, etc. are done with (cf. Karasic & Drescher, 2005). For this reason the most recent *DSM-V* contains the diagnosis of *gender dysphoria* to reflect the fact that being trans per se is not a disorder.

GROUP NORMS

HIERARCHY

Within some circles there is an implicit (or indeed explicit) and problematic hierarchy of perceived legitimacy with cisgender people at the top followed by intersex people; then trans people who have had hormones and surgeries; then people who have 'only' had hormones or no genital surgeries; then people who have not had surgeries or hormones ('dual role' people); and then those with a sexual element to their gender presentation. Of course these also intersect with other demographics such as age, class, race, etc. Some trans women refer to cisgender women as 'real girls' or 'bio girls' – terms which serve to erase the reality and validity of trans women's gender and may be a reflection of low self-esteem on the part of the trans women who use these terms, or internalised transphobia in which the trans woman herself does not like trans people. Similarly, but slightly less commonly, trans men may make reference to 'real men' or 'bio men'. Trans men may also suffer from internalised transphobia, sometimes – but not always – associated with not having a penis and so feeling unable to be a 'real man'.

It is imperative for clinicians to examine their own assumptions and to avoid thinking that someone is 'really' of their birth-assigned gender. If a person has transitioned and appears to be suffering in this way it can be useful to consider the ways in which cisgender people fall short of these targets and yet are still considered to be wholly male or female – for example, many older cisgender women have had hysterectomies and yet are still considered to be fully female, despite not having reproductive capacity; a cisgender man who has his penis removed, perhaps as a result of an accident, would still be a man. Trans, then, may be considered to be just another way of being a woman or a man. For this reason using the terms such as pronouns, name, etc. related to the gender of presentation (except in certain specialised and legal circumstances) is imperative. If in doubt use the *ask etiquette* – and simply ask what form of address is preferred.

PAUSE FOR CONSIDERATION

Take a moment to consider what constitutes a woman or a man in your own mind. Try to think of examples where this is troubled – for example, if men are constituted by being physically strong, what about elderly men?

Some trans people, especially trans women, may move from a position of 'fetishistic' sexualised cross-dressing (see Chapter 11) to a 'dual role' position before deciding to transition fully into the female role. This group may find it especially difficult to accept that they have lived in different roles, due to the different values these are given in the hierarchy. Similarly, trans men may have occupied a place as a queer or butch lesbian and found friends and a sense of community within that, sometimes linked with radical feminist politics, particularly in the case of those growing up in the 1960s and 1970s. It can be especially difficult for such trans men to transition into a male role as they sometimes have to leave friendship groups and communities, and may feel they have betrayed them (or be told they have) as they move to a role which is more personally congruent.

It follows therefore that one of the most useful interventions professionals can make is to impress upon struggling trans people that they are just as male or female as a cisgender man or woman – and that it is okay to be trans. This bears repeating, as many people think that trans people will inevitably fail at life. However, this is not the case. Within the UK there are trans doctors, lawyers, professors and indeed members of just about every profession. Trans people often also have children, partners, etc. and all the accoutrements of what is commonly regarded as a satisfying life. This is not to say that being trans is not sometimes hard, but that it can be quite okay, and exceptional.

'PASSING' AND ABUSE

One particular issue for many trans people endeavouring to live comfortably is that of 'passing' as the gender of their identity. This can be a matter of safety as people who look less uncommon often suffer less abuse. However, some trans people fear that if found out they will invariably suffer abuse when in fact this is not so. A useful question is to ask when the last time was that abuse occurred and ask for a date and details. It may be that the perception is more damaging than the reality. Indeed the act of being 'stealth' – that is passing such that others are unaware that one is trans – can lead to people developing psychological difficulties as they are constantly concerned about being found out. This is called hyper-vigilance and may manifest as people looking at others in the street, thinking people are laughing at them or talking about them. Unfortunately, the very behaviours people use to address this – looking at people to see if they are looking, etc. can cause the effects they are concerned about. Therapeutic methods of addressing anxiety and panic attacks can be effective to address this.

Those people who choose not to 'pass' all the time, or who are unable to, tend to come to terms with their trans status and develop methods of handling any abuse (often through either ignoring or calmly giving information about trans to the abuser) – and consequently may be more content. Those who do suffer psychological difficulties as a result of being abused in this way are subject to *minority stress* in the same way people from other minority groups can suffer from depression and anxiety, etc. It should not be assumed that because of this being trans is psychopathological.

SUMMARY AND CONCLUSIONS

In summary, the following are good practice points when working with trans clients:

- Remember that trans is simply another way of being, albeit one which often involves a major life change.
- Examine one's own gender (whether trans or not) and avoid inadvertently influencing people who are deciding how they wish to be for themselves.
- Reflexively engage with assumptions and encourage staff to do the same.
- Recognise that fundamentally transition is not about becoming a woman or a man, but rather about becoming oneself and making one's peace with that decision.
- Make referral when necessary and involve a multidisciplinary team for any major physiological change.
- Treat people with dignity and respect and use the appropriate pronouns, names, etc.
- Respect confidentiality.
- Normalise trans, and most often simply ignore it when it is not pertinent to the matter under discussion.

FURTHER READING

Barrett, J. (Ed.) (2007). *Transsexual and other disorders of gender identity*. Oxford: Radcliffe.

Bornstein, K. (1994). *Gender outlaw*. London: Routledge.

Ettner, R., Monstrey, S. & Eyler, A.E. (Eds.) (2007). *Principles of transgender medicine and surgery*. New York: The Haworth Press.

Lev, A.I. (2004). *Transgender emergence*. London: Haworth Clinical Practice Press.

ADDITIONAL REFERENCES

Freedman, D., Tasker, F. & Di Ceglie, D. (2002). Children and adolescents with transsexual parents referred to a specialist gender identity development service: A brief report of key development features. *Clinical Child Psychology and Psychiatry*, 7(3), 423–432.

HMSO (2004). Gender Recognition Act.

HMSO (2010). Single Equality Act.

Hoshiai, M., Matsumoto, Y., Sato, T., Ohnishi, M., Okabe, N., Kishimoto, Y., Terada, S. & Kuroda, S. (2010). Psychiatric comorbidity among patients with gender identity disorder. *Psychiatry and Clinical Neurosciences*, 6, 514–519.

Karasic, D. & Drescher, J. (2005). *Sexual and gender diagnoses of the diagnostic and statistical manual (DSM)*. New York: Haworth Press.

Kruijver, F.P.M. (2004). *Sex in the brain*. Amsterdam: Netherlands Institute of Brain Research.

Richards, C. (2010). 'Them and us' in mental health services. *The Psychologist*, *23*(1), 40–41.

Seikowski, K. (2007). Psychotherapy and transsexualism. *Andrologia*, *39*, 248–252.

Serano, J. (2007). *Whipping girl*. Emeryville: Seal Press.

INTERSEX/DIVERSITY OF SEXUAL DEVELOPMENT (DSD)

3

This chapter aims to:

- Examine some of the more common types of intersex/DSD.
- Consider how a diagnosis of intersex/DSD may affect a person.
- Briefly outline surgery for infants with an intersex/DSD condition.
- Consider when referral onwards is necessary and when intersex/DSD diagnosis is irrelevant.

INTRODUCTION

It is often assumed that people come in one of only two types – male or female – and that there is no overlap between these. Culturally we can see that this is not so as there is increasing overlap in clothing, emotional expression, job roles, etc. (see Chapter 4). People's sense of their gender may also not be tied to their anatomy with apparently male-bodied people identifying as women; apparently female-bodied people identifying as men (see Chapter 2); and people identifying as neither and as both (see Chapter 5).

People may also have physiology which does not fall neatly into the categories of male or female. Such people may have an identity which is either at odds with their body; mainly in line with it; concretely either male or female; or something else – as we shall see in this chapter.

TERMINOLOGY

People who have physiology which does not fall neatly into the categories of male or female are sometimes referred to as *intersex* or having a *DSD*. DSD sometimes refers to 'disorder of sex development' – a term which is preferred by many professionals and the Accord Alliance (a DSD support and information society). DSD also refers to *diversity of sex development* – the meaning we have chosen for this chapter. Sometimes *variation of sex development* or *divergence of sex development* are also used.

The reason for the different terms is that some people with an intersex/DSD condition consider themselves to be unremarkably male or female (many with Klinefelter's syndrome consider themselves to be unremarkably male, for example; albeit with an XXY chromosomal makeup). For such people the term intersex does not refer to their sense of identity, which is not intersex. Further, many people who have perfectly well-functioning bodies, albeit ones which are not strictly and completely taxonomically male or female, rightly do not consider themselves to have a disorder. Such people often consider society to be at fault for so rigidly circumscribing what is male and what is female. Having one's urethral opening appear lower on the shaft of the penis in no way affects being a man, albeit that it was caused by a variation in sex differentiation *in utero*. It is important to acknowledge though, that some people with a DSD do prefer the term 'disorder of sex development' and some people have a condition which is threatening to health, which might therefore be called a disorder. Nonetheless as *diversity* seems the kinder, more inclusive, term we have used that here, while retaining intersex for those people who identify somewhere beyond male or female – either physiologically or physiologically and psychologically.[1]

Throughout this chapter we use terms such as 'male', 'female', 'masculinisation' and 'feminisation'. Many people with a DSD do identify with the common gendered understandings of body parts, for example that a penis is a male body part (although this may be less so for people who identify as intersex). For clarity only we have used 'male', 'female', 'masculinisation' and 'feminisation' in line with these common understandings, but professionals should remain aware that it is perfectly possible for a woman to have a penis and to be feminine. The cells that form a penis have no specific gender to them other than that which societies give them (if you are thinking of Y chromosomes read on ...).

There are a number of conditions in which people have some form of physiological variance from strictly male or female. Rates are approximately 1.7% of the population – very roughly 1 in 50 people (Blackless et al., 2000). This chapter provides a brief overview of common conditions. Detailed coverage of all of these is beyond the scope of this book (see Further Reading). We then focus on the issues intersex/DSD people may bring to a professional and how best to approach these.

PHYSIOLOGY AND SEXUAL DIFFERENTIATION

Human beings are typically differentiated in the womb after conception. Genitals are differentiated before brains (which have a limited number of

---

[1] 'Pseudo-hermaphroditism' and 'hermaphroditism' are not used (although the latter is still sometimes in use medically), as both terms are often offensive.

small structural differences between male and female).[2] It has been suggested that when genitals are unremarkably differentiated one way (say female) and brains another (say male) this is the cause of transsexualism (in this case in a trans man – see Chapter 2). This chapter concerns itself primarily with conditions which have observable differences in sexual phenotype and so precludes trans people without intersex/DSD conditions as, at present, trans brains cannot be differentiated from cisgender brains *in vivo*.

In this section we first outline the typical physiological development of primary and secondary sex characteristics, and then outline the ways in which the various intersex/DSD conditions differ from this. This structure will aid reader understanding, however it is more useful to consider all of these (typical and intersex/DSD) to be more/less common diversities of sex development (some of which are medically problematic but many of which are not), rather than taking a 'normal' vs 'abnormal' model. Throughout this part of the book it is apparent that sex/gender development is a complex biopsychosocial process with a huge variety of identities and experiences possible within it.

The causes of differentiation are complex and beyond this chapter to cover in detail, but basically at fertilisation the sperm adds either an X or a Y chromosome to the X in the ovum. This determines the genetic sex of the embryo, with XY being commonplace male and XX being commonplace female. In the first weeks of development, genetic male and female foetuses are extremely similar. In the sixth week of gestation gonads begin to develop and are largely undifferentiated, but then develop into either testes (male gonads) or ovaries (female gonads). Testosterone production by the testis then results in genital differentiation. In the seventh week XX and XY foetuses still basically have identical genitalia and only in the eighth week will an XY foetus' gonads develop (under certain circumstances) into functional testes which primarily secrete testosterone. If the foetus is XX it is in the twelfth week that the gonads become functional ovaries which primarily secrete oestrogens.

Both XX and XY foetuses have a Müllerian duct system. In XY foetuses Müllerian duct-inhibiting hormone causes this to regress. After this androgens secreted by the testes cause the development of the Wolffian duct system, which develops into the seminal vesicles, vas deferens and ejaculatory ducts. In XX foetuses the Müllerian duct system develops into fallopian tubes, the uterus and the inner third of the vagina.

---

[2] These differences are statistical in nature. There are no brain areas that are only female or only male (it is the sizes of some areas which differ) and the overlap between populations of female compared to male are generally larger than the differences.

The external genitalia are also determined by the presence or absence of androgens (however they are derived) from the urogenital sinus which contains the enzyme 5-alpha reductase. 5-alpha reductase converts testosterone to dihydrotestosterone (DHT). If DHT is present the penis and scrotum form, whereas if it is absent female development continues, with the development of a perineal urethra and the formation of a vagina, labia and clitoris.

After this has occurred, the hormones secreted by the testes or ovaries have an organising effect on the brain which, to some extent, differentiates it in a 'male' or 'female' way. Brains are, of course, neuroplastic, meaning that they can physically adapt to stimuli and learn. This means that over-generalisations about 'male' or 'female' brains should be approached with extreme caution as social environment and learning has a marked impact upon people's (especially children's) brains from the earliest stages of human life.

After the effects outlined have organised the body, a second hormone surge at puberty activates various tissues that have formed *in utero* and also triggers the development of others according to genetic make-up, hormonal milieu, etc. These changes further differentiate males and females. Girls typically begin puberty at 10 or so and experience a change in body odour and the onset of acne; have a growth spurt with the pelvis widening and an increase in body fat; develop breasts and pubic hair; begin to have periods (menarche) and so become fertile through the production of eggs (ovulation); as well as enlargement of the clitoris, change of colour of labia minora and some functional changes to the vagina. Puberty for girls typically ends around the age of 15 or 16.

For boys puberty usually begins at 12 or so and involves an increase in testicular size followed by an increase in penis size (the testicles also hang lower sometimes called 'balls dropping') and the start of fertility with the production of sperm; there are more spontaneous erections of the penis; pubic hair develops as well as facial hair – there may or may not be a development of chest hair. There is a marked increase in height, bone mass and musculature; the voice deepens and there are changes in body odour and the development of acne. Puberty usually ends at 16 or 17 although some development, such as facial hair, continues after this.

Various things affect the typical differentiation process outlined above to cause people to become intersex or have a DSD. Some of the more common are detailed below.

CONDITIONS

5-ALPHA REDUCTASE DEFICIENCY

In this condition individuals lack the enzyme 5-alpha reductase which turns testosterone into dihydrotestosterone (a more powerful form of testosterone). People may appear to be female or somewhat feminised at birth but have an XY chromosomal make-up and may have a male gender identity. They have the commonplace internal male genitalia. At puberty further masculinisation may occur which leads to enlargement of the clitoris; the testes descending; hirsutism; and deepening of the voice. It may be that sperm are produced enabling reproduction, however people with 5-alpha reductase deficiency only have a rudimentary prostate and so are often infertile.

ANDROGEN INSENSITIVITY SYNDROME (AIS)

In this condition the individual's cells do not respond to androgens effectively. It is consequently of greater impact for those people who have an XY genotype than those who have XX who may not be aware of having the condition. The degree of AIS varies, with some XY individuals having difficulty producing sperm, but feeling fundamentally male (mild androgen insensitivity syndrome – MAIS); whereas others may have partially masculinised genitalia (partial androgen insensitivity syndrome – PAIS); others may have a fairly unremarkably female body and identity despite the presence of a Y chromosome (complete androgen insensitivity syndrome – CAIS).

CONGENITAL ADRENAL HYPERPLASIA (CAH)

This is a genetic condition in which genetic females are masculinised because the adrenal glands fail to produce cortisol and aldosterone and instead secrete large amounts of androgen during prenatal development. In genetic males this does not affect development, but it can cause clitoromegaly in females to the extent that it resembles a penis. Sometimes the lack of aldosterone results in salt-wasting adrenal hyperplasia which can be fatal and immediate medical assistance is sought when it becomes apparent after birth for this reason.

KLINEFELTER SYNDROME

In this condition people have an XXY genetic make-up. Most commonly people with Klinefelter syndrome identify as male, although some identify as female. Many who do identify as male are unaware of their genetic make-up (as most people are) until they undergo tests for reduced fertility, etc. because genitalia will usually be a penis and testicles in appearance, although these may be smaller than average. People should be reassured that they are not 'less male' because of the extra chromosome, just as those who identify as female should not feel they are 'less female', although they may ask for further physiological assistance.

TURNER SYNDROME

In this condition all, or part, of one of the sex chromosomes is absent – written XO. People with Turner syndrome usually identify as female, but will most usually not have periods and will be infertile. People with Turner syndrome will also have other medical problems including reduced height and heart problems.

MOSAICISM INVOLVING SEX CHROMOSOMES

In this condition some of a person's cells have one genetic make-up and some another. An example might be someone who has partial, or mild, Klinefelter syndrome who has some cells which are XY and some which are XXY. Similarly, some people may have some cells which are XX and some which are XO (Turner syndrome).

These conditions may cause a number of different outcomes some of which are detailed below. Note that not all of the items listed below will be linked to any specific condition.

APHALLIA

The penis/clitoris does not form *in utero* between 3–6 weeks after conception. The urethra opens on the perineum.

CLITOROMEGALY

The clitoris is larger than the 'normal' range sometimes through congenital adrenal hyperplasia if present at birth; or through a hormonal variation if acquired after birth (for example as a result of polycystic ovarian syndrome – PCOS). There is some debate about what constitutes a 'normal' size for a clitoris and when it becomes a micropenis, or penis; and whether it matters if the person is healthy. It is commonly measured using the Prader system which includes other aspects of differentiation; although in terms of absolute size at birth there is some confusion with less than 9mm often being considered an acceptable clitoris, greater than 20mm an acceptable penis and 9mm–20mm often being considered to be atypical (Harper, 2007).

MICROPENIS

Here the penis is smaller than the 'normal' range (see Clitoromegaly above) often through reduced prenatal androgen as a result of Klinefelter syndrome or gonadal dysgenesis. Penises are often strongly linked to maleness and masculinity. The average size for an erect adult penis is about five inches (12.5cm) (although many people mistakenly believe it is substantially more), with micropenis in adults being considered when the erect penis is less than about two inches (5cm). However, as seen in Chapter 2, some people with much smaller penises than this have no trouble regarding themselves as having penises.

HYPOSPADIAS

Here the opening of the urethra from which urine flows is on the shaft of the penis; at the junction of the penis and scrotum; or somewhere in the perineum. It is most likely caused by some variation of pre-natal hormones.

OVOTESTES (PREVIOUSLY CALLED 'TRUE HERMAPHRODITISM')

Here the gonads have developed as either an ovary and a testes, or as ovotestes in which there is both ovarian and testicular tissue in the gonad. With ovotestes there may also be an ovary one side and testis on the other. Ovotestes are sometimes in the form of streak gonads (which are infertile). People may identify as male, female, some other gender or none. General physical appearance is usually commonplace male or female. People with ovotestes may be fertile, but can often have fertility issues. Gonads in this configuration were previously removed as a matter of course (removing all possibility of reproduction) due to the risk of cancer. However, this is not always the case presently. If they are removed, hormones are required at puberty to promote development and to protect bone mineral density.

GONADAL DYSGENESIS

Here the gonads have not developed, either at all (complete) or somewhat (partial). In Turner syndrome the formation of infertile streak gonads is complete gonadal dysgenesis. A number of other conditions beyond the scope of this book may also cause total or partial gonadal dysgenesis.

GENDER ATYPICAL APPEARANCES

CRYPTORCHIDISM

This is the absence of one or both testes from the scrotum. The testes may be undescended and be found elsewhere in the region; or they may be underdeveloped or absent.

HIRSUTISM

This is not truly an intersex or DSD condition, but is included as it may also involve issues pertaining to gender and may be associated with some intersex or DSD conditions. People with hirsutism who identify as female have unusual amounts of body and facial hair growth. This is measured with the Ferriman-Gallwey score which considers both amount and location of hair. It may be caused by hormonal deregulation, or as a result of polycystic ovarian syndrome (PCOS). It is usually addressed by attending to the underlying cause and then removing the hair through standard means of depilation such as shaving, electrolysis or laser treatment. It is important to remember that many cisgender women without intersex/DSD conditions are more hirsute than is commonly believed due to Western cultural tendencies to remove bodily and facial hair. Indeed professionals are well served to consider the cultural aspects of many apparently 'physical' complaints.

GYNAECOMASTIA

People with gynaecomastia who identify as male have developed breast tissue (mammary glands). This may be a side effect of some drugs (including psychiatric drugs)[3]; a metabolic disorder in older people; or an aspect of adolescence where it may disappear after some time (and often involves that person being bullied). Some trans women mourn the loss of this breast tissue in adulthood (see Chapter 2). In the first few years of development gynaecomastia may be addressed endocrinologically, however, after this time surgery would be required for removal of the breast tissue. Professionals should reassure men with mild gynaecomastia that there is a great deal of variation in male chests; often the only chests many men see are those in fitness magazines and in other media which may give unrealistic notions of what is typical.

COMMON CONCERNS

Broadly speaking the reasons why a person with a DSD, or an intersex person, may approach a counsellor, psychologist or other health professional fall into four groups:

- Those for whom this is completely incidental to the reason that they are seeking help or support.
- Those who would like some assistance with their, or their child's, physiology.
- Those who have found out that they have a DSD or intersex condition and have concerns about this.
- Those who are concerned about others' reactions to their DSD or intersex condition.

Those people who fall into the first group may well not mention their intersex/DSD condition and it may well not be apparent. If you are aware that someone has an intersex/DSD condition then, as with trans (see Chapter 2), it is important not to over-emphasise it. It may be pertinent, but in the majority of cases it will not be and should not overshadow your understanding of the rest of the client's world.

---

[3] There is also some suggestion that it may be caused by excess beer consumption.

INTIMATE RELATIONSHIPS

People who are aware that they have an intersex/DSD condition may be concerned about the reaction of others to this (see below). They may feel uncomfortable disclosing this information and so it should be treated sensitively, but in a matter-of-fact manner (as with much else in this book). Other (non-intersex/DSD) people's concerns are often to do with the gender dichotomy: is the intersex person/person with a DSD a 'real' man or a 'real' woman? There may also be concerns about their own identity: what does it mean to be in a relationship with someone with an intersex/DSD condition? Does it mean they are gay? etc. Often education about the physical realities, coupled with information about the primacy of identity over genotype, phenotype, etc. can be extremely useful for everyone involved (see also Chapter 5).

PAUSE FOR CONSIDERATION

Consider your own notions of what makes a 'real' man or a woman. What physiology would they need to have? How might this influence your work with an intersex person/person with a DSD.

Intersex people and people with a DSD may, of course, have any of the sexualities detailed in this book and beyond. There may need to be some open communication if partners are unfamiliar with the physiology of the person. In these cases, as with many matters pertaining to sex, frank and open communication (perhaps with the assistance of a skilled professional) can be invaluable. Some deconstruction of what 'normal' sex 'must' consist of can be very useful as sexual pleasure and intimacy can be gained in a myriad of ways (see Chapters 6, 7 and 10).

People may have reproductive difficulties – indeed this may be the reason the condition became known. Reassurance should often be given that gender role is separate from reproduction for many people (for example women who have had a hysterectomy) as this is a concern of many people. There are many reproductive technologies which may be employed, as with anybody, and similarly adoption and fostering may be options.

PARENTS

Parents may be particularly concerned if they have an intersex child or a child with a DSD. It can be useful to decouple health concerns from those of 'normality', and to educate parents about the diversity of human forms. Further, education about the fact that intersex people may be very successful, with good jobs, families, etc. is often effective at allaying fears. Concerns about immediate genital appearance should be weighed against sexual function and reproductive capacity as an adult. It can be very hard for parents to conceive of their baby as a sexually active adult – but nonetheless that is what they will one day become and any decision taken in infancy will have lasting implications (see surgery below). It is important for parents to have access to a skilled multi-disciplinary team. Privacy (as opposed to secrecy) should be discussed as many people who were diagnosed with a DSD in childhood have said that it was particularly distressing to them not to be given information (despite having treatments) and to have to keep a secret which they felt to be shameful. Just as with any other medical matter or matter concerning genitalia certain people need to be told, without shame, at certain times.

PHYSICAL APPEARANCE

An issue which may concern intersex people and, perhaps especially, those who don't identify as intersex, but who nonetheless have a DSD, is that of physical appearance. This may include hirsutism and clitoromegaly in females; gynaecomastia and micropenis in males as well as various other conditions. In these cases two approaches are available: changing the person's body and addressing the person's psychology. Very often a combination of the two is the most effective approach. As stated above, education about the wide variations in appearance of the general population can be extremely useful as a primary concern of people is often that they are not 'normal'. Additionally, education about other identities, especially those that embrace intersex conditions as part of normal human diversity, can be useful.

Nonetheless some people understandably wish to conform somewhat to common understandings (if not realities) of what men and women look like. It is important that professionals, especially those of a more queer or radical approach, don't expect their clients to be 'poster children' for queering the gender dichotomy. Professionals who belong to minority groups who nonetheless wield significant power (some gay people in the academy or people with LGBT partners for example) should be especially careful not to assume that their experiences match those of others in potentially more difficult situations.

KEY PRACTICES

SURGERY

Some conditions, such as salt-wasting congenital adrenal hyperplasia require immediate medical assistance to prevent illness or death; whereas others, such as a mild hypospadia are usually of no medical consequence, with the men who have them accepting the natural variation of the human form. The necessity of surgery is clearly different.

In some cases surgery of an aesthetic, but not medically necessary, nature is carried out on infants before they have a chance to choose for themselves. This may result in loss of, or reduced, sexual function, reproductive capacity, and possibly incontinence. The surgeries are carried out because both professionals and parents are concerned about the difficulties for children growing up with ambiguous genitalia. These surgeries may include reduction of a large clitoris, removal of a clitoris/penis to form a vagina; and/or removal of gonads (ovaries, testes, ovotestes, etc.). Intersex/DSD activists have often stated that, while they recognise professionals and parents are acting out of a genuine intent to help the child, they would prefer to be given the choice when they grow up – and would like to retain sexual function and reproductive capacity – albeit with unusual genitalia. Nonetheless some professionals remain concerned for the well-being of such children, as well as that of their parents, and believe that surgery is the best option in some cases.

In all cases specialist counselling should be offered to the individuals concerned and a multidisciplinary team involved in any decisions. Professionals should always refer on if the presenting issue is outside of their skill set. This is also the case with adults considering interventions or discovering that they have a DSD. While 'allowing the client space' is sometimes useful, professionals should not hide behind this aphorism as an excuse for a lack of education, or inaction, as it may well slow the process of the client realising an identity and body which is comfortable for them.

For both parents of children, and adult individuals, access to support groups (face-to-face and via the internet) may prove useful. Many of these are specific to the person's condition or diagnosis and may be a useful source of further information and support. As always information from the internet (and indeed other sources[4]) should be checked as bias is often presented as fact.

---

[4] Including (of course) this book.

WIDER SOCIETY

In many areas throughout history people with atypical physiology were treated with some reverence and sometimes as part of a religious system (Herdt, 1996). In some of these cases, as with trans people, it may have been more that it was acceptable for someone else's children rather than one's own – something like many middle class liberal parents' attitudes towards being gay in contemporary Western cultures. This is still the case today in many cultures, although there is also a sense of shame and secrecy (as well as fascination) associated with DSD. For this reason one of the most useful interventions professionals can employ is simply to be matter-of-fact and ensure confidentiality and privacy, while addressing problems with secrecy.

Few countries take account of intersex/DSD legally, instead requiring that people are either legally male or legally female. Of course this is fine for those people with a DSD who identify as male or female, however, it poses problems for some people who identify as intersex and outside of the gender dichotomy. This societal drive to ensure people are part of the gender dichotomy – either male or female – has also put pressure on professionals to select a gender for infants from two possible choices – and for that selection to be done immediately after, or even before, birth, with emphasis on genital surgeries as genitals are so culturally tied to perceived *masculinity* and *femininity* (being about to penetrate or be penetrated, see Chapter 10). In some instances this is simply not possible – leaving professionals and parents alike in difficult positions (see above).

GROUP NORMS

Many people who have a DSD do not identify as intersex and so do not have any group norms as such on the basis of their sex development. Indeed most would identify as cisgender men or women. Professionals should be careful not to endeavour to push 'consciousness raising' on people with DSD such that they 'recognise their intersex identity' as many people will simply wish to get on with their lives, pay the bills, do the shopping, etc.

In contrast some people do, as we have seen, identify as intersex, although – other than an expectation for reasonable languages, respect and appropriate medical care – there are few group norms as such. There is little commercial opportunity in the way there is with some parts of LG culture (see Chapter 9); and few community events (other than online) as there are in some parts of bisexual culture (see Chapter 8). There are a number of conferences available for people within the Western world and, increasingly face-to-face community events are being organised. In some non-Western cultures, intersex/DSD conditions have been integrated into local and national culture and religion – sometimes in a way which is functionally indistinct from what some Western cultures would recognise as transsexualism.

TRANS

As we have seen, intersex people and people with a DSD may identify as cisgender, trans, some form of other gender, no gender, or as intersex as a separate category. The revision to the American Psychiatric Association's *Diagnostic and Statistical Manual (DSM-V)* has 'with or without a DSD' as a specifier for gender dysphoria (see Chapter 2). Some intersex people or people with a DSD find this problematic as they feel that trans people have 'chosen' not to be the gender they were assigned at birth, whereas intersex/DSD has a biological aetiology. As trans is a stigmatised group and often falls lower in a sex/gender hierarchy than intersex (see Chapter 2), it is understandable that some intersex/DSD people would wish to disassociate themselves. However, this does not take into account the emerging evidence for a neurological basis for some trans identities (meaning it may be considered to be a neurological DSD) and also has the effect of dividing groups of people who may be able to profitably work together in many domains. Nonetheless intersex people and people with a DSD who understandably wish to go about their day-to-day business unencumbered (or less encumbered) by prejudice or the need for political activism, may wish to dissociate themselves from trans, and clinicians should generally be respectful of this in order to establish rapport.

SUMMARY AND CONCLUSIONS

The following are good practice points for working with intersex people and people with a DSD who do not identify as intersex:

- Reflexively engage with one's own assumptions around sex development (and encourage all staff within a clinic or organisation to do the same).
- Recognise that intersex people are a different group from those who have a DSD but who do not so identify.
- Recognise that just because a person has a DSD it does not mean they are not a 'real' man or a 'real' woman as there are many and varied constituent factors to these which no one fully embodies.
- Carefully and respectfully investigate any presenting issues, if necessary with a multidisciplinary team and in a matter-of-fact manner, with the acceptance that in many cases someone's DSD status will be irrelevant or incidental.

- Familiarise yourself with the client's condition to a reasonable standard (see Introduction) and do not expect the client to educate you entirely.
- When dealing with someone not able to give consent on their own behalf (for example a child or someone with a learning disability) much thought should be given as to the long-term outcome of the decision.
- Recognise that there are many different cultural understandings of the conditions included in this chapter.

FURTHER READING

Cohen-Kettenis, P. & Pfafflin, F. (2003). *Transgenderism and intersexuality in childhood and adolescence: Making choices*. California: SAGE.

Harper, C. (2007). *Intersex*. Oxford: Berg.

Lee, P.A., Houk, C.P., Ahmed, S.F. & Hughes, I.A. (2006). Consensus statement on management of intersex disorders. *Pediatrics*, *118*(2), e488–e500.

Liao, L.M. & Roen, K. (forthcoming 2014). Intersex special issue. *Psychology & Sexuality*, *5*(1).

ADDITIONAL REFERENCES

Blackless, M., Charuvastra, A., Derryck, A., Fausto-Sterling, A., Lauzanne, K. & Lee, E. (2000). How sexually dimorphic are we? Review and synthesis. *American Journal of Human Biology*, *12*, 151–166.

Herdt, G. (1996). *Third sex third gender*. New York: Zone Books.

CISGENDER – LIVING IN THE GENDER ASSIGNED AT BIRTH

4

This chapter aims to:

- Consider cisgender as a distinct and diverse gender type in its own right.
- Explore the problems that can occur when adhering to normative gender roles too rigidly.
- Examine key practices around cisgender identities.
- Cover societal norms and expectations of cisgender men and women.
- Outline good practice for working with cisgender men and women.

INTRODUCTION

Cisgender is a term used for people who are content to remain in the gender that they were assigned at birth. It may be an unfamiliar term because, of course, it is generally assumed that people will remain in this gender, and it is generally only remarkable when people do not (as in the case of trans and genderqueer people, see Chapters 2 and 5; or when a person sometimes deviates from conventional gender roles, as with some who wear the clothing not generally associated with people of their birth-assigned gender, see Chapter 11). However, it is important to recognise that, as it is possible to change gender, not doing so is consequently a choice – albeit not always an explicit one. The term *cisgender* is used in recognition of this.

For similar reasons the phrase *assigned gender* is used to acknowledge that a baby is often *assigned* a male or female gender at birth or during a scan prior to birth ("it's a boy" or "it's a girl"). This is not a simple matter of observing sexual characteristics such as genitals but is rather a cultural practice (see also Chapters 2 and 3 for details of issues associated with assigning gender on the basis of such observations). In this chapter we use sex to refer to physical attributes associated with being male or female, and gender to refer to psychological and social attributes. However, there are issues with such a simplistic distinction, given that all human behaviours are complexly biopsychosocial. This is covered in greater detail in Chapters 2 and 3. Of note here is that overly simple, particularly neurological, explanations (such as 'left brain/right brain' and 'male brain/female brain') of gender difference are insufficient, and often plain wrong (Fine, 2010) due to the complex interplay of society, psychology and biology, and the neuroplastic nature of the brain.

The, erroneous, idea that there are *only* two sexes – and two genders associated with them – of male and female is called the *gender dichotomy*. This suggests that there are two groups of humanity, men and women, and that they are *dichotomous* in that there is no crossover between them (see Chapter 5). It is of course currently most common for people to fall into one of two rather broad groups (namely men or women) but there is wide diversity within them, as we shall see, and it is increasingly common for people not to fall within these two groups (see Chapter 5).

Within the two broad groups, a *cisgender woman* is someone who has been assigned female at birth as visual inspection has indicated that she has a vagina, and who grows up identifying as a woman and develops secondary sexual characteristics at puberty such as breasts, wider hips, etc., and who conforms to social ideas of femininity. Similarly, a *cisgender man* is someone who has been assigned male at birth as visual inspection has indicated that he has a penis, and who grows up identifying as a man and develops secondary sexual characteristics at puberty such as facial and body hair, a deeper voice, etc., and who conforms to social ideas of masculinity.

Because both sex and gender are assigned at birth, cisgender people will necessarily not have chosen their gender, but will rather have had it assigned to them prior to their earliest memories. This means that cisgender people may well have had more limited opportunity to reflect upon gendered characteristics than people who embrace a gender different from the one that they were assigned at birth. This can lead cisgender people to consider their gendered behaviours to be 'normal' or 'natural' as they are all that they have known. However, many such behaviours are actually culturally determined and shift according to time, place, etc. Examples include women wearing trousers, saris, skirts, or burkhas, or men wearing salwar kameez, suits, kilts, or boubou; and whether women are considered appropriate to vote and to play football, as well as whether men are considered appropriate to look after their children and be involved in caring professions.

Research over the last few decades strongly suggests that the main difficulties explicitly associated with being cisgender occur when people attempt to stick very rigidly to the cultural stereotypes of masculinity and femininity to which they are exposed. For example, in Western culture, 'masculine' men often struggle to express emotions and 'feminine' women are often anxious about their appearance and struggle to tune into their own desires and needs because they are so bound up in their relationships with partners and/or children.[1] Difficulties may also occur when social norms shift and people find that the ways of expressing gender which they are familiar with are called into question or do not fit as well as they previously did.

In the rest of this chapter we provide an overview of the common concerns that cisgender people present to practitioners, consider the key practices associated with cisgender masculinity and femininity, and explore the wider societal perspectives and group norms related to being cisgender. Many of the themes relating to men specifically, and to women specifically, will also be relevant to trans and intersex/DSD people who identify as such. It may be useful, therefore, to consider the issues raised in this chapter as well as the chapter specific to that topic. These groups are also susceptible to the issues associated with cultural pressures on gender (although they *may* have considered these more than cisgender people).

It may be useful to read this chapter alongside Chapter 10 on heterosexuality because many of the gender norms we refer to are intertwined with norms of heterosexuality (for example, ways of demonstrating masculinity or femininity in order to attract a person of the 'opposite' sex). However, it must also be remembered that many bisexual, lesbian and gay people are also cisgender. Gender roles may sometimes differ across sexualities (see Chapters 8 and 9) but rigid expectations may still apply and be problematic for some.

COMMON CONCERNS

Broadly speaking there are four categories of cisgender people who will present to a counsellor, psychologist or other health professional:

- Those for whom their gender identity is incidental to other issues they are dealing with.
- Those who are questioning their cisgender status in some way while remaining in it for the moment (see Chapters 2 and 5 for more about this).
- Those who have a cisgender identity but who question whether they are adequately cisgender in some way, for example wanting to make sure that they are 'normal'.
- Those who do not question their cisgender status at all, but for whom rigidly adhering to societal gender roles is linked to the problems that they are experiencing (for example, an older man whose depression is linked to loss of status on retiring or becoming ill, or a young woman whose body image issues are related to societal ideals of female attractiveness).

---

[1] We have scarequoted these terms to indicate that masculine and feminine need not necessarily mean these things.

If the concerns are incidental it is, of course, important to concentrate on the presenting issue while still holding the notion that there *may* be a cisgender related issue. For many professionals the risk with cisgender, heterosexuality and monogamy, unlike some other identities and practices in this book, is in the assumption that here is no problem where in fact there may be one. Nonetheless, the remainder of this chapter focuses on the latter two groups of people listed above whose presenting concerns can be linked, in some way, to their gender roles, and their expectations about what these involve.

'NORMALITY'

When clients have some worry about whether or not they are 'normal', it is useful to explore what they mean by 'normal' and why it is important to them – this may involve working with them to loosen their attachment to the approval and validation of others, while recognising that such an attachment is common and understandable. It may also be useful to assist them in expanding their understandings of what can be included under 'normality' when it comes to gender, perhaps by pointing to the variety of possible gender roles that are available and exploring which feel most comfortable to them. Such an approach may also involve challenging simple distinctions between cisgender and trans by explaining that most people's gender roles change over the course of their lifetime (see Chapter 5). For example, in some cultures a baby may express masculinity by wearing powder-blue clothes, a toddler by engaging in rough-and-tumble play, an adolescent by seeking sex, a young man by working out in the gym, a middle-aged man by getting involved in home improvement, and a retired person by joining a bowling team.

Several mental and physical health problems are linked to rigid adherence to gender roles. For example, cisgender women are more frequently diagnosed with anxiety and depression than cisgender men and express their distress in different ways, with control over eating and self-harming being particularly prevalent. Middle-aged upper/middle class mothers are at high risk of depression related to the loss of their gendered role as caregiver when children leave home. The 'superwoman ideal' to be career woman *and* wife, maternal nurturer *and* sex goddess can be problematic, with some women retreating to the arena of food and body as one thing that they can control in a world of contradictory messages. Young women are particularly under heavy pressures to be 'attractive' through achieving and maintaining a narrow ideal of feminine beauty. This has been linked to the common experience of 'eating disorders' in this group, with percentages of people in the Western world experiencing anorexia at some point in life around 0.9 for women and 0.3 for men, and bulimia 1.5 and 0.5.

Cisgender men's expression of emotions differs due to strong cultural messages that 'real men' show no fear or pain and are rational rather than emotional. Thus, they are more likely to express distress through alcoholism and drug addiction and more commonly receive diagnoses relating to aggression and anti-social behaviour. Therefore they are often criminalised rather than pathologised and so seen as 'bad' as opposed to 'mad'. This relates to a general tendency for men to be given autonomy that women are not. Women are often disempowered and placed in a victim role, while there are pressures of responsibility on men which means that they may be considered culpable for actions which are equally rooted in distress. There have been calls to address the 'crisis of masculinity' whereby stereotypes of strong, hard men persist despite the decrease in traditional male jobs and roles in the Western world. This has also been linked to high rates of suicide among men with 75% of all suicides in the UK involving men for example.

Those men who are diagnosed with a mental health problem may feel unable to meet stereotyped standards of cisgender masculinity, and may therefore suffer additionally due to this, for example, a young man diagnosed with schizophrenia may feel that the option of a prestigious job is now foreclosed to him, which may affect his sense of himself as a man, and lead to additional distress. In some cases it may literally not be the case that he cannot ever get a prestigious job, but, even if so, wider notions of masculinity can usefully be explored (see below).

PAUSE FOR CONSIDERATION

Write down in two columns what it means to be feminine and what it means to be masculine in mainstream culture (covering all aspects, including behaviour, roles, emotions and appearance – for example 'boys don't cry' and 'good girls don't get angry'). Consider whether anyone you know fits only in one column and how trying to fit in one column only might limit a person.

KEY PRACTICES

One of the key practices of cisgender people is the avoidance of practices associated with people not of their gender. For example, in the West cisgender women will often endeavour to remove body hair, especially facial hair, as this is considered to be masculine, although facial hirsutism of varying degrees is relatively common in women and leg hair is universal. Similarly, cisgender men will often endeavour to avoid very overt displays of emotion outside of certain culturally accepted domains, such as sporting events, as this is considered to be feminine, although again men have a capacity to express emotion in a wide variety of arenas. There are some suggestions that this may be changing in recent years in some specific cultural groups (see Group Norms).

HISTORY

It is important to acknowledge the impact of the history of the treatment of men and women. In most cultures, women have been treated as inferior to men for centuries. In the past, this has impacted upon practitioner views which have held that healthy adults and healthy men are similar, whereas healthy women are quite different, being less independent, aggressive, competitive and persuadable; and more submissive, emotional and conceited about their appearance. This suggests that men are considered the standard of normal humanity against which women and others are compared. This is reinforced by conventions such as presenting data from men first in graphs and tables (Hegarty, Lemieux & McQueen, 2010) or the fact that the common toilet door symbol for a man is the same as the symbol for a person in general (e.g. on warning signs) whereas the symbol for a woman differs. The idea that men are 'normal humans' can lead to a double-bind for women in health services because demonstrating healthy humanity and healthy femininity can still be paradoxical.

The key practices available to cisgender men and women may be constrained by some disabilities which limit their capacity to perform practices which are commonly understood as being vital to the performance of masculinity or femininity. For example, a physically disabled man may struggle to play some sports or to be physically strong and women with some disabilities may not be deemed to be conventionally attractive. A vital issue here is the tension between questioning with clients whether it is necessary for them to be physically strong (if male) or conventionally attractive (if female) and the obvious fact that many disabled men (paralympians for example) are clearly phenomenally strong, and many women with disabilities are beautiful by mainstream standards (a number of models for example). A key issue here is in disentangling cultural norms and learned behaviours (which may or may not serve the person) from personally authentic ways of being

ROMANTIC RELATIONSHIPS

Additionally, there has been a tendency in certain contexts more recently for men to be regarded as incompetent, and for women to be required to 'manage' families including the adult men within them. Common examples of this can be seen in advertisements and sitcoms like *The Simpsons,* and may play out, for example, in problematic dynamics between people in heterosexual couples where the female partner becomes positioned as a 'nag' and the male partner as a 'useless man' – something partners may both collude in and find restrictive and distressing. Other examples of problematic heterosexual cisgender relationship dynamics which can be associated with distress include the female partner being viewed as the 'emotional one', and the male partner as the 'rational one', which can exacerbate experiences such as depression and a sense of disempowerment for the woman; and exasperation, frustration and/or an excessive sense of responsibility for the man.

Abusive dynamics can occur in situations of gender rigidity as well, including female victims feeling too dependent on abusive partners to leave, and cisgender men finding it difficult to tell people that they have been abused due to victim identities not fitting with common notions of masculinity.

Of course, relationships between cisgender people of the same gender are not exempt from gender related difficulties, although they may play out differently in these contexts (see Chapters 8 and 9). People may still have conventional ideas about how men and women should behave, both sexually and non-sexually, and/or more specific ones about the gender identities that LGB men and women should embody in relationships.

SEX

Sexual practices are also very gendered, with (shifting) cultural rules about how men and women should experience and express their sexuality. In the past, and still in some cultural contexts, women have simply not been viewed as sexual beings and there is still a legacy of this in the assumption that men will always want sex and be able to 'perform' sexually, while women will not, or will be more focused on love and romance. Again, this can be problematic for cisgender men and women for whom this is not the case.

Related to this is the double standard of sexuality, whereby men who are sexual, including with many partners, are viewed positively (e.g. as a 'stud' or 'real man') while women who behave similarly are often regarded negatively. More recently there has been a shift to expecting women to be more sexual, but the dividing line between being 'frigid' or 'tight' and being a 'slag' or 'slut' is a difficult one to negotiate, and varies according to class, culture, age and other contexts.

Chapter 10 on heterosexuality describes in more detail some of the problems that can be experienced when heterosexual cisgender people have narrow understandings of how they should feel and behave sexually. Any problems that are experienced can be exacerbated by a sense that one is not a 'real man' or 'real woman' if they are unable to perform sexually in ways that are expected for their gender. For those who identify with, or practice, BDSM (see Chapter 6) there can also be different implications for dominant women and submissive men (going against common gender roles) than there are for submissive women and dominant men (in line with common gender roles). This latter group may need to be especially aware of problematically reproducing gendered power dynamics within this context (Barker & Gill, 2012).

As with relationships, cisgender LGB people may feel somewhat less rigidly defined by their gender identities in relation to their sexual practices, given the sometimes greater flexibility in gender roles in these groups. However, potential issues remain, for example in preferences for 'straight acting', or masculine men in some gay scenes, or lesbians and bisexual women having difficulty negotiating sex with other women if both people involved find it difficult to initiate due to social scripts of femininity (see Chapters 8 and 9).

BODY IMAGE

As much of popular culture represents cisgender people, cisgender people may be considered to be particularly subject to the messages it contains. Increasingly, advertisements, TV, movies, etc. represent an idealised body type which may originally have been surgically 'enhanced' and which is often digitally 'enhanced' post-production. This can lead to cisgender people having unrealistic expectations about their own bodies and how these should fit into the uncommon, and often impossible, 'norms' presented to them (see Chapter 2 for similar issues with regard to trans people).

Historically, women in particular have been judged on the basis of how they look (and men on the basis of what they do), and consequently many cisgender women feel that they need to address how they look in order to be 'normal' and 'proper women'. They may do this, of course, through cosmetics and clothes, but also increasingly through medical means such as Botox, face-lifts, tummy-tucks, liposuction, breast enlargements, etc. Similarly, in more recent years, men have been subject to societal pressures to conform to bodily norms which are sometimes unrealistic and there is increasing pressure on them to address this through clothing, exercise, etc. Additionally, medical interventions such as pectoral implants, liposuction, etc. may be undertaken.

One area in which cisgender men and women may have particular concern is that of their genitals. This is often exacerbated by myths surrounding what normal genitals look like and the use of pornography as a source of information in this regard. Women are increasingly encouraged to have small, 'neat', symmetrical labia when, in fact, there is a massive diversity in vulval appearance.[2] Similarly, men may have unrealistic expectations about what a 'normal' sized penis is (an average non-erect penis being between 2–4 inches (5–10cm) long,[3] and often appearing shorter if the man carries weight around his midriff).

An important recent shift to be aware of in the area of female body image is the common idea that attending to one's appearance is a fun, individually empowering, or pampering activity, where previously it was done more explicitly to make oneself attractive to others (Gill, 2006). This can make it more difficult to challenge even when it is something which is clearly linked to experiences of distress. Relatedly for men, exercise which was previously linked to fitness, health and mastery, has become, in some cases, something which should be undertaken in order to be seen as attractive. For some groups of men (e.g. some younger gay men or *metrosexual* straight men) the body ideal has become much slimmer in recent years. Some groups of women, such as lesbians or those in BDSM or goth scenes, may have more variety in the beauty ideals available to them, although it shouldn't be assumed that this will inevitably be the case.

WIDER SOCIETY

Cisgender is the predominant, and most socially accepted, gender form within wider society. Indeed it is codified within legal frameworks and is assumed within many medical and psychological models (see Chapter 3). Within many countries it is impossible to have a legal status other than male or female and it is not deemed possible to move between these (see Chapter 2). Common identification often reflects a person's birth-assigned gender and so will only reflect a cisgender adult's gender. This expectation that all adults within wider society will be cisgender is also reflected in the lack of a common pronoun which is not gendered in many languages and similarly the lack of non-gendered toilets (see Chapter 5) except, for problematic reasons, in the case of accessible toilets.

Medicolegally, at least, cisgender people are often in a rather more fortunate position than many other groups as their status is easily and universally recognised. However, wider societal expectations of the way in which they present their gender to the world, and indeed to themselves, is subject to a great deal of pressure as we have seen. This gendered performance

---

[2] See www.greatwallofvagina.co.uk/jamie-mccartney and http://thecentrefoldproject.org/

[3] See www.drpetra.co.uk/blog/penis-size-worries/

often feels entirely congruent to the cisgender individual as they have learnt its intricacies from birth and repeated them time and time again gaining praise for acceptable performances and opprobrium for unacceptable ones (of course what are considered acceptable performances shifts over time).

SOCIETAL ROLE IN GENDER

This reinforcing of societal gender norms and understandings can be seen in the way adults interact with babies who are too young to respond in markedly gendered ways. The famous 'baby X' studies found that people presented with the same baby wearing either pink or blue clothing treated them very differently. The baby wearing blue was treated more roughly and seen as being angry if it was distressed, while the baby wearing pink was given dolls and perceived as fearful. This difference in behaviour by adult caregivers can lead to very different developmental trajectories for the infant. This is not to say that biology does not play a role in gender differentiation, but it does draw attention to the complex biopsychosocial processes involved (Fine, 2010).

When people reach a stage at which they are less susceptible to their immediate caregivers' directions and opinions, they will nonetheless remain susceptible to wider societal messages from friends, teachers, co-workers, media, etc. and will have internalised many of these messages such that the wider societal messages may appear to be their own (un)considered opinions. This can lead practitioners to a difficult tension as they may feel that their client is unaware that they are reproducing a societal message regarding gender when their client presents a notion as their own. However, we should be extremely cautious about utilising our power as professionals to suggest that a client has a 'false consciousness' in this regard, as the notion may be indeed their own, albeit in line with wider societal norms (a woman may indeed simply prefer to wear pink) and we should strive to avoid the hubris which may lead us to erroneously assume that we ourselves are outside of the culture which we are most assuredly within.

Practitioners should also be cautious not to unthinkingly reproduce stereotypes of masculinity and femininity within their practice to avoid mistakenly pursuing a line of inquiry simply on the basis of someone's apparent gender. For example, assertive female clients may be misdiagnosed as having emotionally unstable personality disorder, borderline type, while their clinical presentation may not be considered within the pathological range for a male. While standardised ranges are often normalised in a dichotomously gendered fashion, caution should be exercised for the reasons outlined within this chapter (and to include outliers), and considered clinical judgement applied.

It is important for practitioners to remember that they, like clients, live in a world which is saturated with stereotypes of masculinity and femininity, and that they are therefore not immune from making implicit assumptions about gender, or to treating clients differently. As well as their exchanges with the clients themselves it is worth thinking carefully about the pictures on walls, materials available in waiting rooms, etc. with gender in mind, such that all images and materials do not reinforce certain limited understandings of gender.

GROUP NORMS

The gender dichotomy is often monitored by institutions as well as by friends, colleagues, etc. and crucially by the individual themselves. While many heterosexual cisgender people may suggest that their adherence to gender norms is for reasons associated with gaining the approval of the 'opposite gender', very often gender performance is scrutinised more closely by members of the *'same gender'*. For example, groups of male friends telling each other when they are being too emotional or 'feminine', or schoolgirls policing each other on appropriate dress, behaviour around boys, etc. Practitioners should consider their own gender status in relation to their clients and examine how this might impact on their work for that reason.

Here we list some of the overall group norms associated with femininity and masculinity in wider Western culture before exploring some of the diverse forms of masculinity and femininity which have opened up in recent years, in specific groups, which may offer alternatives to rigid ideas about what it means to be a cisgender man or woman.

GENERAL GROUP NORMS AROUND FEMININITY

These include being:

- Nurturing and caring for children.
- Good at social skills.
- Emotional.
- Comfortable expressing sadness and fear, but not anger.
- Bound up, in terms of their identities, with their roles in other people's lives (e.g. mother, wife, daughter, etc.).
- Passive – not initiating things or making big decisions.
- Concerned with their appearance.
- Concerned with being desired by others.

- Vulnerable and needing protection from harm.
- A victim of abuse/violence, but not a perpetrator.
- Cooperative and able to work well with others.
- Good at domestic chores, multi-tasking, etc.

GENERAL GROUP NORMS AROUND MASCULINITY

These include being:

- Competitive and ambitious.
- Independent and capable of making decisions.
- Rational and not easily overcome by emotion.
- A perpetrator of abuse/violence, but not a victim.
- Tough and able to look after themselves.
- Physically strong and good at performing.
- Always ready and keen to be sexual.
- Confident and assertive.
- Dominant and able to lead others.
- Strongly bound up, in terms of identity, with what they do (their career and/or leisure pursuits).
- Risk-taker.

It is worth bearing in mind, of course, that these norms shift over time. For example, prior to the 1920s young boys would commonly wear dresses rather than trousers, and the associations of the colours of pink and blue were reversed with pink being deemed a "more decided colour" appropriate for boys to wear. Similarly, rigid ideas about men being tough and unemotional, and women being hysterical and delicate, were challenged historically during the First and Second World Wars when many decorated soldiers experienced shell shock, and when women had to become involved in hard labour.

When engaging with cisgender clients, it can be useful to consider the reality of some of the assumptions listed above because, as we have seen, they may change over time. Further, bringing into awareness the problems associated with these apparently unassailable 'truths' may be useful in addressing issues related to cisgender as even false assumptions may adversely affect people because they feel they must adhere to them in order to be 'normal'.

In addition to questioning the veracity of such common assumptions, it can be useful to explore, with clients, the diversity of possibilities that currently exist within masculinity and femininity. In recent years these have opened up in many ways. For example, with a cisgender man, it might be worth exploring the different possible kinds of masculinity that are currently available to him, which differ in various ways from the 'dominant' or 'traditional' form (the list above). For example, you might consider together the archetype of the macho hero (from action movies and the like), compared to the kind of masculinity of the computer geek (as embodied in successful men like Bill Gates or Mark Zuckerberg), or the metrosexual man (concerned about his appearance and comfortable being close to other men), the everyday bloke (embodied by the lead characters in bromance movies, see Chapter 10), etc. You could consider fictional characters or celebrities who embody different forms of masculinity, perhaps in a TV programme or set of books or films which are particularly familiar to them.

It is vital to be aware of the way in which cisgender identities intersect with all other aspects of identity such as race, culture, sexuality, age, class, geographical location, disability, etc. For these kinds of explorations, sensitivity should be shown to the client's wider context. For example, it would be better to consider the ways of embodying femininity which are present within a lesbian client's community rather than bringing in heterosexual examples, or exploring what media an Asian client is keen on, rather than assuming that this will necessarily be either only Western, or only Asian, movies.

SUMMARY AND CONCLUSIONS

The following are good practice points when working with cisgender clients:

- Reflexively engage with your own assumptions about gender (and encourage all staff within a clinic or organisation to do the same).
- Be careful not to assume that all clients are cisgender even if they appear so to you.
- Be aware of cultural norms around gender, and recognise the variety of possibilities within cisgender, rather than perpetuating a fixed notion of what cisgender people should be like.
- Be aware of intersections, acknowledging the differences in how gender is experienced across race, culture, class, age, generation, body type, etc. (das Nair & Butler, 2012).
- Encourage client awareness about the expectations and assumptions that they have, and where these come from.
- Ensure that images and materials presented in your workplace do not reinforce limited and rigid norms of gender.

Cisgender, of all the topics covered in this book, is perhaps the most unconsidered way of being, and so great care should be exercised in exploring clients' notions of their gender if rapport is to be maintained. However, because it is unconsidered, much important work may be done in opening up notions of masculinity and femininity.

It may well be helpful to normalise the diversity of ways of being masculine or feminine that are possible with clients, for example by describing different options that people choose appropriately to their context (for those who wish to remain cisgender). This will address the common fear that most cisgender clients will have that they may not be 'normal'. It is important both to broaden out all the possibilities that exist within 'normal' as well as exploring why being 'normal' is valued so highly.

FURTHER READING

Fine, C. (2010). *Delusions of gender: The real science behind sex differences.* London: Icon Books.
Gill, R. (2006). *Gender and the media.* London: Polity Press.
Vincent, N. (2006). *Self-made man.* London: Atlantic Books.

ADDITIONAL REFERENCES

Barker, M. & Gill, R. (2012). Sexual subjectification and Bitchy Jones's Diary. *Psychology & Sexuality, 3*(1), 26–40.
das Nair, R. & Butler, C. (2012). *Intersectionality, sexuality and psychological therapies: Working with lesbian, gay and bisexual diversity.* Hoboken, NJ: Wiley-Blackwell.
Hegarty, P., Lemieux, A. & McQueen, G. (2010). Graphing the order of the sexes: Constructing, recalling, interpreting, and putting the self in gender difference graphs. *Journal of Personality and Social Psychology, 98*(3), 375–391.

FURTHER GENDERS

This chapter aims to:

- Consider the common concerns of those who identify as non, bi-, fluidly or multiply gendered, or otherwise outside of the gender dichotomy of male and female, and who approach counsellors, psychologists and health professionals.
- Provide an overview of common experiences and understandings of these groups.
- Explore wider cultural perceptions, legal and medical perspectives about gender in relation to these groups and the cultural context of dichotomous gender.
- Outline good practice for working with individuals from these groups as clients.

INTRODUCTION

As mentioned in each of the previous three chapters, gender is overwhelmingly regarded as dichotomous: people are viewed as being either men or women, and these categories are seen as mutually exclusive (see Chapter 4). This chapter focuses on those who do not fit within this understanding of gender in various ways. Of course, people who move across the gender dichotomy (permanently or temporarily) may also regard themselves as trans and there will therefore be a good deal of crossover with Chapters 2 and 11.

As covered in Chapter 4, cisgender people are assigned either male or female at birth and then remain in that gender, thus staying within the gender dichotomy. The majority of trans people transition across the gender dichotomy, from male to female, or female to male (see Chapter 2).[1] Also the majority of people who cross-dress spend time in the appearance of, or identifying as, the 'other gender' within the gender dichotomy (see Chapter 11). This chapter covers all other experiences and expressions beyond this. However, it should be noted that there are significant minorities of trans people (mentioned in Chapters 2 and 11) who also do not fit within the gender dichotomy in terms of their understandings and experiences. Those people might perhaps be more properly considered within this chapter, and their inclusion in Chapters 2 and 11 is a necessary artefact of the somewhat arbitrary process of dividing a book such as this into

---

[1] Although even that may be regarded by some uninformed people as challenging of the gender dichotomy.

chapters. The wider category of SGD (sex and gender diverse people) may be a useful term for covering all of the people considered in this chapter.

Some of those we are covering in this chapter also identify as *trans/transgender* and/or *intersex/DSD*, while others do not. It is also important to draw a clear distinction between gender identity and sexual identity here. People who identify with further genders – as with trans, cisgender and intersex people – may be of any of the sexualities/sexual identities covered in the remainder of the book.

IDENTITIES

Many different categories have emerged for those who experience themselves as outwith the gender dichotomy, and new terms and ideas are constantly emerging. Here we cover the main understandings that are currently available, which include people who have elements of 'both' genders; those who have no gender; those who move between genders fluidly; those who are of a specific additional gender; those who are multiply gendered; and those who challenge or trouble the gender dichotomy in more deliberate and/or political ways. The list below includes some of the main terms embraced by people within each of these groups.

- Incorporating aspects of both man and woman: *Mixed gender*, sometimes *pangender, androgynous*.
- Having no gender: *Gender neutral, non-gendered, genderless, agender, neuter, neutrois*.
- Moving between genders: *Bigender, gender fluid*, sometimes *pangender*.
- Being of a specific additional gender (either between man and woman or otherwise additional to those genders): *Third gender, other gender*, sometimes *pangender* (includes both those who have a name for their gender and those who do not).
- Moving between multiple genders: *Trigender*, sometimes *pangender*.
- Disrupting the gender dichotomy: Genderqueer, genderfuck.

As we can see, some of these categories maintain an understanding of dichotomous gender but include the idea that people may incorporate aspects of both male and female, or move between them. Other categories add the possibility of not belonging to either of the dichotomous genders (or any other gender), such as being gender neutral or non-gendered. Some people add on a further gender category, and some transgress or transcend the gender dichotomy more radically.

QUEER

The latter category of genderqueer has roots within both queer politics and the academic area of queer theory. It is not properly understood as an identity, because the agenda of queer is about moving away from identity terms. The term queer generally refers to people who want to get beyond fixed categories of sexual identity; for example, the dichotomy of straight and gay (see Chapter 8). The term genderqueer refers to those who want to get away from fixed sex and/or gender categories such as male/female, man/woman, masculine/feminine, etc.

Many, but not all, people embrace queer and genderqueer simultaneously because they challenge the whole idea of interlinked gender and sexual identity: that we are defined by being a man or a woman and by being attracted to other men or women. It is important to note that queer is a term which has been reclaimed by certain people. It has previously been used as a term of abuse, and indeed still is in some contexts, and consequently should only be used by practitioners when a client uses it themselves. This necessity to use the language of the client holds true for the other terms provided above, but is particularly important in relation to queer given its history as an offensive word.

The remainder of this chapter explores common concerns, key practices, wider societal perspectives and group norms as they pertain to the groups listed above, teasing out specific issues that may differ (e.g. between a non-gendered, bigendered, or genderqueer person) where relevant.

COMMON CONCERNS

As with many of the other identities and practices considered in this book which fall outside mainstream understandings, broadly speaking there are three categories of people who identify with one of the further gender categories who will present to a counsellor, psychologist or other health professional:

- Those for whom this is completely incidental to the reason that they are seeking help or support.
- Those who are experiencing problems related to other people's perceptions of their gender.
- Those who have some concern about their gender which they would like help with.

Again, as with most other groups, it is likely that the majority of clients will fall into the first category and therefore it would be inappropriate for the practitioner to focus on their gender as it is not relevant to the presenting issue. It may be particularly tempting in the case of genders beyond the dichotomy to assume that it is relevant, especially for those who have been trained in approaches which assume gender to be dichotomous. Hence this area is one in which it is particularly important to have reflexively considered one's own understandings around gender in order to be open to experiences which differ from these.

Given that gender tends to be more explicitly visible than other aspects of identity (e.g. sexuality, relationships), practitioners whose clients fall into this first category may need to have explicit conversations about gender in order to use correct terminology, in a way that they would not about other aspects of identity which were irrelevant to the presenting concern. For example, the client may use unfamiliar terminology in an application form or other document, or the name/pronoun used may not fit the practitioner's attribution of gender when meeting the person.

PAUSE FOR CONSIDERATION

How would you currently respond if faced with a client whose gender you struggled to identify? What would your reaction be if they used one of the terms listed in the first section of this chapter?

ASK ETIQUETTE

In such cases the appropriate way of dealing with the situation is what is called *ask etiquette*. In other words, the best thing to do is simply to ask the client what terms they prefer to use for their gender, which pronouns they prefer, what name or names they would like to be called, and respect these wishes as far as possible. If you slip up and use the wrong word, it is best to simply apologise and move on, rather than either making more of it than is necessary, or avoiding mentioning it due to your own embarrassment or anxiety.

As with many of the other marginalised identities and practices in this book, it may be difficult to distinguish clients who fall into the second and third of the categories above. This is because there is so little social recognition of genders outside the gender dichotomy, and so much stigmatisation of them, that most people are likely to experience at least some problems related to other people's perceptions of them. It may therefore be hard to determine what distress is due to such treatment, and what is due to them having their own personal concerns about their gender.

SOCIAL OPPROBRIUM

When the client's presenting difficulties do seem to stem from social opprobrium, it is important to explore with them their understandings of this in a way which is respectful and supportive of their identity (this may be particularly important when working with people who have a learning disability, are on the autistic spectrum, etc.) As with other marginalised identities and practices, practitioner authority may sometimes appropriately be leveraged in order to support the identity, given the general lack of support the person is likely to be experiencing. However, as with all clients in marginalised groups it is worth both professional and client recognising the reality of the wider culture in which they live, and exploring the inevitable tension between freedom of expression and fitting in (e.g. in order to achieve other life goals and/or to avoid daily abuse).

CONCERNS ABOUT ONE'S OWN GENDER

In the third category of clients whose presenting issue relates to their own concerns around their gender there are two subgroups. For one group there may be an awareness of some – sometimes quite ephemeral – issue, but no realisation that it is possible to identify outside of the gender dichotomy. In this situation, the main task of the professional would be to raise awareness of the various possibilities available, and perhaps to point the way to appropriate information and support for further exploration (see Further Reading).

The other subgroup will be clear already on what their identity is, for example gender fluid, gender neutral, etc., and will be looking for help and support around this, for example, in coming out to friends, family or employers; in forming sexual/romantic relationships; or in modifying aspects of their appearance in line with their identity.

As with sexuality, cultural perceptions around gender have a major role which needs to be teased out here as social circumstances may make a person feel that they have to state that they are a gender which is personally uncomfortable for them. Some may try to fit within the gender dichotomy when actually they would be more comfortable outside it, and some may embrace an identity outside the gender dichotomy when actually they would be more comfortable within it, but in the 'other' gender. For example, a person may say that they are transsexual or cisgender when in fact neither of these terms is personally congruent but they are more understandable and/or safer to use with the other people in their lives in a way that, for example, being androgynous or genderfuck are not. Conversely, some people who state that they wish to have physiological interventions in order to make their body more congruent with a non-dichotomous gender may actually feel more comfortable in either a male or female role. They may feel constrained from transitioning into the role that they were not assigned at birth by social factors such as parental disapproval, etc. and thus be taking on a gender neutral or bigender identity, for example, as an alternative to this. It can be useful, when working with such clients, to discuss with them whether they would still wish to be non-traditionally gendered were such social factors to be removed. A useful question here is the "desert island question" – if you were stranded on a desert island with no hope of rescue, but a shipping container of various goods was stranded with you, in what manner would you live?

KEY PRACTICES

As with many other groups who are outside of mainstream culture, the internet has proved to be a useful forum for a sense of community, fun, support, etc. for those who are outside the gender dichotomy. However, it is important to remember that for many people who *do* conform to the gender dichotomy in everyday life, the internet has opened up a space to identify in multiple ways. For example, a great number of individuals have more than one online presence (including avatars, usernames, blogs, social network identities, etc.) which vary in gender, have no gender, etc. The internet appears to offer people who have one gender role in 'real life'[2] the opportunity to comfortably express other, or multiple, aspects of themselves in a virtual environment (this is also the case with regard to sexual identities where people may have multiple and/or varying online sexual encounters or interests).

LANGUAGE AND PRONOUNS

Along with the diversity of ways of experiencing gender listed in the intro-duction, and the terminology that is currently emerging to provide names for these experiences, pronouns have also developed for those who do not fit within dichotomous genders (him/her, he/she, etc.) Here we will focus on Anglophone countries. However, it is important to be mindful of the language of the client here as some languages are even more gendered than English (for example, those which dichotomously gender all nouns), and some already have acceptable non-gendered pronouns (for example, the Swedish 'hen'). Within English it is notable that certain offices have allowed non-gendered pronouns for some time with little difficulty, for example, 'Dr', 'Professor', 'Reverend', etc.

---

[2] This is a common term used to refer to non-virtual environments and is not intended to imply that communication via the internet is any way less 'real' than face-to-face, verbal or 'snailmail', etc. communication. Another, less common, term would be *offline*.

Various pronoun possibilities have developed which clients may want to employ, and ask others to employ, instead of the gendered terms he/him/his/himself or she/her/hers/herself. One possibility, which is grammatically correct (although some do not like the use of the plural) is to use the existing English terms they/their/them/themself. Other popular versions which have been explicitly developed as non-gendered pronouns are Zie/zim/zirs/zirself, Sie/hir/hir/hirself and Per/per/pers/perself.[3]

In addition to pronouns, clients may want to think about how they relate to titles such as Mr/Mrs/Miss/Ms and Sir/Madam, and descriptions such as man/woman, lady/gentleman, girl/boy, guys/gals, etc. For example, words like boi or grrrl may be used as alternatives that capture a less dichotomous sense of gender. People may also decide to change their name to something unisex, to use initials only, or to adopt another word which has meaning for them. They may decide to employ a dual name, to use different names on different occasions, or to change names over time. In all of these considerations it is worth being mindful of the tension between people finding words which suit them well, and also ones which are recognised enough that others will understand them.

APPEARANCE

People outside the gender dichotomy may or may not present in gender dichotomous ways in terms of their appearance. Some may be comfortable simply with gender appropriate names and terminologies, while others may adopt clothing, bodily appearance, voice, and other aspects of presentation congruent with their sense of gender identity.

Examples of this include some non-gendered or gender-neutral people deleting any social cues of masculinity or femininity, for example by wearing unisex clothing, binding breasts if they have them or seeking their surgical removal, concealing or seeking the surgical removal of penises, shaving hair or having a unisex haircut, etc.

Mixed gender or androgynous people may seek to embody aspects of masculinity and femininity concurrently, and may include approximating or obtaining secondary sexual characteristics which they do not have without outside intervention. For example, some may take oestrogens in order to develop breasts and affect a more 'feminine' body contour while retaining the ability to grow facial hair. Others may choose to have their breasts surgically removed or bound while retaining other social signifiers of femininity. Bigender people may utilise some of these means of adjusting their presentation consecutively rather than concurrently. In all cases, clothing

---

[3] See http://forge-forward.org/wp-content/docs/gender-neutral-pronouns1.pdf

and other adornments, make-up, hairstyles, etc. may also be adopted accordingly. It is, of course, important for professionals and clients to consider how any permanent changes may affect the client's future self, especially if that older self will be in a different environment, for example in moving from a supportive college to a formal workplace.

With many pangender, gender fluid and genderqueer people the emphasis is on challenging or transcending the gender dichotomy altogether, rather than on embracing aspects of masculinity and femininity together or on different occasions. Of course because wider society is dichotomously gendered, this can be difficult, and so people may mix gender dichotomous and neutral signifiers in similar ways to those described above. There may also be more deliberate attempts to challenge other people's assumptions around gender in these groups, for example through some of the drag queen/king style performances mentioned in Chapter 11, or through using more than one name, etc. Some (femme) genderqueer people may adopt a deliberately hyperfeminine appearance to reveal how femininity is problematically constructed.

There may be different challenges for somebody who is commonly regarded as female or male in presenting in a genderqueer, neutral or androgynous way. For those commonly regarded as male, almost any 'feminine' presentation (e.g. a little make-up or item of 'female' clothing or jewellery) will lead to them being read as androgynous or feminine. For those commonly regarded as female, far more cues may be required. There may also be restrictions on who is seen as genderqueer, neutral, androgynous, etc. in terms of race and body shape, for example common images of androgynous people tend to be white and slim.

It is of note that cisgender people are also often fluid in their gender presentation, generally within certain socially circumscribed bounds. For example, a cisgender man might foreground his masculinity at a football match, he might be more stereotypically 'feminine' when playing with his two-year-old daughter (e.g. skipping[4]).

POLITICAL/ACADEMIC ENGAGEMENT

Given the lack of recognition of genders outside the gender dichotomy, people in these groups may engage in political activism in order to gain rights and recognition for their groups. Some may be drawn to the discipline of queer theory given that this is a respected academic arena which regards dichotomous genders as problematic and seeks to consider alternatives.

---

[4] Although, of course, were he skipping as part of boxing training it would then be masculine … these things are indeed exceedingly complex.

WIDER SOCIETY

Wider society is overwhelmingly gender dichotomous, with the generally held belief that there are two genders and that they are 'opposite' to
each other in various ways (e.g. men are tough, women are delicate;
men are rational, women are emotional, etc., see Chapter 4). This is
reflected legally and medically from the beginning where birth certificates
state that a person is male or female. It is also reflected in popular culture
in the fact that many magazines are specifically aimed at men or at
women, and in popular books like *Men are from Mars, Women are from
Venus*, or *Why Men Lie and Women Cry* where such 'opposites' are presented
as 'normal' and 'natural'.

On an everyday level, people are often forced to identify as either male
or female, with no alternative option being given. For example, games and
leisure pursuits may be set up as "boys vs girls" or only open to one gender,
toilets are often gendered male or female (except accessible toilets for problematic reasons), children may be asked to line up according to gender in
school, and people may be invited to "stag" or "hen" nights for a wedding,
or asked to get up and sing at a karaoke night with "the lads" or "the girls".
Additionally, many social contexts arbitrarily require people to state their
gender and give the options of male or female. These include such things
as club memberships, job applications and social networking sites, where
gender is irrelevant, or only tangentially related, to the matter in hand.
This can cause difficulties for some trans people (see Chapters 2 and 11),
but may cause particular problems for the groups covered in this chapter.
Such examples highlight the way in which gender is sometimes unrelated
to the pragmatics of living day-to-day and yet permeates the culture in
which people live.

NON-GENDERED PRACTICE

The implications of all this for practice is that clients may want to discuss
how they navigate such examples of the gendered world. For example,
will they tick a 'male' or 'female' box on a form, or add their own category? Will they alternate toilets, use the accessible toilet, or make some
other arrangement? As practitioners it is useful to ensure that our own
documentation and practice does not require gender where it is irrelevant. For example, we may leave the gender option on forms open for
individuals to fill in (or at least provide a number of options), or have
unisex toilets, and ensure that images and materials in waiting rooms are
not all dichotomously gendered. Affirmative practitioners may also wish
to work towards changing gendered aspects of society more widely, for

example by supporting campaigns for removing unnecessary gender markers on paperwork, or contributing awareness-raising information to professional newsletters and websites.

Of course it may be that a client requires interventions specifically related to their physiological sex – and therefore that a male/female category is relevant (for example birth control tailored to their hormonal milieu). However, these instances are relatively uncommon and should not be assumed to refer to the totality of the person in question (there may be an unknown degree of genetic mosaicism, for example, see Chapter 3) and indeed the person's sense of self and/or gender may not be strictly linked to their genotype or apparent phenotype.

SOCIAL OPPROBRIUM

The gender identities and presentations considered here can often be more visible, and so more subject to social opprobrium and abuse, than some of the sexualities and relationship practices considered in this book, which may be more hidden on a day-to-day basis. People can experience a marked sense of disquiet when they are unable to 'correctly gender' a person as either male or female, which may lead to them behaving in a negative way towards that individual, resulting in embarrassment, ridicule, or even violence. This can lead to the usual psychological difficulties associated with being a member of any marginalised group such as *minority stress* and should certainly not be taken as de facto evidence of psychopathology in this group. Indeed there is no evidence that these groups are at higher risk of psychological difficulties, minority stress and discrimination aside, than other groups who conform to the gender dichotomy. Conversely, however, many people considered within this chapter experience discrimination through being made to feel invisible by not being offered an appropriate choice of toilet, for example, or through people using gender dichotomous pronouns to refer to them (albeit without any malevolent intent) when these are not appropriate.

Of course the specific social context that a person is in will have an impact on how easy it is to have, and to present, a gender beyond the dichotomy of male and female. For example, if their background is in a cultural context where gender is differently understood, or their family has a history in such a culture, then they may already have more of a sense that other gender possibilities are available. For example, some South and East Asian, and Native American, cultures recognise multiple gender identities, such as the Hijra identity in India; the Tom, Dee and Kathoey identities in Thailand; or the Bissu, Calabai and Calalai identities in some communities in Indonesia (although of course there may still be stigma around identifying in these ways, and not all people's experiences will fit these specific categories – Herdt, 1996). Additionally, some countries such as India and Australia now have an 'other' option on passports as well as male or female. Within the UK the government has recently recognised the possibility of being non-gendered within the transgender action plan. More locally, it is possible that people who study or work in certain contexts where there is a high awareness of gender diversity will find a greater level of understanding from colleagues and peers.

GROUP NORMS

The groups considered within this chapter are diverse and include people with disparate understandings and experiences. Consequently, there are few norms as such, which would be recognised by all people who move beyond the gender dichotomy other than, perhaps, a recognition of the need to be accepting of other people's experiences and the limitations of the binary gender system.

One of the key difficulties faced by people who identify outside the dichotomous gender system is that there are so few norms which can aid navigation through the social world. For people who identify as gay, at least within contemporary urban Western society, there are a number of under-standings, practices, identities, etc. (sometimes called *scripts*) which can aid a person moving from heteronormative society and assist them in making sense of the world around them albeit, hopefully, with their own take on these new scripts (see Chapter 9). For people in the groups we are consider-ing here, there are a number of internet fora, as well as some face-to-face local meetings within some urban areas. However, there are few wider understandings, and none which have permeated mainstream culture. While it is possible to find gay, lesbian, and even bisexual and trans char-acters and celebrities in mainstream media, there are no prominent exam-ples who have clearly moved beyond the gender dichotomy. Some people may find examples in alternative music, or in science fiction and high fantasy worlds which imagine further genders.

This lack of available scripts within subcultures, as well as in mainstream culture, can lead to difficulties with people negotiating relationships, sexual encounters, etc. as things which might otherwise be assumed are unknown. Professionals may find it useful to encourage frank and open discussion, and indeed may be aided by the fact that people moving beyond the gender dichotomy will generally have done a good deal of thinking about their own preferences and identities, in contrast to people who have not felt the need to directly question other people's assumptions about their gender (see Chapter 4).

SUMMARY AND CONCLUSIONS

In summary, the following are good practice points when working with these groups of clients:

- Reflexively engage with your own assumptions about gender and encourage all staff within a clinic or organisation to do the same.
- Be open to reading/learning more about gender diversity and raising questions with clients (but don't expect them to provide education).
- Become comfortable talking about gender issues and adopting the terminology of the client.
- Normalise genders beyond the dichotomy for clients who are new to this.
- Do not focus on gender when it is not relevant to the presenting issue.
- Do not assume a gender dichotomy or pathologise people who don't experience themselves within it.
- Create a space which is comfortable for people from a diverse range of identities.

FURTHER READING

Bornstein, K. & Bergman, S.B. (Eds.) (2010). *Gender outlaws: The next generation*. New York, NY: Avalon Publishing Group.

Queen, C. & Schimel, L. (Eds.) (1997). *PoMoSexuals*. San Francisco, CA: Cleis Press Inc.

Wilchins, R.A. (1997). *Read my lips: Sexual subversion and the end of gender*. Ann Arbor: Firebrand Books.

ADDITIONAL REFERENCES

Herdt, G. (1996). *Third sex third gender*. New York: Zone Books.

II

SEXUALITY: PRACTICES AND IDENTITIES

BONDAGE AND DISCIPLINE, DOMINANCE AND SUBMISSION, AND SADOMASOCHISM (BDSM)/KINK

6

This chapter aims to:

- Consider the common concerns of those who practise and/or identify with BDSM and who approach counsellors, psychologists and health professionals.
- Provide an overview of common BDSM language, activities and dynamics.
- Explore wider cultural perceptions, legal and medical perspectives about BDSM.
- Outline good practice for working with BDSM clients.

INTRODUCTION

This chapter explores all sexualities which fall under the umbrella of *kink* or *BDSM* (bondage and discipline, domination and submission, and sado-masochism). This covers the whole spectrum from people who occasion-ally fantasise about being tied to the bedposts or who playfully bite their partner during sex, to those who regularly conduct elaborate *scenes*[1] involving role play or who frequently visit a professional dominant to be flogged.

Most important, as mentioned in the introduction, is that we are talking about *consensual* activities where people choose to take – or give up – power and/or to give and receive certain forms of stimulation. We return to this concept of consent several times as it is key.

Sadomasochism *(SM)* is still pathologised by the main psychiatric refer-ence books,[2] and remains criminalised in some contexts, therefore we spend some time considering what it means to work with people affirmatively in

---

[1] A scene is a consensually arranged period of BSDM/kink in which certain agreed activities take place.

[2] Sadism and masochism remain listed within the APA *DSM-V* as sexual sadism disorder and sexual masochism disorder, with slight changes to more clearly dif-ferentiate between that which is 'healthy non-normative sexual behaviour' and that which is a 'psychopathology'.

a culture where they are still widely pathologised and demonised, as well as which diagnostic and legal aspects we should be aware of.

People who practise BDSM often experience biased or inadequate care which puts them off seeking help and/or being open about BDSM. Particularly common are experiences where therapists voice misconceptions and negative judgements about BDSM (such as BDSM being inherently 'sick' or abusive) and/or try to discourage clients or patients from practising it. Such behaviours exacerbate the stigma already felt by someone who is anxious about cultural prejudice against BDSM. It can also make it very difficult for someone who is genuinely concerned about issues within their BDSM fantasies or relationships to be able to talk about those openly.

In order for kinky clients to access services it is important for professionals to have the kind of general, basic understanding of what BDSM involves – which is covered in this chapter – and to have reflected on their own views about these practices and identities. The cultivation of a general atmosphere of awareness of the diversity of sexual practices and identities is very useful; as is responding calmly and respectfully if a client does mention kink activities. Most kinky people would like to feel comfortable sharing their BDSM interests with their practitioner even if it is unrelated to their presenting issue.

A useful BDSM concept to keep in mind throughout this chapter is that of having a *squick* which means a strong negative emotional reaction to an activity which acknowledges that you do not actually judge the activity as wrong or bad.

COMMON CONCERNS

Broadly speaking there are three categories of people who participate in BDSM who will present to a counsellor, psychologist or other health professional:

- Those who practise BDSM but for whom this is completely incidental to the reason that they are seeking help or support.
- Those who have some concern about their BDSM fantasies or practices with which they would like help.
- Those who are looking to engage in counselling or psychological therapy of some kind and who need the practitioner to be aware that they will also be exploring similar issues in their BDSM play as a form of therapeutic or spiritual practice.

PSYCHOPATHOLOGY

The vast majority of people will fall into the first category mentioned here. For many years it was assumed in psychology and psychotherapy that people who were into kink were likely to be particularly emotionally troubled, or that they had been traumatised in their early lives. However, most were operating under the clinician illusion (see Introduction). There are no significant differences between kinky and non-kinky people on any measure of psychological health (Gosselin & Wilson, 1980; Moser & Levit, 1987). Indeed, the most recent large-scale study found that men who had engaged in BDSM scored significantly *lower* on a scale of psychological distress than other men (Richters et al., 2008). Similarly, the assumption that people who practise BDSM are more likely to have been abused as a child has been countered by this and other extensive studies which find no different levels of childhood trauma or childhood attachment styles between BDSM and non-BDSM groups (Nordling et al., 2006).

Of course there will be those who engage in BDSM who have some problems relating to it, as with those who engage in penile-vaginal intercourse for example (see Chapter 10). This second category of BDSM participants falls broadly into two subcategories: those whose anxieties are due to the social stigma attached to BDSM, and those whose fantasies or practices could potentially be problematic for them. For both it would be worth having more education about BDSM than is covered in this chapter, such as taking part in a training workshop and following up some of the further reading. The rest of this chapter, however, gives some initial pointers about how to work in an appropriate way with those who are struggling with social stigma, and how to assess – and work with – those whose BDSM practices are distressing in some way.

ADJUNCTIVE THERAPY

Finally there are those people who want to discuss BDSM with a counsellor or health professional because they see it as part of their own personal therapeutic, health-related and/or spiritual practice, perhaps alongside therapy or counselling, or perhaps separate from it. In recent years there has been an increasing vocalisation, in kink communities, of the potential value of BDSM in terms of personal growth or spiritual transcendence. It is important to be aware that by no means all BDSM participants experience it in this way – there are many different motivations for engaging in BDSM. However, some people experience BDSM as healing, therapeutic or personally useful and may want to talk about what they have discovered about themselves or their relationships during their BDSM practices. Examples of this kind of experience of BDSM would include:

- Someone who finds that the endorphin rush of having clothes pegs attached to their skin and pulled off relieves the pain of a chronic condition.
- Someone who role plays an earlier experience of being bullied in a BDSM scene with a trusted partner who then looks after them gently. This helps them to regain some of the power that they felt they had lost.

- Someone who usually struggles to be assertive and finds the dominant role in a BDSM scene a useful way to practise taking more control and setting clear boundaries.
- An older heterosexual couple who struggle to enjoy penile-vaginal sex due to problems with erection and/or penetration and/or orgasm (see Chapter 10) who have found BDSM scenes to be a good alternative intimate and erotic activity, and have also learnt a lot about their wider relationship dynamics through this.

Members of BDSM and kink communities are clear that they do not want to spend valuable time with a counsellor or health professional explaining the basics of their BDSM practices or kink community. So, while curiosity and openness on the part of the practitioner to the specifics of the individual's world and experience are important, it also behoves us to ensure that we have some basic understanding of these increasingly common practices and identities, as with non-kinky (or 'vanilla') sex practices that our clients may be engaging in. If in doubt refer on to someone with more expertise: perhaps one of the kink-aware professionals listed online, but be cautious of assuming that it will necessarily be a specialist issue simply because someone engages in BDSM/kink.

KEY PRACTICES

BDSM and kink practices are a broad spectrum which frequently overlaps with further sexualities which we will cover in Chapter 12. Some people categorise fetish or voyeurism, for example, under BDSM or kink, and others separate these out as specific – and different – sexualities or interests.

Two useful concepts relating to BDSM are power and sensation. Most BDSM *play* involves some kind of exchange of power and/or some kind of giving and receiving of sensation, with both possible with or without the other. In terms of power this might involve somebody being restrained, tied up, or wearing clothing that restricts movement (*bondage*), it might involve somebody being ordered about or punished if they fail to follow commands (*discipline*), and/or it might involve other forms of dominance and submission such as one person serving others.

PAIN

When it comes to sensation there is a popular perception that kink is all about pain. However, it is perfectly possible for the power aspects of BDSM to take place without any pain being inflicted at all. There is also a continuum to sensation-based play incorporating everything from tickling with feathers, through light scratching or gentle spanking, to more intense sensations such as piercing (very similar to acupuncture needling), heavy flogging, branding, or cutting the skin to create pictures (akin to tattooing). In relation to the most common types of BDSM sensation we might consider the 'pain' in biting your lover in a moment of sexual abandon or a good exercise session – not 'pain' as in being accidentally burnt on a stove. The more extreme levels of pain that some like to experience could be seen as analogous to the pain experienced by long-distance runners or boxers pursuing their sport.

Here we see a distinction between common BDSM activities and those which are less prevalent. Such distinctions are useful to keep in mind in terms of what you are most likely to come across in your professional practice. People unfamiliar with BDSM can often assume, due to media portrayals, that everyone will be in *24/7* arrangements, wearing black leather outfits every day, and regularly engaging in the most extreme acts of cutting and bull-whipping, for example. Actually such practices are rather rare. Of course, this is not to say that it is appropriate to pathologise or question those practising more unusual activities simply for this reason.

EXTENT OF BDSM/KINK

One reason why it is very hard to estimate the number of people involved in BDSM is this diversity. Imagine that we categorise love bites as a BDSM activity. Under this definition we could say that the majority of people had engaged in BDSM at some point in their life. If we define BDSM as experiencing some form of power exchange or pain during sex then the percentage would still be rather high (see Chapter 10 on heterosexuality). Under more conservative definitions some of the following pieces of information may be helpful:

- Two thirds of Canadian undergraduates have enjoyed fantasising about being tied up, and just under half have enjoyed the thought of whipping or spanking someone (Renaud & Byers, 1999).
- 14% of men and 11% of women in the US have engaged in something they would define as BDSM (Janus & Janus, 1994).
- Mainstream sex shops now regularly stock BDSM related toys such as handcuffs and riding crops.
- There are around 153 million web pages dedicated to BDSM.

Of course there is a difference between practice and identity. There are more people who engage in BDSM occasionally than there are people who identify themselves as kinky or as being a *dominant*, a *submissive* or a sado-masochist. Therefore it is important not to assume that somebody who mentions taking part in a BDSM activity is necessarily involved in any kind of kink community or sees this as an important part of their sexual identity.

At the same time, there are many people who see the activities and roles that they enjoy in BDSM as a more fundamental part of their identity than the gender of the people they are attracted to, for example.

INFORMATION

If you have a client who occasionally practises BDSM and who has practical or other concerns about their play, then it might be very useful to point them towards kink communities so that they can gain more information and education about safer practices, as well as the reduction of stigma that can result in realising that others have similar interests. Many big cities hold occasional *fetish fairs* where kinky people can meet, and there are also kink community web pages, discussion groups and mailing lists online (see Further Reading). Unfortunately the kind of equipment sold in high street sex shops is often of poor quality and does not include advice about safer use. While BDSM participants are no less likely to frequent emergency wards than anybody else, there is a real danger that somebody without any education could, for example, beat another person's buttocks too high up and end up damaging their kidneys, or put their hand over someone's nose and mouth to control their breathing without realising that this is often regarded as one of the highest risk BDSM practices.

Table 6.1 US men's BSDM activities by percentage preference

Practice	Tried	Enjoyed	Practice	Tried	Enjoyed
Spanking	82	66	Face slapping	36	31
Bondage	77	65	Group sex	40	30
Humiliation	67	56	Enemas	42	30
Rope	69	54	Ice	41	30
Fetish behaviour	60	51	Hot wax	37	24
Whipping/beating	65	50	Hoods	27	20
Dildos	57	48	Mask	28	20
Kissing ass	59	48	Rubber	31	20
Handcuffs	54	47	Swinging	22	18
Leather	49	42	Pins	18	14
Blindfold	53	42	Piercing	15	11
Chains	53	41	Burns	18	9
Cock binding	46	36	*Scat* (faeces/shit play)	13	9
Gag	49	46	Branding	10	7
Watersports (urine/piss play)	45	33	Tattoos	7	5
Biting	40	32			

In a study by Moser and Levit (1987), men in US BDSM societies and magazines were asked which practices they took part in. Using Thompson (1994) Table 6.1 reproduces these findings showing the most common in descending order of percentage preference.

It is important to remember that all these practices can mean different things to different people, and to the same person on different occasions. For example, someone can enjoy spanking because they like to feel humiliated, because they like the physical sensation, because they like seeing how much they can take, because they like giving up control to another person, because it makes them feel like a child, because it feels taboo, because their buttocks are a major erogenous zone for them, because it feels like an act of great intimacy with a partner, and for many other reasons, or combinations of reasons.

For professionals unfamiliar with BDSM the sense of possible 'danger' in these practices may seem an overriding issue. Indeed that is sometimes the purpose of the practices – a risk-aware and consensual exploration of those feelings between the people involved. However, it is also important to note that the safety of the different practices varies, and appropriate precautions will be taken by responsible people involved in them. Further, for many of these practices there is low, or no, risk of pregnancy or STIs – something which cannot be said for penile-vaginal sex, which is often not considered to be risky.

ROLES

There are a number of possible roles within BDSM. Generally speaking a dominant (*dom*) or *top* takes control and/or gives out sensations, and a *submissive* (*sub*) or *bottom* gives up control and/or receives sensation (see Glossary at the end of the book). However, it is, of course, possible to have different configurations – for example if a submissive provides sensations as part of pleasing their dominant. Some people have a fixed role in BDSM (defining as a bottom or as dominant and never taking a different role) while others take different roles on different occasions (known as *switching* or being *versatile*). Overall, men are fairly equally likely to be dominant, submissive or switches, whereas women are around twice as likely to be submissive than they are to be dominant or switch (see Chapter 4 for more about the societal gender roles which may explain this difference). Of course preferred BDSM roles may change over time just as other aspects of sexual desire can shift and alter. One circulating myth about BDSM is that people will require more and more extreme practices or intense stimulation over time. However, there is no evidence for this. Rather people tend to experience a levelling off after their initial experiences rather in the same way that the vast majority of people who learn to drive do not become racing-car drivers, and most people who drink alcohol do not become alcoholics.

WIDER SOCIETY

The place of BDSM in wider society globally is currently particularly precarious. In some ways kinky practices are becoming part of the 'great' adventurous sex which people are encouraged to seek and maintain in many Western countries (see Chapter 10). Images of mild bondage and discipline, and BDSM-style clothing are commonplace in commercials and music videos, and the BDSM erotica trilogy, *Fifty Shades of Grey*, became an internet phenomena, reaching number one on the *New York Times* bestseller list and being dubbed "mommy porn" for its mainstream appeal. At the same time no other consensual sexual activity is as demonised culturally as is BDSM, with 'full' kinky sex being regarded as an object of ridicule and fear. This can be seen in popular media which either represents BDSM as a spicy part of 'normal' heterosexual sex, or as an utterly deviant activity linked to psychological illness, violence and murder. This can make it difficult for those who are trying to incorporate some kink into their lives as they feel that they have to police a rather unclear borderline between 'fun' kink and 'serious' BDSM.

INTERSECTIONALITY

As with many other practices and identities, people seem much more likely to be stigmatised for their BDSM if they fall outside of the mainstream in other ways as well, which means that a trans, bisexual, gay, lesbian and/or non-monogamous person would be more likely to experience stigma and pathologisation for being kinky than someone who is cisgender, monogamous and heterosexual. Mild kink is also often more generally accepted among young, white, middle-class people who do not have a disability. It is worth being aware of such intersections and how they are likely to impact on the experience of clients. Some more mainstream heterosexual kink clubs and communities can be very intolerant of people who step outside of normative gender displays or fail to conform to conventional ideals of attractiveness (see Chapter 4). However, there are also more alternative kink communities which are more embracing of diversity.

THE LAW

It is useful to be aware of the current legal situation regarding BDSM activities. You might imagine that the law has little role to play in what people consent to have done to their own bodies in BDSM, just as it has little role in the arena of sport and leisure where people can choose to put themselves at risk in the boxing ring or jumping out of a plane. However, there are legal restrictions around BDSM in many countries. For example, following the Spanner case in the UK it was determined that BDSM resulting in marks on the body which were more than "transient and trifling" constituted bodily harm. Those inflicting such marks could be convicted of assault, and those receiving them could be convicted of aiding and abetting assault (Weait, 2007). Also, under recent extreme pornography legislation it is possible to be convicted of owning pornography which realistically portrays acts which are likely to result in serious injury to a person's anus, breast or genitals.

In actuality many cases which come to court do not result in conviction (particularly when they involve otherwise monogamous, heterosexual partners). However it is useful for the kink-aware practitioner to be aware of the potential legal issues that might pertain to their clients if they are fully open about their activities. They may find it useful to talk about how they negotiate levels of outness or self-disclosure in their lives (see Chapter 9). The American legal system has not yet determined the status of BDSM on the national level of the UK so it is worth colleagues in the US and other countries gaining some knowledge of how legal concepts of harm, consent, privacy and protection are applied in such cases. BDSM educational websites often have some information about this.

It is particularly vital to be clear about confidentiality with BDSM clients as many are concerned that confidentiality will be breached because BDSM is assumed by professionals to be harmful per se. It is valuable to be very clear upfront about situations under which you would and would not break client confidentiality and how that would be done, as well as being clear in your own mind about the distinctions between consensual BDSM play and criminal abuse. It can be useful to reflect that most BDSM play is to violent assault, as most heterosexual sex is to rape.

PSYCHIATRIC TAXONOMIES

A further complicating issue with BDSM is the presence of sadism and masochism as 'paraphilias' within the American Psychiatric Association's *Diagnostic and Statistical Manual* (*DSM-V*), and sadomasochism as a "mental and behavioural disorder" in the World Health Organization's *International Classification of Diseases* (*ICD-10*). This is likely to remain the same in upcoming editions, despite members of kink communities and prominent psychiatrists (cf. Moser & Kleinplatz, 2005) criticising its presence and likening it to the previous listing of 'homosexuality' as a mental disorder. The usual caveats exist: that, to be classified as disorders, sadomasochistic urges must recur over at least six months and *either* be non-consensual *or* cause marked distress or interpersonal difficulty (*DSM*) or be the most important stimulation necessary for sexual gratification (*ICD*). However, there is problematic conflation here between activities that are coercive, and those that are merely transgressive of current cultural mores. Also, it may well be that any distress and difficulty is the result of societal stigma around BDSM rather than any individual 'disorder' or problem. Finally, there is no evidence that those who engage in BDSM are any more likely to experience sexual difficulties, as implied here.

Given all of this, how can a professional within services which employ the *DSM* and/or *ICD* best work with the small percentage of people who are engaging in BDSM and who experience it as problematic? We suggest the following:

- Offer a space which is as kink-aware and affirmative as possible (through training all staff), so that the clinic/organisation will not be experienced as yet another place of stigmatisation.
- Work with the client to distinguish between difficulties which are due to not being accepted by wider society, and those which are due to their own concerns about their desires or practices.
- Work with the coercive/transgressive distinction, explaining this to clients. Make it clear that coercive desires should not be acted upon, helping them to locate coercive sexuality within their wider moral codes. Encourage an atmosphere of open curiosity to exploring such desires as *fantasies* so they will be able to bring them out in the open to consider their potential meanings. Attempting to deny that such fantasies exist because they are so threatening may, paradoxically, make it more likely that the client will act upon them, and certainly block potential valuable understanding and self-awareness.
- Where clients have fantasies or practices which are not coercive in any way, but which cause them concern, offer a space to explore what these desires and acts mean to them, what it is that worries them, any relational aspects of their concerns, etc. (just as you might work with any other clients who were disturbed by aspects of their thoughts and/or behaviours).
- As with other sexualities, if a client is not fully able to determine their own life – as in some cases of learning disability, for example – it is important that consensual sexual freedom of expression is respected and that any normative opinions of staff members do not override the individual's own identity.

Being kink-aware and affirmative does not require being completely comfortable with every BDSM practice or relationship which you might encounter as a professional. Rather, it requires us to be conscious of our levels of comfort around such issues, including practices and ideas that might squick us. It is important for therapists to engage in self-reflexivity (reflecting on their own practices, perceptions about BDSM and wider cultural assumptions) as well as engaging in relational reflexivity with clients. For example, the latter might involve asking questions such as: "Is this conversation useful for you?", "Is there any information which you would like me to read so that I don't need to ask basic questions about your practices?", "I notice that you waited before mentioning BDSM. Was this because it was not relevant until now or was this due to something else?." Such conversations can also help to counter previous negative experiences with professionals which BDSM clients are likely to have had.

GROUP NORMS

There are many overlapping kink communities which may have somewhat different norms. There may be little sense of cohesive group community among heterosexual couples who occasionally 'spice up' their sex life with a little kink, while there may be a very strong sense of group cohesion among those who are more strongly identified with an BDSM identity, or who attend kink events (such as parties, clubs or festivals) or online networks.

For example, from the 1940s to the 1980s a gay leather community emerged from motorcycle clubs in many large cities associated with a certain look (black leather) and heightened masculinity, and this became increasingly linked to BDSM. The norms in this community are likely to be different from those among lesbians who practised BDSM during a similar period, whose practices became bound up in the feminist 'sex wars' with debates over whether power imbalances were inherently patriarchal and therefore inappropriate for lesbian sexuality. This group would be different again from a young bisexual who attends kink-related club nights in an urban area and engages in social networking on an alternative sexualities website. The internet has become key, in the last decade or so, for many people who are into BDSM who are now able to make contact with communities and people with similar specific interests even if they are geographically isolated.

However, there are some relatively universal elements of BDSM practice which it is worth being aware of. Most of these revolve around how BDSM play is negotiated, conducted and ended, particularly in relation to informed consent.

INFORMED CONSENT

Key terms which have evolved as ground rules of BDSM play are *safe, sane, consensual* (*SSC*) and *risk-aware consensual kink* (*RACK*). The latter relates to the former in a similar way to the way in which the concept of *safer sex* replaced that of 'safe sex' in penile-anal and penile-vaginal intercourse. It recognises that few activities in life can be completely 'safe' due to uncontrollable and unpredictable factors. It also rejects the notion of 'sane' given the problematic line-drawing which takes place in relation to this term. Just as in any other sexual activity or identity, there will be kinky people who have mental health diagnoses, who have been in abusive relationships, who self-injure, who suffer from mental distress, etc. The important thing is to recognise that such things are no more common within BDSM than in any other group, and not to assume that this necessarily makes the BDSM activities problematic if the client or patient does not experience them as such. However, RACK does suggest that all BDSM participants should be *aware* of any potential risks and vulnerabilities before playing, and it also maintains the same strong emphasis on consent as SSC.

Consent is negotiated in various ways within BDSM. One way is for all parties to engage in discussion before they play together to ensure that they know what they are doing and are aware of each others' limits and what they have to offer. One way of doing this is for people to complete a BDSM checklist of activities to which they can answer Yes, No or Maybe about whether they would like this activity, and add further comments and ratings to signal how enthusiastic they are.

PAUSE FOR CONSIDERATION

For reflexivity purposes (and interest) you might find it interesting to complete a BDSM checklist yourself (many can be found online). Sex therapists find an adapted version of this to be a useful activity to conduct with clients, BDSM or not. Ask the client to make a list of every sexual or erotic activity that they have ever heard of, and then go through this rating how much they are excited by them. Joint compiling of such lists can be a valuable part of relationship therapy.

SAFEWORDS

In BDSM there is an understanding that consent is not a fixed thing which remains in place once it has been given. Rather it requires continual checking in and renegotiation as situations change. People cannot always predict how they will feel once a scene is underway. During BDSM play various *safewords* and signals can be used to ensure that all parties are keen to continue. Safewords are words which would never be accidentally used as part of the scene. Sometimes people want to be able to say "no" or "stop", for example, during the scene and to have that ignored. However, as this is a consensual encounter, they know that if they say "Midnight", for example, the scene will stop immediately.

A common form of safeword is the traffic light system: Red for "stop now", amber for "ease up a bit", and green for "go, go, go!". Some tops might check in regularly where their bottom is on a scale of 1 to 10 in terms of how difficult they are finding the stimulation to take. Some bottoms, some of the time, may wish to be pushed to the limits of their endurance, while others may never want to go near that (another thing which should be negotiated in advance). Finally, if someone is wearing a gag or taking part in a non-verbal role play (acting as a puppy or a baby, for example) it is worth having a non-verbal signal instead of a safeword. They might hold a ball, for example, and dropping the ball means they want it to stop, or they may have agreed hand gestures or other body language.

When play is more public (at a club or party) there may also need to be negotiation of consent with those around the scene. It is generally accepted that people should not find themselves witnessing something that they are likely to be uncomfortable with.

In a more ongoing BDSM relationship there is unlikely to be negotiation before every scene, and consent may become more implicit as people come to know each other better. However, it may well be useful (as in all relationships) to occasionally check whether people still have the same desires and limits, and whether they still feel able to stop things if they are not enjoying them.

Just as the means of ensuring informed consent vary from individual to individual and group to group, so do other rules. For example, many groups would have rules that people do not play when they are drunk or intoxicated, some would have norms about play with known people or strangers. Certain rules may be put in place, or suspended, for a particular agreed scene, party or event. Within a relationship there may be rules about which activities people do with each other, and which they are allowed to do with people outside that relationship (see Chapter 14). Also, specific forms of commitment may be used, for example a *collaring ceremony* where a submissive agrees to commit to a specific dominant and wear their collar to signify this.[3] It is important to remember that such artefacts may well be as significant as, for example, a wedding ring to a married person (this may be relevant if requiring it to be removed for a physical examination). Another

---

[3] Such collars are available from fetish fairs and online. They are often lockable but vary from the obviously kinky leather collar to metal hoops which more closely resemble mainstream jewellery.

common anxiety among professionals is around BDSM-identified people who have children and the potential impact on them. As with any parental sexual activity this is not necessarily problematic in any way, and locks on bedroom doors are often a good idea so that parents have control over what children are told and when.

As mentioned previously, the meaning that BDSM practices have for people can also vary between groups, for example those focused on more D/S (dominant/submissive – usually power based) or S/M (sadism/masochism, usually sensation based) play, between relationships, between individuals, and within the same individual on different occasions.

BDSM is often assumed to be a sexual practice, however, it may veer so far from being sexual that it becomes something more akin to a sport, an art form or a spiritual experience. For some people genital contact and orgasm is an important part of BDSM play, for others there are alternative forms of climax (reaching a pinnacle of endurance, for example, or breaking down in tears), and for others there is no need for a climactic moment at all.

Below are some common reasons given for engaging in BDSM:

- Giving up control and responsibility and letting go.
- Having fun, being playful, enjoyment, creativity, imagination.
- Exploring different roles, identities, maybe genders, being somebody else for a while.
- Reaching a state of calmness and relaxation, or even bliss or meditation.
- Feeling in control and powerful. Doing something you do well.
- Showing how much can be endured. Building self-confidence.
- Intimacy and closeness with another person, sharing emotions.
- Confronting the stuff you find scary or difficult.
- Getting really looked after, treated well and cared for.

Of course, as with everything, there may be multiple reasons going on within the same person, and these may well change over time. Many theoretical orientations in counselling and psychotherapy have attempted to provide one 'explanation' for sadism or masochism, so this fact of multiple meanings and motivations is a very important point to keep in mind and to relate back to your training in a challenging way if necessary.

AFTERCARE

Many in BDSM have a concept of *aftercare*, which is the importance of the period following a scene where those concerned connect in a different way and come back to their everyday life. This might be more important following a heavy scene, or ones involving quite different psychological *headspaces. Subspace*, for example, is a state of mind (and body) which people can go into when being very submissive for a period. It may take some time to return from this to a more everyday way of being. It is important to remember that tops and dominants can require just as much looking after and reassurance as bottoms and submissives, although it is usual for the bottom or submissive to get looked after first. For some people aftercare is the whole point of BDSM. For others it is not necessary.

SUMMARY AND CONCLUSIONS

In summary, the following are good practice points when working with BDSM clients (cf. Kolmes, Stock & Moser, 2006):

- Reflexively engage with your own assumptions about sexual practices/identities (and encourage all staff within a clinic or organisation to do the same).
- Be open to reading/learning more about BDSM and raising questions with clients (but not expecting them to provide lots of education).
- Treat with respect 24/7 relationships, collars, etc. and consider your clinic's policy on appropriate dress.
- Show comfort in talking about BDSM issues.
- Normalise BDSM interest for clients or patients new to BDSM.
- Do not focus on BDSM when it is not the focus of treatment.
- Recognise the multiple meanings for BDSM practice and be curious about the meanings for this particular person/relationship (where relevant).
- Understand and promote RACK.

FURTHER READING

Barker, M., Iantaffi, A. & Gupta, C. (2007). Kinky clients, kinky counselling? The challenges and potentials of BDSM. In L. Moon (Ed.), *Feeling queer or queer feelings: Counselling and sexual cultures* (pp.106–124). London: Routledge.

Connan, S. (2010). A kink in the process. *Therapy Today, 6* (21).

Easton, D. & Hardy, J.W. (2001). *The new bottoming book*. California, US: Greenery Press.

Easton, D. & Hardy, J.W. (2003). *The new topping book*. California, US: Greenery Press.

Kleinplatz, P. & Moser, C. (Eds.) (2006). *SM: Powerful pleasures*. Binghamton, NY: Haworth Press.

Langdridge, D. & Barker, M. (Eds.) (2007). *Safe, sane and consensual: Contemporary perspectives on sadomasochism*. Basingstoke: Palgrave Macmillan.

ADDITIONAL REFERENCES

Gosselin, C. & Wilson, G. (1980). *Sexual variations: Fetishism, sadomasochism and transvestism*. London: Faber and Faber.

Janus, S.S. & Janus, C.L. (1994). *The Janus Report on sexual behavior*. New York, NY: John Wiley & Sons, Inc.

Kolmes, K., Stock, W. & Moser, C. (2006). Investigating bias in psychotherapy with BDSM clients. In P. Kleinplatz & C. Moser (Eds.), *SM: Powerful pleasures* (pp. 301–324). Binghamton, NY: Haworth Press.

Moser, C. & Kleinplatz, P.J. (2005). DSM-IV-TR and the paraphilias: An argument for removal. *Journal of Psychology and Human Sexuality, 17*(3/4), 91–109.

Moser, C. & Levit, E.E. (1987). An explanatory-descriptive study of a sadomasochistically oriented sample. *The Journal of Sex Research, 23*, 322–337.

Nordling, N., Sandabba, N.K., Santilla, P. & Alison, L. (2006). Differences and similarities between gay and straight individuals involved in the sadomasochistic subculture. In P. Kleinplatz & C. Moser (Eds.), *SM: Powerful pleasures* (pp. 41–58). Binghamton, NY: Haworth Press.

Renaud, C. & Byers, E.S. (1999). Exploring the frequency, diversity and content of university students' positive and negative sexual cognitions. *Canadian Journal of Human Sexuality, 8*(1), 17–30.

Richters, J., De Visser, R.O., Rissel, C.E., Grulich, A.E. & Smith, A.M.A. (2008). Demographic and psychosocial features of participants in bondage and discipline, 'sadomasochism' or dominance and submission (BDSM): Data from a national survey. *The Journal of Sexual Medicine, 5*(7), 1660–1668.

Thompson, B. (1994). *Sadomasochism*. New York: Cassell.

Weait, M. (2007). Sadomasochism and the law. In D. Langdridge & M. Barker (Eds.), *Safe, sane and consensual: Contemporary perspectives on sadomasochism* (pp.63–84). Basingstoke: Palgrave Macmillan.

ASEXUALITY 7

This chapter aims to:

- Consider the common concerns of those who identify as asexual or who do not experience sexual attraction and who approach counsellors, psychologists and health professionals.
- Provide an overview of common asexual experiences and understandings.
- Explore wider cultural perceptions, legal and medical perspectives about asexuality and the context of an imperative to be sexual.
- Outline good practice for working with asexual clients.

INTRODUCTION

Within counselling, psychology, health and social care, and particularly within psychosexual therapy and sexual health, it has often been assumed that being sexual is a necessary and inevitable part of being a healthy human being. However, just over 1% of the population report not experiencing sexual attraction (Bogaert, 2004), and this percentage would be larger if we also included all those not currently experiencing sexual attraction in addition to those for whom this was a lifelong experience. Indeed, most people at some point in their lives are not sexual, and some people explicitly identify as asexual. Linking to Chapters 6 and 12, there is some questioning of the notion of what 'counts' as sexuality and asexuality in the context of the cultural imperative to be sexual.

PAUSE FOR CONSIDERATION

Before going on, take some time to consider what your view would currently be of a client who said that they did not experience sexual attraction (without using the word asexual). Then, consider what associations you have with the word asexual if someone explicitly identified in this way. Is that different from or similar to the associations you have with celibacy?

The standard definition of being asexual (sometimes shortened to *Ace*), as provided by asexual communities such as AVEN (the Asexuality Visibility and Education Network – AVEN, 2009) and by researchers in this area, is "not experiencing sexual attraction". There are some people, however, who define as asexual and do experience sexual attraction, but who do not wish to act upon it for a variety of reasons, and may sometimes therefore be referred to as celibate.

In this chapter we mostly focus on those who identify as asexual, but we also consider people who do not experience sexual attraction but who don't use this label. Like bisexuality (Chapter 8), it is useful to think of asexuality as an umbrella term under which several identities and experiences cluster. We consider some of the different groups who define in this way in the Key Practices section.

COMMON CONCERNS

Broadly speaking there are four categories of people who identify as asexual who will present to a counsellor, psychologist or other health professional:

- Those for whom this is completely incidental to the reason that they are seeking help or support.
- Those who are experiencing problems related to other people's perceptions of their asexuality.
- Those who are concerned about being asexual.
- Those who are content being asexual, but who nonetheless have some difficulty associated with it.

As seen elsewhere in the book, the vast majority of people of any sexuality are likely to fall into the first category, and indeed professionals may not find out about their sexuality at all. However, many professionals include explorations of sexual experience at some stage of the process (e.g. because of sexual health implications, or because they try to cover all aspects of experience in their practice). Therefore, it is important to be informed enough about asexuality not to respond in a negative and/or pathologising way upon finding that a client is asexual. Also, again as in other chapters, the less well known and understood a sexuality is in wider society, the more likely that people will present in categories 2 and 3 when they might otherwise be in category 1, and this is certainly the case for asexuality at present. It is important that people in category 4 (who may present feeling that they are happy being asexual, but wish to have children for example) do not have their identities unnecessarily questioned. Rather an exploration of possibilities given their identities, as with a 'same-gender' couple for example, is the best way forward.

Societal pressures to be sexual, explored more fully in the section on Wider Society below, may impact asexual people in multiple ways; for example, asexual people may feel a sense of abnormality and not fitting due to the obviousness of the sexual imperative in the world around them (conversations, mainstream media, etc). In this case professionals can identify asexuality as another valid sexuality (perhaps citing this book) and can suggest asexual resources and groups in order to find support. Quite often education of friends and family in a non-confrontational way can serve to allay fears about the person not being 'normal'.

Some asexual people may wish to have a romantic, but not sexual relationship but may feel that they will have to be sexual in order to maintain it even if they don't want to be. Again, education about the sexual imperative and asexuality can be very useful here. Some asexual people are content to have sex with their partners in order to satisfy them, although this would need to be carefully negotiated in order for the asexual person not to be uncomfortably acceding to their partner (who may have unexplored notions about what a 'proper' relationship should be).

Some asexual people may face stigma from people in their lives, including friends, family and co-workers, if they are open about their asexuality. This may be implicit or explicit (see below) and may include intersections with gender such as the assumption that they are gay or not a 'real man' if they are male, or stereotypes of frigidity if they are a woman. Gender roles are explored more fully in Chapter 4 – but professionals can often usefully decouple gender roles from societal expectations around gender in order to focus on what feels comfortable and personally authentic for the person involved.

Of course, as asexuality is a relatively new sexuality in terms of labelling and community it can be especially difficult for people to consider it a valid identity, meaning that societal messages may have been internalised such that, even when asexuality is recognised as personally authentic, it may still be regarded as 'wrong' or 'not normal'. Professional power can be leveraged here to explain that it is not 'wrong' or 'abnormal' per se, but that it may or may not be right for that client at that time. The de facto assumption should be that it is a perfectly acceptable possibility.

For those who are explicitly concerned about being asexual it should be determined whether, as above, this is a concern about being 'normal' or whether there is a specific issue, either medical or psychological that needs addressing. Some people may be asexual and simply need reassurance that it is okay (it is); whereas others may have a difficulty they would in fact like resolved and do not identify as asexual, or use the word in a different manner from members of asexual communities. Impressing upon a non-asexual man who genuinely wishes to have an erection for penetrative sex that it is okay to be asexual is equally problematic as suggesting to an asexual man that he *should* have penetrative sex. As ever, fully exploring the client's world is paramount.

KEY PRACTICES

The asexual communities are very new – the main online network, AVEN, was only set up in 2001 – so many people may not be aware of the label. Also some may not use it due to the stigma surrounding it, or for other reasons such as not wanting a static identity label (see Chapter 5).

TERMINOLOGY

As with all of the sexualities covered in this book, it is best for the practitioner to determine the terminology that the client themselves uses and to employ this. As we have seen, it may also be useful to explore what possibilities people are aware of, and to open up alternatives if they are not aware of them (in this case asexual identities/communities). However, the rule should be to go with the person's own language rather than imposing a language upon them, exploring terms and understandings that are familiar in their cultural context or which make sense to them.

It is important to think carefully about the assumptions underlying your own talk. For example, you might find yourself referring to someone's "lack of sexual attraction" rather than them having "no sexual attraction". While those phrases might seem very similar, the former implicitly suggests that not having sexual attraction is negative (a 'lack') in a way that the latter does not.

CELIBACY

Asexuality is not the same thing as celibacy. Celibacy refers to a choice not to be sexual, while asexuality is about not experiencing sexual attraction. Celibate people may or may not be asexual, and asexual people may or may not be celibate. As we will see later, some people have sex despite not experiencing sexual attraction (for various reasons including pleasing a partner and maintaining a relationship), whereas others do not. While celibacy and asexuality are both stigmatised socially, celibacy is usually more understood and accepted, at least for certain groups (such as religious leaders, monks and nuns, and teenagers where abstinence movements are in place).

DESIRE

Professionals may also wonder why asexuality refers to attraction rather than desire. Partly this is a historical artefact of the networks which found international visibility (such as AVEN) and the terminology which their founders preferred. Also, some asexual people do report feeling desire, but not attraction. For example, several have non-directed sexual desire but do not find themselves attracted to people. They may enjoy sexual fantasies, watching pornography and/or masturbating, for example, while not wanting to take part in sexual encounters with others or to form sexual relationships.

Not all asexual people even concur with the definition of not experiencing sexual attraction: just under half of the asexual people in one study said that they did have sexual attraction but that they defined as asexual because they didn't want to act on this with any form of sexual behaviour (Scherrer, 2008). In addition to this, some asexual people enjoy some forms of physical intimacy (e.g. cuddling, kissing, or even pleasing a partner sexually). People draw the lines around being sexual in different places. This is reflected in the terms *Grey-A*, which refers to being asexual to some extent, and *demisexual* for those who only feel sexual when there is a very strong emotional attraction.

ROMANCE

Many asexual people want to form intimate romantic relationships, just not sexual ones, and they may have romantic attractions to certain genders. Consequently, asexual people can also be lesbian, gay, bi, queer or straight, for example. They may use a term like *biromantic* rather than *bisexual* though, to emphasise that it is a romantic identity rather than a sexual one. Other asexual people are *aromantic*, and may prefer to be on their own and/or to prioritise other kinds of relationships.

Asexuality is therefore experienced in a number of different ways. Asexual people may or may not also be celibate; they may or may not experience sexual desire. Some may experience sexual attraction but not wish to engage in sexual behaviour; some may engage in some intimate physical closeness. And asexual people may or may not wish to form romantic/intimate relationships. Asexuality is frequently lifelong but may also be a useful term for periods of not being sexually attracted.

DEVELOPMENT

Some asexual people report an initial stage of experiencing something different about themselves (for example, realising that sex is important to other people in a way it isn't for them). This is often followed by a period of self-questioning and self-clarification when they ruminate on these issues internally. At some point they are likely to speak to others (for example, searching online and finding asexual communities and/or speaking to people around them who may well dissuade them from an asexual identity). Some then claim an asexual identity (Carrigan, 2011). Of course, people may not all follow this model and may exit it at different points.

AETIOLOGY

Some research has searched for explanations of why people are asexual. As with such research on other sexualities we can question this on two levels. First, the search for explanations only tends to happen with sexualities outside the cultural norm (see Chapters 9 and 10), implying that they are requiring of explanation due to being problematic in some way. Second, it is likely that there are multiple, rather than singular, reasons for a person being of any sexuality, often incorporating a complex mixture of biological, psychological and social factors. This makes a search for one universal 'cause' or 'explanation' problematic. Just as there are multiple routes to asexuality, sex has multiple meanings across asexual people and at different times for the same person. It can be regarded, for example, as unpleasant, repulsive, boring, neutral, vaguely pleasurable, or with ambivalence.

WIDER SOCIETY

There is a societal assumption that it is normal, natural and healthy to be sexual – or at least to have sexual thoughts, within certain situations – and abnormal, unnatural and unhealthy not to be. Often the only exceptions to this rule are people deemed to be 'other' or 'different': people with disabilities, older people, children, etc. Consequently, people who are asexual may face opprobrium or incomprehension, and may simply feel excluded from common conversation. This is partially codified within the diagnostic texts which make little distinction between asexuality and pathological difficulties.

DIAGNOSIS

Like BDSM (Chapter 6) and some of the further sexualities we consider in Chapter 12, there are still diagnostic categories which relate to the experience of not having sexual attraction. However, these are classified under 'sexual dysfunctions' rather than under 'paraphilias' in this case. For example, the *DSM-V* includes hypoactive sexual desire disorder (HSDD); and the *ICD-10* additionally includes 'lack or loss of sexual desire'. Both nosologies include diagnoses which imply sense of fear, anxiety or repulsion around sex, rather than just not being interested. While some asexual people do report such feelings, it seems likely that most asexual people will be labelled with the disorders relating to low/lost sexual desire than with those relating to aversion. Asexual community engagement with the APA around the most recent edition of the *DSM* (*DSM-V*) has certainly focused on these categories (Hinderliter, 2010). Whether one is a practitioner who diagnoses or not, it is, as ever, worth being cautious with any diagnoses and using them as a tentative bureaucratic tag (often for funding purposes), rather than as a concrete means of formulation. The standard practice of finding out what is going on *for that client* is, as always, paramount.

RESEARCH

Research and expertise in this area overwhelmingly supports the view that asexuality is not the same thing as HSDD as asexual people do not suffer from 'marked distress' and 'interpersonal difficulty' (Bogaert, 2006); in general do not lack physical arousal (Brotto & Yule, 2010);[1] and do not have disproportionate rates of depression, alexithymia, social withdrawal or personality disorders (Brotto et al., 2010). It is, of course, inherently problematic to pathologise a newly emergent sexual identity and practitioners should be wary of making clients feel that their identity is not acceptable through the act of diagnosis. Further, the assumption that it is abnormal not to be sexual reaches far beyond the medical profession, so – as with other minority sexualities covered in this book – it is vital to explore whether any distress a person does experience is related to external pressures and is consequently *minority stress*. As usual, this requires the practitioner to reflect on their own assumptions and practices. It is vital to refer on if you are not able to work in a way that is affirmative of asexual identities.

---

[1] Of course, a lack of physiological arousal need not necessarily indicate a problem in any case.

THE SEXUAL IMPERATIVE

Asexual communities have been at the forefront of questioning the imperative to be sexual, which has negative impacts beyond asexual people (see, for example, Chapter 10). The sexual imperative privileges sexual relationships over other ways of relating such as friendships, family, collegiate relationships, etc. It sees our sexual identities as core aspects of our self-identities, and it views sex as healthy for individuals and necessary for romantic relationships. This is often reflected in the media which conflates sexual and romantic success in relationships, often without considering vitally important aspects of such relationships such as shared interests, financial arrangements, values, goals, etc. Similarly, friendships of long standing may be put to one side when a person gains a new sexual partner due to this privileging of sex over friendship. Within Western societies sex is sometimes so central that up to a third of people engage in unwanted sex which they consent to (O'Sullivan & Allgeier, 1998). This sexual imperative is also reflected within laws where marriages are required to be consummated and lack of sex can be the focus of divorce proceedings.

This focus on sex occasionally leads to explicitly phobic attitudes towards asexual people where they are given sex toys or told they need therapy etc. More frequently there are less extreme responses, and people may be told they "haven't met the right person yet", etc. However, the past decade has seen a number of articles and occasional documentaries about asexuality, so it is hopeful that discrimination will eventually decrease as people become more familiar with the idea. However, the sexual imperative is still so entrenched that it is unlikely that asexuality will become an easy identity to claim any time soon and professionals may wish to work towards this both politically and in their work.

GROUP NORMS

Multiple asexuality communities are currently coming into existence around the globe which differ in their understandings of asexuality and their politics. At present, AVEN is the biggest online asexual community with over 30,000 members worldwide. This is useful because, as with many minority sexualities, the internet means that geographically isolated people can get support and find out about asexuality. Online and face-to-face communities tend to form around different languages. It is consequently worth finding which – if any – communities a specific client is tapped into and the ways in which asexuality is understood there. However, it should not be assumed that simply because a client is asexual that they will be a member of an asexual community.

LABELLING

As mentioned, there are group norms in asexual communities which may not fit all asexual people. There may be a sense, as with many communities, that some people are more 'properly' asexual than others. Norms include viewing asexuality as a necessarily lifelong identity. Many people view asexuality as having a biological aetiology (something fixed that they 'naturally' are), so those who do not experience it in this way (for example, those for whom it feels like a response to life experience, or a choice) may feel a pressure to conform to this biological–essentialist understanding. In common with many sexual identities, the idea that it is natural and fixed may be used as part of a fight for equal rights. In the case of asexuality though, there is a tension if – on the one hand – people are questioning the assumption of sex as natural, but – on the other hand – they are presenting asexuality using 'natural' arguments.

One risk of an asexual label (as with all the identity labels mentioned in this book) is that people might feel fixed in it and unable to move out of it if things change for them. This is problematic given increasing evidence on the fluidity of sexuality (Diamond, 2008). Practitioners can be an important force in shifting cultural views of sexuality so people feel less need to rigidly fix it and more possibility for movement.

RELATIONSHIPS

As previously mentioned, asexual people can have all kinds of relationship structures, including being single, and monogamous and non-monogamous relationships which may or may not be focused on one gender. Partners may or may not be asexual. If they are not, then the relationship may or may not include sexual practices, and this may or may not be difficult for the asexual person (some are quite happy to have sex if a partner wants it, while some find this a terrible pressure).

Some find that openly non-monogamous structures enable non-asexual partners of asexual people to have relationships that are both sexual and non-sexual. There is also some overlap between asexual and trans communities, with some trans people being lifelong asexual, and others experiencing asexual periods, for example, connected with unhappiness with their bodies pre-transition; while undergoing physical treatments; or once they feel more contented and under less pressure to conform when they are happy in their identity and/or body.

SUMMARY AND CONCLUSIONS

In summary, the following are good practice points when working with asexual clients:

- Reflexively engage with your own beliefs about sex (and encourage all staff within a clinic or organisation to do the same).
- Be open to reading/learning more about asexuality and raising questions with clients (but not expecting them to provide lots of education).
- Show comfort in talking about asexual issues.
- Normalise asexuality for clients or patients new to it.
- Do not focus on asexuality when it is not the presenting issue.
- Do not assume a sexual imperative.
- Be careful in diagnosing people who don't experience sexual attraction.
- Consider asexuality within modes of speech and bureaucracy.

Asexuality highlights the importance of not assuming that clients and patients are either sexual *or* asexual, and of not pathologising people simply on the basis of wanting too much or too little sex. All too often professional definitions of sex addiction or hypersexual desire equate to people having more sex than the professional themself is having, while asexual/hyposexual desire often equates to people having less sex than them. Individual distress, rather than 'normality', should be the criterion under consideration.

Beyond people who identify as asexual, we might also expand out the respect and reflection that we have given to asexual people here to question the ways that we work with people who are having unwanted sex (see Chapter 10). This might involve opening up the possibility of asexuality and related understandings rather than (often unwittingly) supporting the sexual imperative by trying to force bodies to have sex through psychological and physical means, when that is not, at that time at least, appropriate.

FURTHER READING

Carrigan, M., Morrison, T. & Gupta, K. (2013). I do not miss what I do not want: Asexual identities, asexual lives. Special issue of *Psychology & Sexuality*, 4(2).

ADDITIONAL REFERENCES

AVEN (2009). Asexuality Visibility and Education Network homepage. Accessed from www.asexuality.org/home on 11 January 2012.
Bogaert, A.F. (2004). Asexuality: Its prevalence and associated factors in a national probability sample. *Journal of Sex Research, 41* (3), 279–287.

Bogaert, A.F. (2006). Toward a conceptual understanding of asexuality. *Review of General Psychology, 10*(3), 241–250.

Brotto, L.A., Knudson, G., Inskip, J., Rhodes, K. & Erskine, Y. (2010). Asexuality: A mixed methods approach. *Archives of Sexual Behavior, 39*(3): 599–618.

Brotto, L.A. & Yule, M.A. (2010). Physiological and subjective sexual arousal in self-identified asexual women. *Archives of Sexual Behavior, 40*, 699–712.

Carrigan, M. (2011). Spotlight on asexuality studies. Accessed from http://sociologicalimagination.org/archives/7938 on 11 January 2012.

Diamond, L.M. (2008). *Sexual fluidity: Understanding women's love and desire*. Cambridge, MA: Harvard University Press.

Hinderliter, A. (2010). Pathology and asexual politics. Accessed from http://sociologicalimagination.org/archives/1224 on 11 January 2012.

O'Sullivan, L.F. & Allgeier, E.R. (1998). Feigning sexual desire: Consenting to unwanted sexual activity in heterosexual dating relationships. *The Journal of Sex Research, 35*(3), 234–243.

Scherrer, K. (2008). Coming to an asexual identity: Negotiating identity, negotiating desire. *Sexualities, 11*, 621–641.

BISEXUALITY   8

This chapter aims to:

- Consider the common concerns of bisexual people who approach counsellors, psychologists and health professionals.
- Provide an overview of experiences, identities and practices related to bisexuality, including invisibility.
- Explore wider cultural perceptions, legal and psychological perspectives about bisexuality.
- Outline good practice for working with bisexual clients.

INTRODUCTION

Bisexuality covers a broad range of sexual identities and experiences where there is attraction to more than one gender. Of all the common sexual identity groups, bisexual people have been linked to the worst mental health problems compared to heterosexuals, and to LG people, and have reported the most negative responses from professionals (King & McKeown, 2003). This is related to the wider societal understanding of sexuality as an either/or binary (people can only be *either* gay *or* straight) and the troubling position of bisexuality in relation to this. For these reasons it is particularly important for professionals to gain good understandings about bisexual experience, and to work affirmatively with bisexual clients.

It is useful to read this chapter alongside the following two chapters (9 and 10) because bisexual people share many experiences with LG people (due to all three groups having 'same-gender' attraction in a world which generally regards heterosexuality as the norm), and because of the issues faced by heterosexually identified people who have some 'same-gender' attraction or encounters. However, there are also many aspects which are unique to bisexual experience, and some which may have more in common with transgender and genderqueer experiences (see Chapters 2 and 5) because they are about transgressing binaries of gender (man/woman) and sexuality (gay/straight).

When people have revealed 'same' and 'other' sex attraction and experiences it is also important to be very cautious of assuming sexual *identity* on the basis of them. Some people identify as straight but have sex with women and men – thus if that person was a woman the sexual health term for the practice would be WSWM (woman who has sex with women and men) and the identity would be straight. The term for a man would be MSWM, the identity still being straight (see Glossary). Further, it is important to note that a significant minority of bisexual clients rarely or never disclose their bisexuality to clinicians due to concerns about how they would be treated.

COMMON CONCERNS

Broadly speaking there are three categories of bisexual people who will present to a counsellor, psychologist or other health professional:

- Those for whom bisexuality is incidental to other issues they are dealing with.
- Those who are experiencing problems related to other people's perceptions of their bisexuality.
- Those who are concerned in some way about their sexual attraction towards more than one gender, who may or may not use the label 'bisexual'.

As with so many of the genders, sexualities and relationship structures in this book, the majority of bisexual people coming to a professional will fall into the former of these three categories: their issues having nothing or little to do with the fact that they are bisexual. It is important, in such cases, not to assume that bisexuality is more relevant than it is.

Professionals should reflect upon two things in order to practise affirmatively with bisexual clients, as with many other groups in this book. First, they need to interrogate their clinical approach, and second they need to consider their own experiences and assumptions relating to bisexuality.

PAUSE FOR CONSIDERATION

Consider how the approach you were trained in understands sexual identity or orientation. What did you learn about this in your training? What are the understandings of your peers? How is bisexuality understood – if at all? What are your own personal beliefs and understandings about bisexuality – and where have these come from?

There is a history in many training approaches of pathologising same-sex attraction and/or of theories which assume that people will form heterosexual relationships (see Chapter 9). Obviously this impacts on bisexual clients as well as on lesbian, gay and heterosexual ones. However, more specifically, both psychoanalysis and mainstream psychology and medicine have generally viewed sexuality as a binary (people are either heterosexual or homosexual). In psychoanalysis there is the notion of normal development involving fixing on one sexual object (male or female) from an original 'polymorphous perversity'. This means that those who do not fix in this way are often viewed as pathological or immature. In mainstream psychology, most theories of sexuality are rooted in an assumption that people are born gay or straight (Barker, 2007), an assumption which may well influence other approaches. Bisexuality is rendered invisible by such perspectives, meaning that professionals who draw on them are likely to view it as unreal, or perhaps as a phase on the way to a lesbian, straight or gay identity. Bisexual clients often report having links made between their sexuality and an extant mental health problem; or – under the guise of empathic support – being told that one bisexual experience didn't make the client bisexual.

It is important that professionals do not draw upon only their own or a friend's experience and then generalise that to all bisexual people, and for gay, and gay-affirmative, professionals (see Chapter 9) to ensure that their practice is also bi-affirmative. Some questioning of sexual identity is common on the journey towards gay and lesbian, and bisexual, identities. There is a risk that questioning will always be read as the former, rather than the latter, and so the impression will be given that it is acceptable to be gay/lesbian but not bisexual. There is a real danger of professionals reinforcing the same prejudices which their clients encounter in wider society.

As with other sexualities and genders, bisexual clients should not have to spend time they, or the taxpayer/insurance company/charity, have paid for educating professionals about bisexuality. This chapter provides the basics for a reflective professional to work with bisexual clients who aren't struggling in relation to their bisexuality. The suggestions in the Further Reading section below give the kind of detail necessary for a professional to work affirmatively with bisexual clients who wanted to explore their sexuality and bisexual experience in more depth.

Returning to the three groups of bisexual people who might present to a professional, there may well be overlap between the latter two groups (those whose problems are related to other people's perceptions of them, and those who are concerned about their own sexuality) because people might feel confused and distressed in themselves due to a knowledge that they are socially stigmatised or that significant people in their lives struggle with their sexuality. Here is a summary of some of the common problems that bisexual people might have in these two categories:

- Issues around discrimination, or fear of discrimination, in work/educational/community and personal settings. Here professionals may be well served by educating those settings if it is within their remit. Within the UK and many other countries bisexuality (defined in this context as being attracted to women and men) is protected under law against discrimination. This includes discrimination regarding parenting as bisexual people are, of course, just as good at parenting as people of other sexualities.
- Concerns about coming out, or being open with family, friends and others (see Disclosure, later in the chapter). Here professionals may wish to allow space to discuss concerns, paying particular attention to the specifics.
- Worries about attracting partners and maintaining relationships when there are such negative perceptions of bisexual people in relationships. Professionals may wish to link bisexual people to community groups and also point to the large numbers of people who are bisexual, but may not say they are.
- Desire to find support or spaces where they 'fit'. Again, community resources can be of great assistance here, as well as exploring the notion that because one is bisexual one will necessarily not fit in mainstream spaces. Some people fear that others will ostracise them for their bisexuality, and while this does happen all too often, quite frequently people are more concerned with themselves than with other people's sexualities.
- Explorations of one's relationship to 'normativity', e.g. in what ways do they want to 'pass' or to challenge normativity, to be outside or inside of it (see Queer, in Chapter 5)? Simply offering space to discuss this, and normalising the range of available experiences, is extremely useful. Being matter of fact takes very little time and can have great benefits.

Common concerns individuals have with their own sexual attractions:

- Being confused about sexuality and exploring what they want and how they might identify to others. Here the knowledge of the professional is paramount. It is important that many avenues are open and limited understandings of professional and/or client do not curtail a comfortable authentic identity.
- Knowing that they have bisexual attractions but feeling uncomfortable with this, perhaps relating to gender as well as to sexual identity (what it means to be a man or a woman). Here an exploration of the client's own views as well as widening the understandings that are available to them is useful.
- Having bisexual desires but a relationship which doesn't allow for them to act on this, or to be open about it. Here it is important not to assume that bisexual people will necessarily be either monogamous or non-monogamous (they may be either), but to explore possibilities within their current relationship structure (see Chapters 13 and 14).
- Being comfortable in their bisexuality but feeling isolated and alienated from anyone other than other bisexual people due to negative experiences in the past. Gently re-exploring other spaces can be of use in this instance as well as identifying the boundaries around the negative experiences and how closely they map onto the delineation of sexuality (as opposed to the place they happened for example).

KEY PRACTICES

Bisexuality is generally understood to mean people who have attraction to, or sexual contact with, both men and women. However it is actually rather more complex than this. First, many who identify as bisexual would not accept this definition. Second, many people who would fall under this definition would not identify as bisexual. The practices and experiences of bisexuality vary markedly across these different groups.

THE UMBRELLA OF BISEXUALITY

If we look at people who apply the label *bisexual* to themselves and see themselves as members of wider bisexual communities, we find that the preferred definition of bisexuality is something like a changeable "emotional and/or sexual attraction to people whose gender may not be a defining factor". In other words, bisexual people themselves often don't see bisexuality as being attracted to *both* men and women, but rather that the gender of a person is not particularly relevant to whether or not they are attracted to them. It is similar to something like eye colour – noticeable and people may have a vague preference, or not – but not the defining area of attraction. Bisexual people often mention other qualities, such as intellect, sense of humour, creativity, kindness, etc. as being more important. Bisexual people also often see attraction as something that can change over time, and as something that incorporates sexual and/or emotional aspects. Also, many within bisexual communities question the idea that there are 'both' men and women, seeing gender as more complex than that (see Chapter 5).

The identity 'bisexual' can be considered to be an umbrella term which includes all of the following groups and more:

- People who generally have relationships with one gender, but who know that they can be attracted to another one (they may also use terms like 'bi-curious' or *metrosexual*).
- People who see other people in terms of men and women, and know that they are attracted to both (maybe more to one or the other, or equally to both).
- People who don't see gender as a defining feature of their sexual attraction (some may also use terms like *pansexual, omnisexual* or *ecosexual* – see Glossary).
- People who do not believe that there are two binary genders or two binary sexualities (some may also use the term queer).

BISEXUALITY BEYOND BISEXUAL COMMUNITIES

For various reasons which we explore below, only a very small minority of people who have attraction to more than one gender actually identify as bisexual or see themselves as members of bisexual communities. In the 1940s when Alfred Kinsey measured sexuality on a continuum, rather than using labels (as most statistics do), he found that many people fell somewhere between being exclusively heterosexual or homosexual. Even this way of measuring has been criticised because it doesn't allow for people changing over time, it is based on a two-gender model, and it suggests that more attraction to one gender means less attraction to the other (a useful analogy is chocolate: just because you like milk chocolate a lot does not mean you don't like dark chocolate as much). Similarly, there is a good deal of evidence that many people who identify as heterosexual, gay or lesbian have had sexual encounters with men and women, in some cases to the same extent that bisexual people have.

INTERSECTIONS

This is an area where the intersections between sexuality, gender, race and culture become very relevant because stigmatisation of those who are married or who identify as heterosexual, but have sex with people of the 'same' sex varies across cultures. For example, among white people in the UK such behaviour is often viewed in a sensationalist manner and regarded as a reason to mistrust – for example – politicians, who are viewed as 'really gay' but lying about it. Among some African–American people, some people in such situations reject potential LGBT identities due to a perception that these are part of white culture (Boykin, 2005). Some authors have suggested that there is greater allowance of sexual fluidity (outside dichotomies of heterosexual/homosexual) in South and East Asian contexts (Gosine, 2006). As usual it should be remembered that such cultural categories are extremely broad and that there are multiple meanings attached to bisexual behaviour and identity within each group, related to class, religion, generation, geographical location, personal experience and many other factors.

WIDER SOCIETY

As we have already mentioned, wider Western society, as well as many others, generally understands both gender and sexuality to be dichotomous (you are a woman or a man and you are attracted to women or men) and to be fixed (the gender and sexuality you are will remain the same throughout your life). This explains why bisexuality has generally been either completely invisible or the object of stigmatisation (because it is deeply troubling to both of these understandings). *Biphobia* is therefore something different from *homophobia* or *heteronormativity* (although these things impact on bisexual people as well) because it involves being ignored or discriminated against specifically for being bisexual.

BISEXUAL INVISIBILITY

We see the invisibility of bisexuality in the way in which the B is often added to lesbian and gay groups, policies and events (as in LGBT), but then missed off throughout (see *The Bisexuality Report* in Further Reading for a full exploration of this). For bisexual people listening to a talk at an LGB event, or reading a document purporting to be about LGB people, is often painful as it involves hearing only silence about their experiences. For example, much of the writing about LGB people in education or at work only mentions homophobia and not biphobia as a separate, and equally important, issue. Bisexual invisibility can also take the form of people asking whether someone is "gay or straight", or of assuming this on the basis of someone's current partner. Bisexual people may have to come out to friends, family and colleagues more than once because of the frequency of people hearing "gay" when someone says "bisexual", and then being confused if the person mentions an "opposite sex" partner. The stereotypes of bisexuality being "just a phase" or a "confusion" or "fence-sitting" are also related to this invisibility and sense that bisexuality isn't a real sexual identity.

The more active form of biphobia frequently takes the form of assuming that bisexual people are greedy, promiscuous, or will leave partners for a person of a different gender. We will see in Chapter 14 that there are bisexual people who are openly non-monogamous (which is not necessarily the same as being promiscuous). However, there are also many who form monogamous relationships (see Chapter 13), although very often they are not recognised as bisexual due to the invisibility mentioned above.

DOUBLE DISCRIMINATION

A major difficulty for many bisexual people is the double discrimination they can face from both heterosexual people and from LG people. They are sometimes seen by heterosexual people as amoral, untrustworthy, hedonistic spreaders of disease and disrupters of families, *and* viewed by LG people as possessing a degree of privilege not available to them. LG people may also feel threatened if they have any attraction themselves to people who aren't of the 'same' gender – and are faced with the tough prospect of a second *coming out* if they identify with bisexuality. Also, some can feel that the existence of bisexuality 'muddies the water' in a way which calls into question the basis which they have fought for their rights.

All this can easily mean that bisexual people feel that they don't belong anywhere, and that they struggle to access support. It can be particularly harsh if somebody plucks up the courage to go to an LGB group only to find that they are discriminated against there too (bisexual people often cite being refused entry to gay nightclubs, or having people sing "making your mind up" at them during the LGBT Pride event). The sense of isolation has eased somewhat with the internet, which helps people to find bisexual communities at a distance, and there are also increasing numbers of local bisexual groups. However, it is also important to ensure bisexual inclusion in groups and places (including professional environments) that are not specifically bisexual.

Discrimination around bisexuality often plays out differently according to gender. People who are both trans and bisexual are often either doubly invisible, or doubly discriminated for threatening assumptions about the gender binary. Recent years have seen widely publicised research conducted claiming to reveal that bisexual men do not exist, so bisexual men may have particular problems with invisibility and not being believed, despite more recent (less publicised) research overturning this finding (Conway, 2007). Also, heterosexuality and masculinity are so interwoven that bisexual men may find others, or themselves, questioning their masculinity on the basis of their bisexuality, as well as heterosexual men feeling that their security about their own sexuality is called into question by the bisexual man's existence. Professionals can profitably explore the meanings and veracity of these concerns with clients.

Bisexual women are more frequently depicted in the media, but generally in the form of titillation for men, and may well be perceived as promiscuous and perhaps as 'only' being 'bi-curious' in order to turn men on. There have been tensions in the past between lesbian and bisexual women, particularly in radical feminist contexts where there may be a perception of 'sleeping with the enemy'. It can be particularly difficult for women who move from a lesbian to a bisexual identity, as they may face rejection from friends and community in a similar way to some trans men (see Chapter 2).

Bisexual invisibility, biphobia and double discrimination have all been put forward as likely reasons for the high levels of *minority stress* and mental health problems among bisexual people mentioned earlier. It is striking that bisexual people are less likely to be out to others, including health professionals, and are also more likely to be psychologically distressed than lesbian and gay people. Clearly it is vital that professionals do not reproduce any of these experiences with clients. It is important to include bisexuality fully, rather than just adding the B as lip-service. This could include promoting bisexual groups, publications and events on notice boards, using bisexual images and examples in literature (e.g. images from pride events of bisexual groups, or of prominent bisexual figures), and ensuring that equality and diversity training includes bisexuality fully rather than as an adjunct to LG.

Despite bisexual invisibility, bisexuality is covered within the UK in the relevant legislation regarding equal treatment in relation to 'sexual orientation'. There is prohibition of discrimination on the grounds of sexual orientation, which is taken to mean: 'an individual's sexual orientation towards: people of the 'same' sex as him or her (gay or lesbian); people of the 'opposite' sex (heterosexual); or people of 'both' sexes (bisexual) (see Chapter 9).

GROUP NORMS

Experience is likely to differ greatly between the different groups under the umbrella of bisexuality, and even more so in relation to those who are attracted to, or sexually active with, more than one gender but who don't identify as bisexual.

There is an explicit bisexual community in many countries which is active in organising bisexual events and online bisexual spaces. There is no commercial bisexual scene in the same way that there is for gay men and, to a lesser extent, lesbian women, but rather more of a grassroots community. There are also therefore fewer of the identifiable identities within bisexuality that there are within LG scenes (see Chapter 9). However, there is overlap between bisexual communities and many other 'alternative' groups including trans (see Chapter 2), kink (see Chapter 6), polyamory (see Chapter 14), goth, geek and paganism (see Glossary). The bisexual community is also generally very welcoming of *allies* and *SOFFAs* (those who are not bisexual themselves but have partners or family who are, or who just find bisexual spaces to be comfortable, as do many trans and queer people, for example). There is generally a high level of awareness of mental health issues and diversity of ability and body forms which, again, can be a very positive experience for those who have found commercial heterosexual and gay scenes less welcoming. However, bisexual spaces, at least in the UK, tend to be very white and with the majority of people highly educated, meaning that some people of colour as well as those without high levels of education may feel less comfortable there.

Due to overlaps with kink and polyamorous communities, there is also often a strong ethos of consent within bisexual spaces, with people encouraged to check before any kind of physical contact with another (even hugs), and aware of language and behaviour that may be triggering to others (although again this can be experienced as excluding for those who are less well versed in such matters or whose cultural mode of communication involves a lot of touch). Many bisexual people speak of events like BiCon and BiFests in the UK and internationally as places where they feel more at home than in their daily life, due to them being able to be out, to mention their bisexuality without it being questioned or made an issue of, and also because of the generally welcoming and accepting atmosphere. However, events can feel very emotionally charged for the same reasons, and people are often encouraged to reflect on, and talk about, their self-care needs during them.

DISCLOSURE

As with LG people, issues of outness and self-disclosure are likely to be of relevance to bisexual people, with people coming to different decisions about who to tell and how to do this. Past psychological theories have often viewed *coming out* as an essential part of developing a healthy, mature sexual identity. However, more recently this has been questioned, for example by those who have pointed out that the concept of sexual identity may not be relevant across all cultures and that disclosure can open people up to discrimination, exclusion and violence, particularly within some cultural contexts. Of course there are stresses involved both in being out and in remaining closeted, which we explore further in Chapter 9. Therefore, while professionals should aid clients in coming out where a clear identity is held, they may usefully also explore degrees of outness and self-disclosure in such cases and be careful not to rush clients towards an identity label that does not feel comfortable to them.

RELATIONSHIP NORMS

There may be clashes of norms within relationships where one person is bisexual-identified and the other person (or people) is/are not. Perhaps particularly common, in terms of presenting to professionals, are married and long-term couples where one person has come out as bisexual later in the relationship, either after the discovery that they have been non-consensually non-monogamous (see Chapters 13 and 14) or because they have come to this realisation and disclosed to their partner. It is useful to explore, with both partners separately, what bisexuality means to them, how it is currently manifesting, how they see it being in future (following the disclosure) and whether they want to continue being in the relationship. After they have come to an awareness of their own feelings on these matters it is useful to bring them together to discuss it and find out where they are in agreement, where they can compromise and/or where they have irreconcilable differences.

It is worth being aware that partners may well have concerns about sexual rejection, losing the relationship, and worries about what this means for their own sexual identity and their knowledge of, and trust in, their partner. There may be challenges around accepting what has happened and letting go of the hope that the relationship could go back to how it was, as well as worries that it may be 'their fault' in some way, and anger at the partner for changing. Of course the experience of people in such situations is likely to vary depending on age, generation, culture, background, and many other factors.

SUMMARY AND CONCLUSIONS

Much of the good practice for working with bisexual clients is similar to that of working affirmatively with LG clients (see Chapter 8). In addition to these points, the following are pertinent.

- Professionals should reflect on their own sexuality, particularly the potential for fluidity.
- Examine your own attitudes towards bisexuality, recognising that biphobia and homophobia are culturally dominant and so people are likely to reproduce these to some extent, whatever their own sexual identity.
- Don't assume a person's sexual identity from information (like gender of partner) and be open to them choosing whatever label works for them, including no label or a shifting label.
- Recognise the social context rather than simply individualising the client's problems (e.g. if they fear prejudice or feel isolated).
- Be affirmative in ways that counteract shame, isolation, heteronormativity and biphobia. For example by gently challenging stereotypes, valuing the courage needed to claim a bisexual identity, and increasing the visibility of bisexual people (by giving examples or mentioning famous bisexual people).
- Be aware that community support may well be as valuable, or more so, than therapy or professional input (but also be aware that specifically bisexual communities may not always be the best place for everyone. For example, it is useful to be aware of other support which is available for older and younger people, queer people of colour, etc. as well).
- Include the B throughout your service and in any training, and challenge biphobia and bisexual invisibility more broadly.

FURTHER READING

Barker, M., Richards, C., Jones, R., Bowes-Catton, H., Plowman, T., Yockney, J. & Morgan, M. (2012). *The bisexuality report: Bisexual inclusion in LGBT equality and diversity*. Milton Keynes: The Open University Centre for

Citizenship, Identities and Governance. Available to download from www.biuk.org.

Firestein, B.A. (Ed.) (2007). *Becoming visible: Counseling bisexuals across the lifespan.* New York, NY: Columbia University Press.

Fox, R. (Ed.) (2006). *Affirmative psychotherapy with bisexual women and bisexual men.* Binghamton, NY: Harrington Park Press.

ADDITIONAL REFERENCES

Barker, M. (2007). Heteronormativity and the exclusion of bisexuality in psychology. In V. Clarke & E. Peel (Eds.), *Out in psychology: Lesbian, gay, bisexual, trans, and queer perspectives* (pp. 86–118). Chichester, UK: Wiley.

Boykin, K. (2005). *Beyond the down low.* Avalon.

Conway, L. (2007). Straight, gay or lying? Bisexuality revisited. http://ai.eecs.umich.edu/people/conway/TS/Bailey/Bisexuality/Bisexuality-NYT%207-05-05.html.

Gosine, A. (2006). 'Race', culture, power, sex, desire, love: Writing in 'men who have sex with men'. *IDS Bulletin, 37*(5): 27–33.

King, M. & McKeown, E. (2003). *Mental health and wellbeing of gay men, lesbians and bisexuals in England and Wales.* London: Mind.

LESBIAN AND GAY SEXUALITY

9

This chapter aims to:

- Consider the common concerns of lesbian and gay (LG) people, and 'same-gender' attracted people, who approach counsellors, psychologists and health professionals.
- Provide an overview of experiences, identities and practices of LG people.
- Explore wider cultural perceptions, legal and psychological perspectives about LG identities and experiences, including the history of pathologisation and criminalisation.

INTRODUCTION

This chapter considers identities and experiences based on 'same-gender' attraction. This encompasses people who explicitly identify as LG as well as those who have such attractions, encounters and/or relationships, who don't necessarily define as LG. This latter group are sometimes referred to using the sexual health terms men who have sex with men (*MSM*) and women who have sex with women (*WSW*) – the differentiation of practice from identity that we have seen elsewhere in this book.

The term *gay* can be used to refer to both men and women, whereas the term *lesbian* generally only refers to women. Of course it is always worth checking with each person which term they prefer. Many younger women prefer 'gay' to 'lesbian', while for some 'lesbian' is an important identity. It is problematic to use the term 'homosexual' rather than *lesbian* or *gay* (LG) to describe people because it is not a neutral term, but one loaded down by a history of pathologisation (see below). Additionally, people should be referred to as a gay man, for example, not as 'a gay' and then only when their sexuality is pertinent (otherwise just 'a man'). Some terms are offensive in some contexts (such as dyke, queer and queen), but may be used by the people themselves. Professionals should only use such terms if the client uses them, even if the professional uses such terms to refer to themselves.

It is somewhat questionable to cover the issues of LG men and women together in the same chapter because, as we will see, there are certainly many differences between the experiences of lesbian/gay women and gay men. Also, these issues have frequently been lumped together in the past in problematic ways which erase these differences. However, the same could also be said for covering bisexual, or heterosexual, women and men together in the same chapters (Chapters 8 and 10) as their experiences also differ greatly according to gender. We have consequently included women and men together here for consistency and also because there are several ways in which people with 'same-gender' attraction/relationships are treated similarly, meaning that they are likely to have some similar experiences (hence the history of LG politics frequently being a unified movement).

It will, however, be useful to read this chapter together with the chapter on cisgender (Chapter 4) to consider how wider perceptions of femininity and masculinity may impact on women and men differently, as well as with the chapter on transgender (Chapter 2) to consider the specific issues faced by LG people who are trans. Those who see themselves as gender-queer (Chapter 5) are less likely to identify as LG due to positioning themselves, and their attractions, outside binaries of gender (see Chapter 8).

COMMON CONCERNS

Broadly speaking, as with bisexual people (Chapter 8), there are three categories of 'same-gender' attracted people who will present to a counsellor, psychologist or other health professional:

- Those for whom their sexual identity and attractions are incidental to other issues they are dealing with.
- Those who are experiencing problems related to other people's perceptions of their sexual identity/practices.
- Those who are concerned in some way about their sexual attraction towards the 'same gender', who may or may not use the label *lesbian* or *gay*.

The majority of work with LG people, will of course fall under the first category where sexuality should not be the focus of the work. It may, of course, be that sexuality, as with any other identity or practice, will enter into the work at a later stage, but, as with heterosexual people, it should not be the first order of business.

COMING OUT

LG people may become open about their sexuality quite comfortably, but for some, being open in a heteronormative society can cause difficulties which bring them into contact with professionals. This may be the case, for example, if a person is older and so feels the need to reorganise several parts of their life due to the disclosure. As coming out is a common LG practice we have included it under Key Practices below.

EXPLANATIONS

Before and during coming out people often explore their sexual identity, and so it is probable that many clients will engage with the various explanations that have been put forward for LG sexualities. They may well present to a professional for precisely this reason.

PAUSE FOR CONSIDERATION

What explanations of sexuality are you aware of? Which are you drawn to? Consider: What caused your sexuality? How is it for you speaking to people who have very different explanations? Does there need to be a cause?

Much problematic theorising and research has been conducted in this area: problematic because it is overwhelmingly assumed that LGB sexualities require an explanation in a way that heterosexual ones do not, and also because most of the explanations which have been put forward suggest some abnormality or deficiency on the part of LGB people. However, many people desire such explanations in order to make sense of their experiences, to feel that their 'difference' is not 'their fault', and/or to prove their legitimacy to others. Currently biological explanations are often assumed to confer more legitimacy in these ways, so many may be drawn to the notion that they were 'born gay', while those who align themselves with queer activism (see Chapter 5) may be drawn to more sociocultural understandings.

As we have previously seen with trans and cisgender (Chapters 2 and 4), sexual and gender identities are likely to be the result of complex interactions between biological, psychological and social factors, with each influencing the other, all playing out in a certain sociohistorical context which structures the sense that is made of them, and how they are experienced. Additionally, even if such complexities were untangled, it is likely that explanations would differ vastly between people, for example the woman who took up a politically lesbian identity in the 1970s, compared to the teenage boy who knows that he has been attracted to other boys all his life.

As professionals it is important that we are open to multiple accounts of sexual identity, and to clients expressing beliefs and explanations which may not fit with our own. As with sexual identity labels themselves, a useful way to practise with explanations is to encourage clients to consider the various possibilities, what they offer, and what their drawbacks are. It is worth including consideration of what is lost and gained by having an explanation in general (including the possibility of not having one), as well as gently questioning whether explanations rooted in choice are the same thing as someone being 'to blame' (and the assumption behind this that being LG is somehow problematic in itself – it is not).

While coming out, and looking for explanations, are quite common experiences across LG people (as well as for many bisexual and queer people), experiences may well differ on the basis of gender in terms of the explanations and perceptions which are readily available to them. For example, the focus of explanations for 'same-gender' attraction has generally been on men rather than women and, as we will see, stereotypes and prejudices around 'same-gender' attracted men and women's sexualities differ.

'SEX ADDICTION'

The concept of 'sex addiction' has become more prevalent in recent years, and has particularly been applied to some gay men (by professionals and sometimes by men themselves). This concept can be particularly problematic in the contexts detailed in this chapter, especially concerning consensual non-monogamies (see Chapter 14), and should be used only with caution and if brought up by the client. Almost all diagnoses are culturally construed and behaviours which in some cultures are seen as quite acceptable (talking to spirits for example) may be seen as psychopathological in others. We can see the similarities between these diagnoses and those of 'sex addiction' in which, within certain gay subcultures, having had sexual partners numbering in the hundreds is not unusual, but may be considered so by someone used to a culture which expects heteronormative *serial monogamy* with some infidelity (see Chapter 13). As with other 'disorders' attention should be paid to whether the client deems there to be a problem (or in rare cases significant numbers of others do) and if that problem is individual to the client or socially derived (does the problem stem from his sister being angry with him for bringing men home, is that then the sister's problem?). Of course gay men also commonly have monogamous relationships – see below and Chapter 13.

HIV

In some countries there has been an historic association between HIV and gay communities, as with bisexual communities, which continues to the present day. While there are high rates of HIV among gay men, rates among heterosexual people are higher.[1] It is nonetheless worth practitioners being familiar with the treatments for HIV, such as antiretroviral medications, both globally and local to them as well as common experiences of being HIV positive as a gay man (cf. Flowers, Duncan & Knussen, 2003).

Experiences of HIV may be affected by this historic association in a way which is not present for some heterosexual people. Professionals should be particularly careful not to reinforce this, as HIV is, of course, a matter for people of any sexuality (although many asexual people and some BDSM practitioners and people who identify as furries are at a much lesser or zero risk, see Chapters 6, 7 and 12). When appropriate, practitioners may wish to refer people to LGB support groups and STI clinics for assistance with HIV and STIs more generally. However, as with other sexualities, LG specific support should be offered, but not assumed necessary, as many people may feel comfortable accessing general services.

ABUSE

LG people may seek assistance for abuse, as may people of all the sexualities and genders in this book. Physical and sexual abuse in 'same-gender' relationships can be particularly hard to acknowledge due to assumptions that it only takes place in a male–female context, pressure to present relationships in a positive light to others, and fears of ongoing contact with abusers due to small communities. Also, for women, there is the wider perception that they are not violent or abusive which can exacerbate difficulties in speaking out about such abuse, or for abusers in acknowledging what they are doing.

For men there is the additional complexity of the common link between masculinity and aggression. This is not to say that all gay men will be aggressive, indeed many gay men may have thought through these issues rather more carefully than their heterosexual counterparts who may have not been required to subject themselves to the same degree of introspection. However, in many societies, aggression and masculinity are inextricably intertwined and some gay men may access this as part of their masculinity.

Professionals should be aware of various forms of abuse with people of all sexualities, recognising that while physical violence can be traumatising,

---

[1] 38% of diagnoses in gay men compared to 57% in heterosexuals. See www.hpa.org.uk/NewsCentre/NationalPressReleases/2009PressReleases/090326NewHIVdiagnosesshowburdencontinuingingay/.

sexual abuse, social ostracism, emotional abuse and neglect, etc. can all also be so. It is important not to be overly cautious about alerting the proper authorities for fear that something is a 'minority matter'. If a person needs protection they should be protected.

COMMON MENTAL HEALTH PROBLEMS

Common mental health problems, such as depression and anxiety, are more prevalent in LG people than among heterosexuals (King & McKeown, 2003), probably related to the common experiences of, and anxieties about, homophobia, discrimination and loss (e.g. of family/ friends following coming out). Self-harm and suicide are particularly prevalent among LG youth who may feel lacking in support and role models offered by popular or traditional culture. Any mental health problems should be dealt with as with any other client, but with the added recognition that there may be stresses from society which are exacerbating them. Caution not to pathologise LG sexuality by proxy should be exercised if people present in very confused states and state they are gay or lesbian. All too often non-heterosexual sexualities are considered to be acceptable provided that clients are not in some other minority – otherwise there can be a problematic pursuit of 'normality', including heterosexuality. Staff should be advised that if they or other clients are uncomfortable then they nonetheless must accept the LG person's rights.

DISCRIMINATION (HETEROSEXISM, HOMOPHOBIA, BULLYING, ETC.)

Of course, one of the key issues which brings LG people to professionals is that of discrimination in its various forms. This is covered under Wider Society more fully below. Briefly, however, education can be extremely useful, whether by the professional involved or another professional. Support from the appropriate services and institutions can be effective at regaining the LG person's sense of equilibrium. Some LG people also find political activism useful in addressing these inequalities and in gaining a personal sense of satisfaction.

RELATIONSHIPS AND PARENTING

LG people may, of course, have relationship difficulties, much as people of other sexualities do. These are covered within parenting, relationship structures and sexual practices below.

ALCOHOL AND DRUG USE

Alcohol and drug use can be particularly common among some LG people as many LG social events, especially those on the gay scene, involve alcohol and/or drugs. In addition some sexual practices may involve drug use (see below). It is important for professionals to offer tailored services as some drug and alcohol use can be a means of dealing with discrimination and failing to address this could exacerbate the drug/alcohol use. Professionals should also be cautious around services which prioritise identifying as an 'addict' one's primary identity, as this can be deeply problematic for those with an LGB identity.

GENDER IDENTITY AND SEXUAL ATTRACTION

There is also, perhaps, a further category to the three outlined at the start of this section: that of a gay man who states that he is a woman because he is attracted to men. This is uncommon in people from Western cultures, but more commonly happens with men from some parts of the Middle East, Asia and Africa. Some people so presenting may, of course, actually be trans (see Chapter 2) and/or this may be related to different levels of discrimination of trans and 'same-gender' attracted people in some countries. In cases where people feel that their sexual attraction defines their gender it is worth emphasising that one may be a man and be attracted to another man, and exploring whether the client feels they 'should' transition in such cases and whether they would still do so if they were stranded on a desert island (without the influence of others). Education about the everyday reality of most gay men's lives can also be helpful as some people have stereotypical ideas.

KEY PRACTICES

COMING OUT

When LG people do come to a practitioner specifically to talk about sexuality, one key practice that may well be of relevance is *coming out*, that is, the disclosure of sexual identity to other people. Because it is still generally assumed that people are heterosexual unless otherwise stated, coming out is necessary in many contexts if people want others to be aware of their LGB identity. Only perhaps in specifically gay contexts, or contexts with high numbers of LGB people, would this situation be reversed. Thus, the decision to actively come out, or to remain *closeted* and allow people's assumptions to go unchecked, is an everyday reality for most, with both options having stress associated with them. If a client comes out to you for the first time this involves great trust and should be treated as such. Tentative enquires as to what assistance is required (if any) rather than immediate lectures on safe sex, HIV, etc. are appropriate.

Coming out is not a single event, but rather an ongoing process as new people enter a person's life. There are often stages in an initial coming-out process: coming out to oneself (recognising your own sexual identity), coming out privately to a few friends and family, coming out publicly to more people, and sometimes coming out politically in order to be recognised as an LGB person. However, not everyone will pass through all of these stages, they may occur in different orders and people may return to previous stages (for example, with new family members). Of course issues of class, culture, religion, geography, gender and age all intersect with sexuality meaning that coming out can be a highly individualised experience.

Common, but by no means universal, emotions around coming out are concern for other people's reactions (including rejection and/or attack), feelings of self-doubt, relief at being authentic, and the opening up of new possibilities. Sometimes the decision to be out is taken out of the individual's hands, for example if others gossip about their possible sexual identity, or if they are publicly outed by those who think they should be open about their sexuality. The lack of control in such circumstances can be very difficult, as can the sense that others are talking about you and viewing you in a certain limited way. Many LGB people go through coming out for the first time as a life stage like many others, with attendant difficulties, but with no undue distress. Some people do have difficulties, however and, especially if they come out later in life, may seek assistance. Professionals should assist clients to consider the implications as well as seeking to affirm a nascent identity against the vicissitudes of what is still usually a heterosexist culture.

While coming out has frequently been seen as *the* critical life experience in the development of LG people, it is important to be cautious about assuming this. Some younger people, particularly, may be more likely to perceive their sexual identity as fluid (see Chapter 8), and possibly not the most salient aspect of themselves. The experience of coming out is likely to be very different today than it was when LG sexualities were criminalised and pathologised (which may still be an important part of the life experience of many older LG people). It may be important to challenge assumptions that coming out is necessarily an all-consuming struggle, as well as common ideas that 'same-gender' sexual experiences, or embracing of community, are necessary parts of the coming-out process for everyone. As professionals it is obviously important that we protect the level of disclosure each client has chosen and that we make the process of coming out to us as positive as possible.

SEXUAL PRACTICES AND RELATIONSHIPS

Stereotypes often relate to sexual practices, based on misconceptions that lesbian/gay women exclusively/predominantly practise *oral sex* and gay men *anal sex*. In reality there are a range of sexual practices (including penetration with strap-on dildos among over half of lesbian/gay women), and oral and anal sex are both at least as common among heterosexual people (although what counts as sex is relevant here, as penetration being considered a *sine qua non* of sex may mean that some kinds of sex between men and between women is counted and some is not).

There are few differences between relationships involving LGB and heterosexual people in terms of satisfaction, longevity, or the kinds of everyday issues to be negotiated, but there may be less social support around the relationship for LGB people, depending on the extent of community that the relationship is located in. The subsections below outline some sexual practices and aspects of relationships which are worth being aware of, but diversity is the rule, as with heterosexual people, and an exploration of the client's own life is, of course, vital.

GAY MEN AND 'SAME-GENDER' ATTRACTED MEN'S SEXUAL PRACTICES AND RELATIONSHIPS

Gay men may have a variety of sexual practices when with a partner or partners including all of the possible forms of sexual contact. Non-monogamous relationships are comparatively common (see Chapter 14). There is also some overlap between gay and BDSM communities, particularly in relation to those who were involved in the 1970s' and 1980s' leather scenes (see Chapter 6). It is therefore useful for professionals to familiarise themselves with all of these things, both to be aware of possible intersections, and also so as not to elide them with gay men's sexuality inappropriately (as many are not non-monogamous or BDSM practitioners). It is also important that practitioners reflect on their own assumptions about what constitutes 'normal' sex so as not to pathologise clients or show discomfort around discussion of the variety of practices.

As with heterosexual people, gay men's sex, whether partnered or casual, may include barrier protection (condoms) for penetrative sex (for STIs – as there is, of course, no risk of unwanted pregnancy) and usually some form of lubricant if the people are having anal sex. As with heterosexual people some gay men may opt not to use condoms (sometimes called barebacking). This can have many different meanings (as for heterosexual people who do it) including being a demonstration of trust in a committed relationship or because it is experienced as more exciting or pleasurable. The meanings for a particular individual and/or couple can be useful to explore in the context of safer sex conversations.

Some, especially younger, gay men in urban areas may use poppers or crystal meth to enhance sex. Poppers (alkyl nitrates) can create a head rush and increased sexual pleasure and crystal meth (crystal methamphetamine) can increase arousal. Both, of course, have side effects and crystal meth addiction is a growing problem among some parts of the young urban gay communities, especially among sex workers (sometimes known as 'rent boys'). Education where necessary can be useful, although professionals should be wary of assuming clients are uneducated in these areas. The opportunity for specialist help can usefully be offered in cases of crystal meth addiction.

Other practices some gay men engage in are:

- *Cruising* (looking for other gay men or *MSM* to have sexual encounters with. These days this increasingly involves the use of phone apps which show where other gay men are, such as Grindr).
- *Cottaging* (having sexual encounters with other gay men or *MSM* in a public place, not uncommonly a park or a public toilet, not in use by other patrons – late at night for example).
- Attending bath houses for sex.
- *Cybersex* (having sexual encounters via the internet).

LESBIAN AND 'SAME-GENDER' ATTRACTED WOMEN'S SEXUAL PRACTICES AND RELATIONSHIPS

Women in long-term relationships with women may have less sex than those of other sexualities (often known as 'lesbian bed death'). However, it is important not to assume that will be true of all in such relationships, and to remember that sex is often heteronormatively defined as penetration, meaning that forms of sex in woman–woman relationships may not be captured by some studies (see Chapter 7 for more on how sex is defined).

While non-monogamous relationships are not as common among lesbian/gay women as among bisexuals or gay men, there are those who engage in this, and also in BDSM (see Chapters 14 and 6). For those lesbian/gay women whose sexual identities are related to political feminism, there may be tensions here as some feminists have regarded both non-monogamy and BDSM as inherently sexist.

Sometimes it is assumed that safer sex issues will not be of relevance to lesbian/gay women, but they also pass on STIs during sex of various kinds and should be aware of screening and protection possibilities such as condoms for sex toys and fingers, and dental dams for oral sex. As we saw in

Chapter 8, there is evidence that quite a large proportion of those who identify as lesbian have had some sexual activity with men, so it is important not to assume that all sex will be 'same-gender'. Consequently, screening and other health considerations, including birth control, may still be necessary, but should be addressed outside of discussions about sexual identity.

The general invisibility of lesbian sexuality mentioned above impacts on how easy it is for women to take up a LG identity, and may lead to some focusing on female friendships and fitting into 'companion' models, while others may project lesbian identities strongly, including visible markers (such as short hair), in order to speak above the silence. There are also increasingly recognised varieties of lesbian/gay women's appearances (beyond the butch/femme binaries of the 1950s and 60s).

In terms of relationships, most research finds little difference between relationships between women, and between men and women (on measures of satisfaction, longevity, etc.). However, relationships between women are often more equal, in terms of sharing household tasks and finances, but often also have less social support around them in times of difficulty. Some women settle quickly together (sometimes called 'U-Haul lesbians' after the US transport firm) and this can work out well, but will often need significant negotiation about the management of everyday life, as with people from other sexualities. It is important for professionals to be aware of their own assumptions about how soon people should settle and endeavour to see the client's worldview (if this is the matter before them) rather than, even implicitly, imposing their own.

WIDER SOCIETY

PATHOLOGISATION

The backdrop for the vast majority of gay or lesbian people approaching a practitioner will likely be an awareness of the history of pathologisation of 'homosexuality' within psychiatry, psychology and psychotherapy. Homosexuality was listed as a mental illness in the *DSM* until 1973 and as a disease in the *ICD* until 1992. 'Egodystonic homosexuality' remained a category in the *DSM* until 1987 (unwanted and distressing 'homosexual arousal') despite the likely involvement of sociocultural factors in this distress and the lack of a category of 'egodystonic heterosexuality'.

There is also a history, in many therapeutic approaches, of viewing 'same-gender' attraction and relationships as abnormalities or disorders, as in many of the psychoanalysts who built on Freud, Ellis' initial form of Rational Emotive Therapy, and the heterosexual assumptions of early forms of systemic family therapy. While many have moved away from such stances, there is still a vocal minority of therapists advocating 'conversion' or 'reparative' therapies aimed at making people heterosexual.

REPARATIVE OR CONVERSION THERAPY

The American Psychiatric Association position is that they oppose "any psychiatric treatment, such as 'reparative' or conversion therapy, which is based upon the assumption that homosexuality per se is a mental disorder or based upon the a priori assumption that a patient should change his/her sexual ... orientation", as well as finding lack of evidence for any efficacy of such therapies (APA, 1998). The American Psychological Association, Australian Psychological Society, UK Council for Psychotherapy, British Association for Counselling and Psychotherapy, the British Psychological Society, the Royal College of Psychiatrists and many other bodies, have released similar statements. For example, the United Kingdom Council for Psychotherapy advises therapists whose clients request 'conversion' to heterosexuality that such desires generally mask other pressing issues. It is useful, in such cases, for the practitioner to explore with the client why they consider their sexual desires or behaviours to be problematic, where and when this perception began, what others around them think, and the wider cultural and subcultural context of their lives. If at all uncertain, clients should be referred to those with expertise in LGB therapy. Under no circumstances should any attempt be made to engage in therapy based on heterosexism.

PROBLEMATIC PROFESSIONAL PRACTICE

Away from such extreme examples of homophobia and heterosexism, problematic professional practices also still occur with alarming frequency. Many LG people have had difficult experiences with health professionals because of their sexuality – often for matters quite unrelated to it. As with several of the other marginalised groups considered in this book, prevalent forms of problematic practice include:

- Viewing clients' LG sexuality as pathological.
- Assuming that sexuality is relevant to presenting problems.
- Lack of knowledge of LG issues, often meaning reliance on stereotypical assumptions due to not having other resources to draw on.
- Underestimating the impact of prejudice and discrimination.

This latter point is why it is worth being cautious about the use of the term 'internalised homophobia'. While certainly some with 'same-gender' attractions have anxieties, discomforts and other difficulties around their sexuality themselves, it is vital to contextualise this in the culture they are living in which still overwhelmingly views heterosexuality as the normal, and ideal, way of being. The idea of internalised homophobia risks pathologising and individualising the distress experienced rather than viewing it as a political and cultural issue requiring social change.

Even when a practitioner manages to avoid all of the problems above, it is still possible to engage in practices which unwittingly reinforce the idea that being LG is somehow problematic. For example, some heterosexual therapists used more pejorative emotion words when talking about LGB clients than LGB therapists did (aggressive, frightened, venomous and shameful; compared to assertive, proud, isolated and vulnerable – see Moon, 2008). Some professionals even express concerns about LGB, but not heterosexual, clients becoming parents when there is no evidence to support such concerns (Golombok, 1999).

PAUSE FOR CONSIDERATION

Dominic Davies, the founder of the organisation Pink Therapy, has suggested that heterosexual therapists do the following 'homowork' to experience – albeit briefly – something of what it is like being LG.

- Buy an LG magazine and read it in public.
- Go for a drink in an LG club or bar.
- Wear an LG shirt or badge.
- Hold hands with a 'same-gender' person in public.
- Keep your heterosexuality in the closet for a week by ensuring that you don't give it away in conversation (e.g. don't mention a partner's gender when talking about what you did at the weekend or when talking on the phone with a tradesperson).[2]

LGB PROFESSIONALS

It is important to be aware that LGB practitioners are not immune from problematic practices here. For example, it may be difficult to work with client accounts of their sexuality which differ widely from our own experiences if we are of the same identity (see Chapter 8). It can be difficult to

---

[2] Other useful activities along these lines are the heterosexuality questionnaire (www.pinkpractice.co.uk/quaire.htm) and homoworld (www.bps.org.uk/downloadfile. cfm?file_uuid=035DD3B4-1143-DFD0-7EBA-89C49CB6637E&ext=doc).

recognise intersections of sexuality with socio-economic status, race, culture, class, age, gender, etc. which mean that identity labels, spaces and resources which are positive for the professional may not be for the client. Finally, there are issues around self-disclosure and dual relationships specific to being an LGB professional with an LGB client which are covered in the Introduction to this book.

MATCHING CLIENT AND PROFESSIONAL

Some LG clients prefer to be matched with an LG practitioner (as can also be the case with gender, race, religion and ethnicity) so it is worth having this available where possible, raising it with clients to help them to make such a request, and being aware of local LGBTQ services for referral where it is not possible within an organisation. That said, client concerns about seeing non-gay or lesbian professionals should often also be attended to as sometimes simple reassurance regarding discrimination may be sufficient to allay fears. It may be that the most skilled professional is not one of the same sexuality.

SELF-DISCLOSURE OF PROFESSIONALS

Attention should also be paid to issues of self-disclosure. Many (although not all) LG clients want to know the sexuality of their practitioner and consider this important for the work. In terms of countering heteronormativity, self-disclosure can be useful in terms of therapists modelling comfort with their own sexuality (particularly if they are LGB themselves) and demonstrating that these issues are important for everyone to be aware of (if they are heterosexual). Of course, heterosexuality is generally assumed and quite often communicated to clients (via married names, wedding rings and/or pictures of spouse/family) so it is quite appropriate that other sexualities be communicated in similar ways. Sexualities may well be assumed anyway, particularly if practitioners are listed on LGBTQ-friendly websites. However, self-disclosure should *only* be done if it is in the client's interest otherwise the professional is at risk of co-opting the client's space. It is also worth thinking about what professionals do and do not disclose generally and whether sexuality should be paramount. If professionals do disclose, it should always be done thoughtfully, and with awareness and possibly exploration of what it means to a client. For example, self-disclosures may be heard as encouragement for 'questioning' clients to take up the practitioner's identity, rather than an alternative one.

DUAL RELATIONSHIPS

There are specific challenges for both heterosexual, and LGB professionals, when working with LGB clients, as we have seen. A final issue for LGB practitioners to negotiate is that of dual relationships. Communities are small and therefore it is likely that practitioners will occasionally find themselves meeting clients in social or professional spaces and/or find that they are linked by friends-of-friends or lovers-of-lovers. This is another reason to consider up-front self-disclosure and discussion of how such meetings and links will be navigated. Practitioners may feel pressure to be 'poster children' for their sexuality when out-and-about, and/or they may feel they have to restrict themselves and perhaps lose some of their own sources of community and social support. These are all issues which could be well-addressed with an LGB supervisor and are certainly worth being aware of from the outset. LGB professionals may find it useful to create smaller safe community-within-community groups of similarly positioned professionals for support.

HOMOPHOBIA

Perhaps the most important commonality between lesbian/gay women and gay men is their shared experience of *homophobia* (including *institutionalised homophobia*), *heterosexism* and *heteronormativity* (see Glossary). It is important to recognise that, even when there is no overt homophobia, people are subject to heterosexism in common beliefs that 'same-gender' couples shouldn't express affection publicly, or have precisely the same rights, as heterosexual people. Heteronormativity can be seen in everyday assumptions that a person's partner will be of the 'other gender' (so they either have to correct this, or let the wrong assumption go unchallenged), or the fact that anniversary cards, commercials, and men's and women's magazines assume heterosexual relationships.

Experiences of homophobia, heterosexism and heteronormativity are not unified. The onus is not *just* on heterosexual practitioners to interrogate their assumptions. LG practitioners may be just as likely as heterosexual ones to make biphobic or cisgenderist assumptions (if they are cisgender) which are negative for bisexual clients (see Chapter 8) or trans LGB people (see Chapter 2).

RACE, CULTURE, ETHNICITY AND HOMOPHOBIA

White practitioners of all sexualities need to reflect on white privilege, which can include coming out as LGB. The double discrimination of racism

and homophobia impacts hugely on *queer people of colour* and those in ethnic minorities with 'same-gender' attraction, as does the view in some (but
by no means all) racial contexts that LGB identities are a white thing (see
Chapter 8), and the potential loss of the family and community who are
vital for dealing with everyday experiences of racism and discrimination.
Professionals can usefully reflect on what the experience of 'same-gender'
attraction would be like for those with a cultural background where it is
illegal (Iran, for example), where certain sexual practices with 'same-gender'
people are comprehensible within heterosexuality (e.g. men who penetrate
men in some Latin and Arab countries), or where there is a non-dichotomous
model of gender (see Chapter 2).

AGE AND GENERATION AND HOMOPHOBIA

Age and generation impact on the lived experience of discrimination that
people have: whether, for example, they were ever convicted or treated for
their sexuality. Practitioners should be especially careful not to alienate
clients who may have had extremely bad experiences with professionals
before. Also it should not be assumed that a person is heterosexual, just
because they are older. Careful exploration of understandings, which may
differ from some younger people's understandings of sexuality, is necessary.

GEOGRAPHICAL LOCATION AND HOMOPHOBIA

Geographical location impacts on experiences of prejudice and discrimination. For example those in cities with a gay area (like London, Manchester
and Brighton in England; San Francisco or Boston in the US or Paris in
France) are likely to have very different experiences from those in more rural
settings (with the notable exception of Hebden Bridge, a small, rural Yorkshire
mill town in the UK with a high proportion of lesbian inhabitants). Professionals should therefore be wary of recommending 'community support' in
areas where there is none. The internet is, as ever, invaluable in this regard.
Those people without internet access via a computer or mobile phone may
often access it in a library or community centre, although it is worth being
mindful that some may feel uncomfortable in such a public setting.

GENDER AND HOMOPHOBIA

Clearly there are also gender differences in experiences of homophobia
and heterosexism. As we have seen, there are a number of misconceptions
about LG people's sexual practices. Common to stereotypes relating to

both lesbian/gay women and to gay men is a confusion of gender and sexuality, such that lesbian/gay women are often stereotyped as masculine or 'butch', and gay men as feminine or 'effeminate'. While some LG people do claim butch or camp identities, for various reasons, by no means all do and it should not be assumed. Similarly, the stereotype that there are 'masculine' and 'feminine' partners in 'same-gender' relationships is not the case, although some lesbian/gay women understand their relationships in 'butch/femme' terms.

Lesbian/gay women are generally less visible than gay men (in media, policies, events, etc.) which means there may be more difficulties being recognised as lesbian as well as double discrimination due to being a woman and being 'same-gender' attracted. However, gay men may be more frequently recognised and regarded with suspicion (with stereotypes about being predatory and/or promiscuous). All this means that professionals should be cautious in reproducing received stereotypes about LG people and should make a concerted effort not to perpetuate such stereotypes themselves, even though questioning whether these things are true for their clients.

HATE CRIME

Homophobic hate crimes remain a common occurrence. Very many LGB people have been the victim of physical violence or bullying and the word 'gay' is used as a casual insult in UK school playgrounds with homophobic bullying in this context being commonplace. There are 85 UN countries that still view same-sex sexual practices as criminal and 'unnatural' acts, and they are even punishable by death in some. Clearly, that will impact on the experiences of many who now live in the UK. Professionals should strive to reassure clients that they work in an affirmative manner and that clients are protected under UK law. Careful consideration should be given as to the passing on of information and records where there are concerns.

LEGAL RECOGNITION

Legally, protections for LG people and others with 'same-gender' attraction differ across countries and it is consequently important to find out about these in your own legal context. There are two main pieces of UK legislation which protect LG people, which are well worth being aware of. The Equality Act (Sexual Orientation) Regulations (2007) prohibits discrimination on the grounds of sexual orientation, in the provision of goods, facilities and services. The Civil Partnership Act (2004) allows legal partnerships between two people regardless of gender, with equal rights to married spouses regarding pensions, immigration, next of kin and tax. LGB people are free therefore to have 'same sex' civil partnerships. These are quite often ceremonies something similar to weddings with people in suits and dresses, etc. Of course, as with heterosexual people, there may also be much diversity, but in general they are elegant celebrations of love.

However, marriage between 'same-gender' partners is not allowed at present meaning that equality is not total, and that some trans people have to divorce post transition as this puts them in a 'same-gender' relationship.

On the back of the legislation listed above, guidelines have been put in place by key bodies for training of health professionals regarding sexuality (e.g. Department of Health, 2006).

GROUP NORMS

In this section we consider some norms among lesbian/gay women, and among gay men. Bear in mind that LG group norms differ across cultural and regional contexts (see above). Generally professionals working with LG clients should familiarise themselves with LG culture broadly (for example, by watching LG movies and TV programmes and reading LG magazines) as well as with their more local LG communities (what support exists, what terminology is current, etc.).

THE SCENE

The scene is a term for the commercial products, clubs, pubs, restaurants, etc. which cater for a gay, and to a lesser extent, lesbian clientele. For some people it is a comfortable place as it offers a sense of community and home, however access will be determined by socio-economic constraints as well as other factors considered below.

CLASS

Class and socio-economic factors may affect people's access into certain spaces. Further, understandings and acceptances of sexual diversity differ across class contexts, and middle class LG people may be more likely than working class ones to have access to positive representations of people like themselves in the media, and educational resources around sexuality. Practitioners can strive to address this through affirmative practice, while still recognising the reality of the situation for clients needing to find an income, social group, etc.

DISABILITY

There are LGBT networks for some – but not all forms – of physical and learning disability. There are often issues in accessibility of services as there can be lack of recognition of any sexuality of disabled people – particularly those who are LGB. Also the idealisation of certain body types in some, but by no means all, LG spaces can impact negatively on some disabled LG people.

Professionals should strive to provide services which are equally available for heterosexual and LGB people. It can be tiring at best, and impossible at worst, for people seeking services to also have to negotiate heterosexism. For example, a person coming on to a ward should not have to explain to all staff that his next of kin is his male partner where a female partner would be assumed.

HEALTH ISSUES

Women's health issues, such as menopause, breast cancer, hysterectomy and infertility may impact differently on lesbian/gay women than on bisexual and heterosexual women. For example, infertility may compound other barriers in the way of lesbian/gay women becoming pregnant. Also, some may have particular issues around their femininity which are challenged through medical interventions such as hysterectomy and mastectomy or menopause. Professionals should be careful to support and assist lesbian/gay women attending to both gender and sexuality (as well as other aspects of their identity).

Notions of masculinity and what it means to be a man may be particularly relevant to gay men, especially in the context of the wider stereotype of gay men as feminine and passive. Gay men may therefore be especially concerned about health issues which affect masculinity. Issues such as erectile dysfunction should be attended to carefully as well as any relationship implications. It is worth being aware (and possibly making clients aware) that there is not just one masculinity but multiple masculinities, and that these are changing and dynamic processes rather than being fixed within people (see also Chapters 2, 4 and 5). Of course, as we have seen, HIV has particular connotations for gay men which should also be sensitively addressed.

PARENTING

Around a third of lesbian/gay women parent. In the past, and sometimes still currently, this occurs through them having previously become parents in relationships with men. Some become pregnant through donor insemination (either as couples or single parents). This may be with an unknown donor, or a known person who is involved in family life to some extent. Some adopt or foster. There may be one parent, two parents, or multiple parents involved in all these situations. It is worth practitioners being well informed about the possibilities, as well as aware of the potential hetero-normativity that will be faced by women in this situation (for example, assuming that male friends are the father or failure to recognise the co-parent). It is also important to be aware of common myths around lesbian parenting and to be able to dispel these. For example, evidence is strong that children with lesbian parents fair as well in every way as those with heterosexual parents, and concerns that such children will be bullied are homophobic in a similar way to an argument that black people should not have children because of racism would be racist (Clarke, 2001).

Around 13% of gay men have children. As with lesbian/gay women, this is either through previous relationships with women, various kinds of co-parenting arrangements, adoption/fostering, or occasionally surrogacy. It is worth practitioners being well informed about the options and potential barriers to parenting, which may of course, include prejudice which practitioners can address through their own work and advocacy on behalf of their clients as needed. Within the UK, LG parents are protected under law from various types of discrimination, but this is by no means the case globally.

HOMONORMATIVITY

In recent years, gay rights activists have fought for equality in terms of relationship recognition, adoption rights and other rights that heterosexual people have access to. It is important to recognise, however, that while many embrace these developments, others prefer to remain outside such heteronormative institutions. Some have proposed that, in addition to heteronormativity, there is also a homonormativity, particularly in more commercial gay (and, to some extent, lesbian) scenes, whereby those who are most similar to heterosexuals are seen as most worthy of rights. This can be seen, perhaps, in the preference in many personal ads for 'straight-acting' gay men, in the privileging of gender conformity and conventional coupled relationships, and in the othering that occurs in some gay contexts around attraction to different racial groups ('queen slang'). Some have also criticised the focus on appearance in gay communities, particularly around youth and gym-toned bodies, although this is complicated, to some extent, by subcultures which have emerged for specific appearances, notably bear culture (chunky, hairy, gay men), which has led to further subgroups such as otters (sleeker), cubs (younger) and silver foxes (mature, grey-haired). These community terms should be used with caution by practitioners as, while they should not be offensive as such, they require significant nuance to be used correctly.

SUMMARY AND CONCLUSIONS

Since the 1980s a great deal has been written on gay-affirmative therapy. This developed due to evidence of harmful therapeutic practices mentioned previously. Some have challenged the term 'affirmative', questioning whether practitioners have the authority to determine what should be affirmed. For example, as we have seen, affirming a gay identity poses serious problems if it means disaffirming a possible bisexual identity (Chapter 8) or if race, cultural and religious contexts are not taken into account. However, given the omnipresence and pervasive power of heteronormativity, it is necessary for practitioners to use some of the weight of their authority to counter this (as much as is possible), for example: by raising awareness of heteronormativity in clients, by attending to the wider world of the client rather than focusing on their individual experience, by providing education and resources, and by aiding them in countering prejudice. This is in addition to valuing 'same-gender' attraction and LGB identities as much as 'other-gender' attraction and heterosexuality, which should be part of all ethical practice.

Good practice with lesbian, gay and 'same-gender' attracted clients includes the following points, whatever clinical approach. Most of these points apply equally to the other marginalised sexualities, genders and relationship structures covered in this book:

- Practitioners should gain an awareness and comfort with their own sexuality through self-reflection.
- There should be respect for the client's sexuality, culture and beliefs, including openness to the diversity of ways in which they may, or may not, self-identify.
- Professionals should not implicitly or explicitly reinforce the pathologisation or stigmatisation of client sexualities.

Professionals should also demonstrate:

- Awareness of heteronormativity, heterosexism and homophobia in clients' lives.
- Awareness of the history of the treatment of people with 'same-gender' attraction and the diversity of people and communities under this umbrella.
- Understanding of the power differences between client and practitioner, particularly where practitioners occupy positions of privilege which the client does not (e.g. heterosexual, cisgender, white, male, upper/middle class, etc.).

It is also worth ensuring that everyone in a clinic/organisation is trained in these issues – including administrative staff – and ensuring that literature, images and materials are not exclusively heteronormative.

FURTHER READING

Clarke, V., Ellis, S.E., Peel, E. & Riggs, D.W. (2009). *Lesbian, gay, bisexual, trans and queer psychology: An introduction*. Cambridge: Cambridge University Press.

King, M., Semylen, J., Killaspy, H., Nazareth, I. & Osborn, D. (2007). *A systematic review of the research on counselling and psychotherapy for lesbian, gay, bisexual and transgender people*. Leicester: BACP.

Kort, J. (2007). *Gay affirmative therapy for the straight clinician*. New York, NY: Norton.

Peel, E., Clarke, V. & Drescher, J. (Eds.) (2007). *British lesbian, gay and bisexual psychologies*. Binghamton, NY: Haworth Press.

Ritter, K.Y. & Terndrup, A.I. (2002). *Handbook of affirmative psychotherapy with lesbian women and gay men*. New York: The Guilford Press.

ADDITIONAL REFERENCES

American Psychiatric Association (1998). Reparative therapy [Position Statement]. Washington DC: APA.

Clarke, V. (2001). What about the children? Arguments against lesbian and gay parenting. *Women's Studies International Forum, 24*(5), 555–570.

Department of Health (2006). *Core training standards for sexual orientation: Making national health services inclusive for LGB people*. London: Department of Health.

Flowers, P., Duncan, B. & Knussen, C. (2003). Reappraising HIV testing: An exploration of the psychosocial costs and benefits associated with learning one's HIV status in a purposive sample of Scottish gay men. *British Journal of Health Psychology, 8*, 179–194.

Golombok, S. (1999). Lesbian mother families. In A. Bainham, S. Day Sciater & M. Richards (Eds.), *What is a parent: A socio-legal analysis*. Oxford: Hart Publishing.

King, M. & McKeown, E. (2003). *Mental health and wellbeing of gay men, lesbians and bisexuals in England and Wales*. London: Mind.

Moon, L. (2008). Queer(y)ing the heterosexualisation of emotion. In L. Moon (Ed.), *Feeling queer or queer feelings* (pp. 36–53). London: Routledge.

HETEROSEXUALITY   10

This chapter aims to:

- Consider heterosexuality as a distinct and diverse sexuality in its own right.
- Explore the problems that can occur when adhering to normative sexuality too rigidly.
- Examine key practices around the relationships and sexual encounters of heterosexual people.
- Cover societal norms and expectations of heterosexual people, and the social and psychological categories which they may be placed in if they fail to meet these expectations.

INTRODUCTION

This chapter considers heterosexuality, which is attraction to the 'other gender' (as opposed to the 'same gender' or more than one gender, covered in Chapters 8 and 9). The word *straight* is also frequently used for this sexual identity. It is important to note that people in a romantic relationship between a man and a woman may not, themselves, be heterosexual, as one or both of them may be bisexual (see Chapter 8). This chapter specifically considers heterosexuality, although some aspects may also apply to bisexual people in such relationships. Generally we are speaking about heterosexual individuals and heterosexual people in a relationship.

HETERONORMATIVITY

This idea of heterosexuality as the 'norm' – which has other assumptions associated with it such as (in many Western cultures) being a couple, getting married, having a family, owning a car, wearing the 'right' clothes, and meeting key landmarks in life – is often known as 'heteronormativity'. Often, heterosexual people's issues do not pertain directly to their sexuality, but rather to wider concerns around what it means to be (hetero)normative.

PAUSE FOR CONSIDERATION

Try listing the ideal version of sexuality which is portrayed in the media. Think about the kinds of relationships and sex which are depicted in billboard advertisements, women's and men's magazines, Hollywood movies, and/or in pop songs.

Heteronormativity means that the issues faced by those identifying as heterosexual are often quite different from those of LGB people because they are more about fitting into this norm, rather than about experiencing difficulties due to being placed outside of it. For example, as with other normative identities such as cisgender (Chapter 4) and monogamy (Chapter 13), problems might consist of:

- Trying to conform to a very narrow set of practices rather than appreciating the diversity of possibilities within the identity.
- Thinking that being 'normal' in one way means having to buy into a whole package of normativity (for example, also conforming to conventional gender roles, relationship structures, and life events such as getting married, having children, etc.).
- Not seeing one's identity as something that can be spoken about or considered because it is taken for granted.
- Feeling trapped within the norm if it is not something that completely fits.
- Fearing what will happen if one strays from the norm in any way because of not having experienced being outside of the norm, and because of how people on the outside are treated.

For these reasons it is worth reading this chapter alongside Chapters 4 and 13 because often the three identities (cisgender, heterosexual and monogamous) present together, and the issues with them overlap. This is particularly the case with cisgender because sexuality and gender are strongly culturally interwoven. For example, being a 'real man' is associated with being attracted to women, and vice versa. In this chapter we focus mostly on the sexual aspects of being within the norm, while in Chapter 4 we focus on gender roles more broadly, and in Chapter 13 on common relationship structures. However, it is important to bear in mind that there may be other intersections with heterosexuality. For example, many people with a trans history (see Chapter 2) will also be heterosexual and monogamous, and have normative gender roles, and there are many heterosexual non-monogamous people (for example this is particularly common among swingers, see Chapter 14).

COMMON CONCERNS

Broadly speaking there are three categories of heterosexual people who will present to a counsellor, psychologist or other health professional:

- Those for whom their identity or sexual attraction is incidental to other issues they are dealing with.
- Those for whom heterosexuality is their primary identity, but who nonetheless experience some attraction to people of the 'same gender' (this group is dealt with in Chapter 8 on bisexuality, which covers all variations of 'same- and other-gender' attraction).
- People who experience attraction only to the 'other gender' but define heterosexuality very narrowly, causing them to have difficulties because – for example – they assume that they have to have a very specific kind of sex, relationship or family.

The remainder of this chapter will focus on the latter group of people whose presenting concerns can be linked, in some way, to their heterosexuality, and to their expectations about what this involves. People are very unlikely to present to a practitioner as having issues with their heterosexuality, and indeed many practitioners may inadvertently assume that because a client is heterosexual no exploration need be undertaken. However, examination of what their assumptions are (about the 'normal' way to have sex, relationships, families, etc.) will be a vital exploration in many cases. As with most other sexualities, having a questioning whisper at the back of one's mind as to whether this sexuality may be relevant can be useful rather than assuming it will necessarily be the case.

NORMALITY

One of the potential benefits of identifying as heterosexual is that it offers a set of relatively common understandings of what appropriate or 'normal' behaviour is (although this will vary across time and culture – see below), which can be very reassuring and should therefore be carefully addressed by the practitioner when relevant. A difficulty with this is that these understandings are generally received (from wider society, parents, peers, etc.) rather than created by the individual, and consequently sometimes lack the personal fit of other sexualities where an individual can determine their own identity and practices to a greater degree. Practitioners should therefore weigh up possible interventions, considering potential benefits of personal authenticity against possible costs of ostracism and alienation.

Almost every heterosexual person in this latter category, presenting to a practitioner, will at some point say something along the lines of "I just want to be normal" or "Am I normal?". The key concern, in all areas of life, is about matching up to an assumption of what 'normal' is, and the key anxiety is that one might not be 'normal' (in that culture, time, place, etc.).

Often an important thing that a professional can offer is to widen out the concept of what normal is, for example by pointing out that people often present themselves in life as being very normal, but that – as professionals – we see the diversity of differences and experiences that there are among seemingly 'normal' individuals, couples, families, etc. This kind of normalising, for example, might be about letting a woman know how many other women struggle to experience orgasms from penetrative sex, or telling a couple how common conflicts of the kind they are experiencing are, bringing in the idea of 'good-enough' child-rearing, or citing statistics on divorce and/or infidelity.

SPECIFIC ISSUES

For the remainder of this section we will briefly summarise some of the common specific issues brought by heterosexual people in relation to sex, relationships, gender, family, and the lifespan.

SEX

Most of the 'sexual dysfunctions' listed in the *DSM* and *ICD* are related to attempts to have a certain form of (penis-in-vagina) heterosexual sex (Barker, 2011a). Briefly these include lack of desire or aversion to sex; 'female' and 'male' forms of both orgasm disorder and sexual arousal disorder (in men the latter is more commonly called 'erectile dysfunction', ED); 'premature ejaculation' (PE) for men; pain disorder; and vaginismus (for women who experience uncomfortable vaginal muscle spasms when penetrated). In addition to these, the *ICD-10* also lists forms of 'excessive sexual drive' (nymphomania and satyriasis). There is also a common cultural category of 'sex addiction' which is about people wanting 'too much' sex.

From this, we can see that 'normal' sex is often viewed as requiring enough, but not too much, sexual desire, and that it is necessary, when applied to heterosexual people, for men to be erect and to penetrate women vaginally, for women to be penetrated, and for both to orgasm. Heterosexual people are likely to present to a GP, sex therapist, or sexual health practitioner, if their sexual experience does not map on to this.

Professionals should be cautious in uncritically accepting the versions of sex suggested by these categories as the normal/only ways of having sex, and may benefit from considering other possibilities within it (see below) and outside of heteronormative sex (see Chapters 6, 7 and 12). This is not to say that heteronormative sex may not be quite the right thing for a particular client, but rather that it should be a considered choice, rather than an unconsidered one which causes enough distress to bring them to a professional.

RELATIONSHIPS

Heterosexual people may experience problems if they are single for any length of time beyond adolescence, since a norm of heterosexuality is to be in a couple. Also, there are specific ideals about how to meet a partner and what it means to be in a couple, and people often experience problems if these are not met. Relationship conflicts can be difficult when the norm of relationships is that they should easily run smoothly and break-ups can be experienced as a personal failure.

Again here the professional may wish to gently challenge some of the assumptions, especially those from the movies, which generally stop at a drive into the sunset and ignore 40 years of picking up pants afterwards. Careful consideration of the reality of the client's life, rather than an unconsidered expectation, is key.

GENDER

Because heterosexuality often involves people of different genders living together, their gender expressions can be curtailed because the person of the other gender feels inadequate if 'their role' is taken over. For example, if a woman earns more than her husband or if a male partner enjoys cooking, the other partner may feel inadequate in terms of their own gender. There can also be other issues around gender expectations, for example in the common situation of male partners struggling to see their female partners as both mothers and sexual beings. Here it can be useful for clients to consider who wrote the roles they are adhering to and how variable those roles are across time and cultures. Careful exploration can be useful while widening out the notion of 'still being normal'.

FAMILY

There are often ideas that 'normal' heterosexuality involves having one's own family at a particular point in life (although this point varies across generations, cultures, etc.) Therefore problems can be experienced if there is infertility, or ambivalence about what having children will mean, or if the economic situation makes it very difficult to have children. Additionally, people can be traumatised, in terms of their own identity as well as in terms of the loss, if their children are removed. There are cultural and class variations in terms of whether a nuclear or extended family model is expected, and difficulties experienced when the situation makes it difficult to conform to the expectation.

It can be useful for professionals to assist people to consider their own motivations for a family and what, independent of social (or other) constraints, they would wish for, before returning to the reality of the social (or other) constraints to consider those. As usual 'of course' and 'should' phrases should be carefully attended to as they often point the way to received assumptions which may not be helpful in this client's case.

LIFESPAN

Heterosexuality often brings with it certain other assumptions about points in life at which certain rites of passage need to take place. For example, it may be expected that somebody will have a job by a certain age, get married at a certain point, that children will leave home at a particular age, and that any retirement will take place at a certain time (and what this will mean). There can be a lot of stress if it looks like these 'checkpoints' will not be reached, or if couples have different views about what their key points are and/or when they should happen.

Again careful consideration of these expectations, especially considering whether the expectations of others such as parents etc. are reasonable can be useful in unpicking the problems for the client and the problem other people have with the client. People will often have to live with others' opinions of their actions and that can usefully form part of the consideration as to what people wish to do.

EVERYDAY LIFE

Beyond specific life goals, heterosexuality often brings with it certain assumptions around wider aspects of everyday life, which are perpetuated by mass media. These may include assumptions that it is necessary to have a certain type of car, house, body, kitchen, etc. Some groups (for example those who are marginalised, poor, disabled, who have mental health problems) may not be able to acquire all the possessions, aspects of appearance, and such, which are considered necessary to be 'properly' heterosexual. For example, there may be constraints around the ability to earn money or to have a specific body type if one is on certain medications. A further aspect of everyday life which is often linked to heterosexuality is the set of assumptions around shared time, space, etc. For example, heterosexual couples may feel that they always have to eat dinner together, go on holiday together, or sleep in the same bed, even when it is impractical to do so due to health problems, different interests, financial constraints, etc.

In all of these arenas of life, feelings of loss, failure or distress can result when it is perceived that an individual, couple or family is not fitting the 'norm' and that this may be seen by others. Professionals, especially those working with marginalised groups, should be especially careful if their interventions impact upon people's wish to adhere to the 'norm', opening up discussion of this when necessary.

It is important that professionals do not only question the norm in their clients when it is appropriate to do so, but also consider ways in which they themselves may adhere to these (as most people do to different extents). For a professional with a car, for example, to question a client's wish to have one as part of heteronormativity would be a potentially problematic intervention, unless they themselves had carefully considered the matter.

KEY PRACTICES

In this section we will consider, in more detail, the sexual, relationship and friendship practices of heterosexual people.

SEX

Heterosexual people may have a variety of different types of sexual encounters. Common practices include oral sex (sometimes known as *going down* or *cunilingus* where a man licks a woman's vulva, or a *blow job* or *fellatio* where a man puts his penis in a woman's mouth), *anal sex* (in which a man puts his fingers or penis into a woman's anus, or when a woman penetrates a man anally using fingers, a dildo or strap-on, also known as *pegging*), and vaginal sex (where a vagina envelops a penis, often called 'penetrative' sex). Of course, what is considered 'usual' sexually changes over time, and is influenced by media including pornography and mainstream depictions of sex (see Wider Society section below). So, for example, practices such as *pegging* (see above), *teabagging* (taking a man's testicles in one's mouth), *tit-wank* (a woman masturbating a man between her breasts), *intercrural sex* (stimulation between lubricated thighs), *pearl necklace* (a man ejaculating on a woman's upper body), *rimming* (licking the anus), etc. may move from being stigmatised practices to being mainstream, or even expected, as might sexual fashions such as Brazilian waxes (the removal of pubic hair), genital piercings or decorations, etc.

There are various different positions associated with oral, anal and vaginal sex. It is often assumed that the most common type of vaginal sex is missionary intercourse (where a woman lies facing up underneath a man who faces down with their heads at the same end). However, there are many different positions in which sex can take place, and others may well be more conducive to pleasure and/or orgasm than the *missionary position* (for example, penises often become erect more easily when standing up, and most women require some clitoral stimulation in order to orgasm, which is easier if the clitoris can be touched by hands or vibrators and/or if their legs are together rather than separated).

It is often assumed that heterosexual sex should generally follow a specific trajectory, moving from kissing and cuddling, to 'foreplay' (touching and kissing parts of the body which are considered erotic such as breasts and genitals), to penetration once both people are aroused, to orgasm, to afterglow. The 'sexual dysfunctions' covered above are related to one or more of these stages not happening in the expected way (such as penetration being painful or orgasm being impossible). Sex therapy often involves taking the pressure off the expected trajectory (hence the problem with the 'fore' in foreplay) to focus on the here-and-now sensations. It also involves improving communication about what people find sexually exciting (covered below).

PREGNANCY AND STIs

One of the particular risks associated with sex between a man and a woman, most commonly in heterosexual sex, is that of unwanted pregnancy – which does not occur in other forms of sex. When considering safer sex, heterosexual people will need to be aware of the risk of both sexually transmitted infections (STIs) and unwanted pregnancy. This means that, for example, contraception may be necessary even in a monogamous partnership where neither partner has an STI. *Safer sex* may also be related to the taken-for-granted trajectory of sex as it may be viewed as 'getting in the way' of this flow. It may be helpful for health practitioners to help people to find ways of incorporating condoms or other barrier protection into their *sexual scripts* (something that has been done to some extent in sexual health literature for LGB people, but less so in relation to heterosexuality).

RELATIONSHIPS

The common practices in relationships between men and women vary over time and across cultural groups. So, for example, there may be differences in the rituals around dating, when it is considered appropriate to have sex for the first time (from the first meeting to after *marriage*), what is expected of the different genders, when certain rites of passage should take place, etc.

Since around the 1950s, Western societies have accepted as common practice a trajectory from dating/courting (usually with the emphasis on the male partner initiating and the female accepting or rejecting the invitation), through to marriage (with sex taking place either before or after this, again with the expectation that the man will push for sex and the woman will withhold it until there is a clear commitment to an ongoing relationship), to producing a nuclear family. Here it is important to be aware of intersections, however. For example, in some cultural groups, there will be an expectation that parents take an active role in suggesting partners for their children (sometimes known as *arranged marriages* which differ markedly from forced marriages), while others emphasise the choice of the individuals or a 'natural' process of falling in love. Different classes and religions will have different expectations around the number of children that is appropriate, whether grandparents are involved in child-rearing in a more extended family model, etc.

MARRIAGE

Heterosexual people may often get married – which is a legal and some-times religious ceremony which bonds a man and a woman together for life, and often involves a celebration and the exchange of some physical token such as a ring in the sight of friends, family, etc. (see Chapter 13).

These older expectations now coexist with newer expectations, meaning that heterosexual people may have to negotiate some contradictions when managing their relationships. For example, marriage is not always seen as inevitable and many decide to cohabit and/or have children without hav-ing such a formal commitment.

In relation to dating and sex, in *hook-up culture*, which may be common in universities and colleges and among younger heterosexual people, it is expected that people will have several casual heterosexual encounters with-out forming committed relationships with those people (perhaps including *friends-with-benefits* or *fuckbuddy* arrangements where people have sexual friendships which are not romantic and/or sex with relative strangers and *one-night stands*). Chapter 14 also covers the ways in which some relation-ships are opening up in terms of their rules around monogamy.

Given the shifting trajectory of heterosexual people it is important that professionals do not assume that clients will necessarily follow that trajec-tory. When clients are from another culture or subculture to the profes-sional, it is important for the professional to educate themselves about it to a basic extent. Heterosexual people who are generally the 'norm' may feel especially ostracised by having to explain elements of their identity or practices to professionals.

FRIENDSHIPS

Another important set of heterosexual practices to consider are those around friendships with 'same-gender' and 'other-gender' friends. 'Other-gender' friendships are still often regarded as threatening to a relationship and may be dissolved or given a low priority for this reason. However, close relationships of this kind may be negotiated, particularly where there are children from a previous relationship, strong connections between ex-partners, or old friends (see Chapters 13 and 14).

The issues of 'same-gender' friendships have become more visible in recent years with a number of films, books and television programmes exploring the close bonds between heterosexual women (such as the *Sex and the City* books, television programme and movies) or heterosexual men (for example, the *bromance* phenomenon of movies about close friendships between men). For men, in particular, the expectations around heterosexual masculinity often make it difficult to express strong feelings for another man (as heterosexuality is often 'proven' by men as being in opposition to being in any way feminine or gay), although such constraints may be loosening in some class/age contexts (McCormack, 2012). Once a romantic relationship has formed, there may be a sense of loss of these important male–male or female–female relationships as it is expected that more time and space is shared with one's partner or spouse than with friends.

Professionals can usefully work with this loss as it may be difficult for heterosexual people to grieve for a lessening or lost relationship as the primacy of the new love relationship is commonly an accepted norm. The value of all sorts of relationships (friendships, collegiate, parental, etc.) can be explored. It may be that reassurance will need to be given to the romantic partner as transgressing the norm of an 'all encompassing' and 'all fulfilling' love may make them feel inadequate or betrayed. Of course no one person can ever be 'everything' for another in all domains and the belief that they can be is linked to relationship distress and dissatisfaction.

WIDER SOCIETY

The key societal message regarding heterosexuality is that it is 'natural' and/or 'normal' (this can be seen in Chapters 8 and 9 from the fact that a person has to *come out* if they are not heterosexual). Indeed, this normativity is reflected in most legal frameworks which consider heterosexuality to be the 'standard', or even only, relationship form, and consequently affords relationships between people of different genders greater protections than other (e.g. 'same-gender') relationships. This has also historically been the case in many other domains where partners of the 'other gender' have been more readily afforded rights relating to medical cases, as co-parents, by organisations, in relation to property, etc. (see Chapter 9).

It follows that people who identify as heterosexual often do not feel the need to discuss, or reflect upon, the meaning of their sexuality, or to consider any alternatives, in the way, for example, that an LGBTQ person will when considering coming out or which identity term to use. Thus, if an issue arises, people generally don't think to look to their heterosexuality as a potential part of the situation (for example, the (hetero) norms they have internalised about what makes good sex, a good relationship, a good life and so on).

SHIFTING NORMS OF HETEROSEXUALITY

Such issues can be particularly problematic for people when cultural norms and expectations pertaining to heterosexuality shift. A common example of this is that of a heterosexual woman who followed societal expectations and got married when young, before raising children. When these children left home, she felt a loss of identity as her identity was primarily that of a mother, while societal shifts created expectations for heterosexual women to have additional, or other, identities, for example that of a professional (see Chapter 4).

SEXUALISATION OF CULTURE

Another important example of this relates to what has been termed the *sexualisation of culture* (Attwood, 2007): the idea that depictions of sex have become much more prevalent in mainstream media, and that sexuality has taken up a greater role in people's lives (in determining who they are as individuals – their sexual identity – and the quality of their romantic relationships). A key element of this shift is that, as well as wanting to have a 'normal' sex life, there is also pressure to have 'great' sex. Often this means dipping a toe into some of the more marginal sexualities covered in this book (e.g. non-monogamy, BDSM, bisexuality), and/or taking up some of the sexual practices depicted in pornography, while still policing the boundaries against being considered 'abnormal' or 'freaky'. This adds a new element of pressure for heterosexual people, to be precisely adventurous enough, and may make it even more difficult for them to tune into their sexual desires as they are more concerned with having expected kinds of sex (Barker, 2012).

CHILDREN OUTSIDE OF MARRIAGE

Heterosexuality has also shifted in relation to wider society in terms of having children outside of marriage, previously called 'illegitimacy'. Whereas in the past, pregnancy outside of marriage was almost universally decried, in many areas it is now quite accepted. However, intersections of class, age and race often come into play here. For example, the figure of the working class teenage mother is still highly stigmatised and frequently used as a scapegoat for all kinds of social problems in media reporting.

OPENING UP DIVERSE POSSIBILITIES WITHIN HETEROSEXUALITY

It is precisely because the norms, expectations and assumptions about heterosexuality shift over time, and vary between groups and cultures, in this way, that we know that it is not a fixed and static, 'natural' and universal thing. More broadly than these recent shifts, we can see vast differences between the sexual relationships and practices that were considered 'normal' and ideal in, for example, Ancient Greece and modern America (in the former case, these often being based around people having higher and lower positions of power, rather than around gender – Weeks, 2003). Additionally, there are many animals which are not heterosexual (Roughgarden, 2004), suggesting that, while heterosexuality is an entirely legitimate sexuality, it is not the only, 'natural', sexuality.

Just as with any other sexuality, heterosexual people need the opportunity to reflect upon their sexual identity, to check that it is right for them, and to decide what it means for them, and the manner in which they want to embody that heterosexuality (from the diversity of possible ways). Because culturally heterosexual people are rarely afforded that opportunity due to the societal assumptions mentioned here, it may well be something that is worth opening up with them as a practitioner. This might involve gently challenging ideas of fixed, 'natural', 'normal' forms of heterosexuality, and offering more diverse ways of being heterosexual, as well as the idea that this sexuality could be fluid and changing over time. As a very simple example, if a heterosexual couple feel that they have to share a bed, but have very different sleeping patterns, a professional might mention other heterosexual people who have separate beds or separate rooms, cultural differences in sleeping arrangements, or ways of separating out sexual aspects of sharing a bed from aspects relating to sleep.

GROUP NORMS

As mentioned, one of the key aspects of heterosexuality is that the group norms are assumed to be 'natural' and 'universal'. It follows therefore that people assume that other heterosexual people will be aware of precisely the same norms and values as they are. Many of the difficulties with this sexuality arise because the group norms are in fact rather varied and key work in this area is associated with exploring an individual's understanding of these norms, and possibly assisting them in communicating these understandings.

The list below sets out some of the common group norms shared by most heterosexual people, and also mentions some of the variations which may occur within each norm, depending on intersections with gender, age, generation, race, culture, class, background, etc. In each case, the first point refers to the most 'normative' version of heterosexuality within the Western world – that presented in the mass media of women's magazines, soap operas, Hollywood movies and so on, which tends to also be reflective of young, white, middle class, non-disabled, slim, heterosexual people.

- It is vitally important to find a partner of the other gender. However, for many men this may be expected to follow a time of playing the field and having many sexual encounters, whereas many women still experience the sexual double standard – meaning that having too many such encounters can result in being labelled a 'slut' or 'slag', and there is often more pressure on women for relationships to be their main goal in life (see Chapter 4).

- Multiple partners will be had consecutively rather than concurrently, and serious relationships will be monogamous (see Chapters 13 and 14).
- After a certain age it is not really acceptable to be single.
- Having a serious partner means living together, planning a future together, sharing a bed, deprioritising other people in one's life (except children), and combining finances (however, these things may differ in certain communities, for example in the military where couples are expected to be apart for lengths of time).
- Partners should be in love with each other (although some groups and individuals may see love more as something that develops over time).
- Sex with the right partner will be naturally great, without requiring any communication, and will remain great throughout the relationship. Diminished sex is a 'bad sign' (although some groups and individuals may be more accepting of less sexual relationships, and there is an expectation that older people will no longer be sexual, see Chapter 7).
- The right partner will meet all of one's emotional, physical, sexual, social and intellectual needs, and will understand one almost telepathically such that conflicts will not arise.
- After a certain time the relationship should be committed to permanently via a marriage ceremony (although some choose not to marry, and there are different forms of marriage in different cultures and religions).

It is important to establish whether clients are aware that they are adhering to these norms and, if so, whether they are content with that. Further, it is important to establish whether that contentment lies solely in confirming to wider society (and fitting in), or whether it is an aspect of this norm ringing true for the client. Upon establishing this, practitioners will be able to consider whether further exploration, or even challenge, is required, and will also be able to be guided by the client's wishes with greater clarity. For example, clarification of the reasons behind some women wishing to be penetrated is vital in determining whether they have fully considered the matter, or whether they are simply acceding to cultural norms. Only when this has been established, can we consider what further intervention is required (Barker, 2011b).

PAUSE FOR CONSIDERATION

Now that we have considered heterosexuality in depth, pause to think about how your own sexual identity might impact on your work with heterosexual clients. Might you have your own expectations about what it means to be heterosexual and how flexible or fixed the possibilities are for heterosexual people?

SUMMARY AND CONCLUSIONS

In summary, the following are good practice points when working with clients.

- Be careful not to assume that all clients are heterosexual (even if they have a partner of the other gender, see Chapter 8). Also be aware that some clients have a *heterosexual* identity while also having sexual attraction to and/or encounters with people of the 'same gender' (see Chapter 8).
- Be aware of cultural norms around heterosexuality, and recognise the variety of possibilities within heterosexuality, rather than perpetuating a fixed notion of what heterosexual sex and relationships should be like. This involves some reflexive exploration of their own assumptions.
- Be aware of intersections, acknowledging the differences in how heterosexuality is experienced across race, culture, class, age, generation, body type, etc.
- It may be useful to work with wider family and/or social structures.
- Encourage client awareness about the expectations and assumptions that they have, and where these come from, and to encourage communication between partners about these rather than assuming that their expectations will be shared. The assumption that ideals around heterosexual sex and relationships will be the same has been linked to relationship distress and sexual problems.

It may well be helpful to normalise the diversity of styles of sex and relationship that are possible with clients, for example by describing different options that people choose. This will address the common fear that most heterosexual clients will have that they are not, or would not be, 'normal'. It is important both to broaden out all the possibilities that exist within 'normal' as well as exploring why being 'normal' is valued so highly.

FURTHER READING

Barker, M. (2012). *Rewriting the rules: An integrative guide to love, sex and relationships*. London: Routledge.

ADDITIONAL REFERENCES

Attwood, F. (Ed.) (2007). *Mainstreaming sex: The sexualization of culture*. London: I.B. Tauris.
Barker, M. (2011a). Existential sex therapy. *Sexual and Relationship Therapy*, *26*(1), 33–47.

Barker, M. (2011b). De Beauvoir, Bridget Jones' pants and vaginismus. *Existential Analysis, 22*(2), 203–216.

McCormack, M. (2012). *The declining significance of homophobia: How teenage boys are redefining masculinity and heterosexuality.* Oxford: Oxford University Press.

Roughgarden, J. (2004). *Evolution's rainbow.* Berkeley, CA: University of California Press.

Weeks, J. (2003). *Sexuality.* London: Routledge.

CROSS-DRESSING

This chapter aims to:

- Explain the difference between cross-dressing, 'autogynephilia'/'autoandrophilia' and transsexualism.
- Explore the various reasons people may practise cross-dressing.
- Consider the medical and cultural contexts of cross-dressing.

INTRODUCTION

When we think of someone who *cross-dresses* (sometimes defined as 'transvestism' – see below) the first thing that may spring to mind is the tragi-comic figure portrayed in much mainstream culture: someone apparently clearly male, perhaps with a beard and deep voice, dressed in overly feminine attire, often with an undertone of sexuality and an overtone of defiance. Indeed the *DSM IV-TR* required that the person under consideration was male – there could be no female transvestites in this taxonomy – and that the purpose of wearing female clothing was for sexual release.

This stereotyped and prejudicial understanding misses the greater part of this practice/identity and does disservice to the men, women and others for whom it is a satisfying and unharmful pursuit. Indeed, although diagnoses of this sort are understandably contested (see below), the current *DSM-V* allows the diagnosis to apply to women; and the *ICD-10* has a second category alongside 'fetishistic transvestism', that of 'dual role transvestism' in which there is no sexual component.

It is clear that people may wear a variety of clothing and present in diverse ways for a variety of purposes, from a man wearing a pair of knickers for sexual release, to a person assigned male at birth wearing female clothing at the weekends as this feels more congruent, to a woman expertly presenting as a *drag king* in a stereotyped male role for purposes of entertainment.

These complexities may lead us to ask whether it is appropriate for such people to be pathologised through inclusion in a psychiatric taxonomy. How does one assist a client who is concerned about such practices and, commonly, possible repercussions from those around them? It is these questions that this chapter seeks to address.

A NOTE ON TERMINOLOGY

We use the term cross-dressing and *presenting in a way not societally usual for a person of that birth-assigned gender* in this chapter rather than 'transvestism', also known as 'transvestitism' (terms a number of specialist and compassionate practitioners continue to use), as 'transvestism' is a term originally derived from the medical literature which has a history of pathologisation associated with it (as seen above). The term 'transvestitism' should not be considered to be a safe term, and should certainly not be used as a noun, as in 'a transvestite'. Instead, and only when relevant, the term *trans person* should be used. Thus, if a male person is talking about wishing to tell his girlfriend that he would like to wear her clothes then the fact that he is (or wishes to be) a trans person is relevant. However if a man who wears his girlfriend's clothes is talking about being nervous about a forthcoming job interview in which they will wear their own, masculine, clothes they are simply a man – albeit that they may have other qualifiers to that at other times such as father, teacher, trans person, cook, son, best friend, goalkeeper, etc. Additionally, the term *trans** is increasingly being used online – with * being a wildcard character used in programming, search terms, etc. to refer to an unknown string. In this case it acts as a means of inclusion, encompassing transsexual, transgender, transvestite, etc. without being pejorative.

There are some people who have reclaimed the word 'transvestite' and may also use the word 'tranny' or 'TV' to refer to themselves and others. Of course, it is important to respect the client's own terminology, but it should be remembered that these words are not safe to use with all clients – even if you use them to refer to yourself. Some people who were assigned male at birth and who have had an augmentation mammoplasty and/or feminising hormones such that they have breasts and a penis use the term 'she-male' to refer to themselves. It is imperative that professionals do not use this for others, or other terms such as 'HeShe', etc. as they are very offensive to most people with such presentations as well as to many other people.

The term cross-dressing too is somewhat outdated and problematic as not only do many fashions allow any gender to wear them – at least in many contemporary Western societies – but it also suggests a strict dichotomy being reinforced by the person who uses it. If a professional states that a person is 'cross-dressed' it may suggest that they are making a judgement about the appropriateness of the attire for that person and are, perhaps, placing undue weight on the person's birth-assigned gender: the person may be identifying at that time as the sex they are presenting as.

Note that we are using the term 'he' and 'she' here to refer to people's birth-assigned gender – usually based upon an inspection of people's genitalia just after birth. This is because for most people this chapter refers to identify primarily as that sex. However, for reasons of rapport, you should generally address a person with reference to their mode of gender presentation, irrespective of whether you are aware of their birth-assigned gender. You may need to keep records relating to birth sex and certain medical and legal letters and documents may need to pertain to birth sex, but in face-to-face encounters the gender of presentation should be respected. If you are unsure, then asking to be reminded of a first name is a useful tactic, or otherwise simply asking if a person has a mode of address they prefer (*ask etiquette*) will suffice. Thus, if a person is presenting in a female role with a dress, make-up etc., yet as their GP you are aware that they are male, it will usually not be necessary to make reference to cross-dressing as such, although questioning about name and pronoun use and any support needed may be useful. If it is the first time you have seen them presenting in such a manner then referring to Chapter 2 on transgender with reference to *coming out* may be of assistance.

AUTOGYNEPHILIA AND AUTOANDROPHILIA

Cross-dressing, as stated above, refers to presenting in a way that is not societally usual for a person of that birth-assigned gender, usually through clothing, gesture, speech, etc. and is often used to refer to sexual excitement associated with that. Some authors (e.g. Blanchard, 1989; Lawrence, 2007) have suggested a second category – that of 'autogynephilia' and 'autoandrophilia' – being the state of being erotically aroused at the thought of oneself as a woman or a man respectively. The difference is a subtle one, perhaps best construed as 'outside sourced' arousal versus 'inside sourced' arousal. Someone who is aroused at the thought of others seeing them in clothing not normally associated with their gender could be regarded as erotically cross-dressing, whereas someone who is aroused at the thought of *themselves* as a person not of their natally assigned gender would be 'autogynephilic' if they were male or 'autoandrophilic' if they were female.

If this seems confusing, never fear – it is. Even experienced professionals struggle to differentiate between erotic cross-dressing (sometimes called 'fetishistic transvestism' – see above) and 'autogynephilia'/'autoandrophilia'. The terms are included here due to the common confusion of the two categories, particularly in US literature. However, a recent study has shown that if the common US mode of defining autogynephilia is used, then 93% of cisgender women would also be so categorised (Moser, 2009). Clearly this is therefore not useful as a means of categorisation for service provision etc.

In the UK, understanding of the terms 'transvestism' or erotic cross-dressing is relatively common, but 'autogynephilia' and 'autoandrophilia' are rare. Most practitioners will never meet someone who would fit the criteria, but *will* most likely meet people who present in a way not societally usual for a person of that birth-assigned gender: people who cross-dress whether for reasons of sexuality, for comfort, for the release of stress, as play, as a social practice, or for some other reason.

TRANSSEXUALITY

Transsexuality is not the same as cross-dressing and is consequently considered independently in Chapter 2. People who define as a cross-dresser in some way necessarily do not actually wish to be the gender that commonly presents in the way they occasionally do, and are instead content to remain the sex they were assigned at birth. In contrast, transsexual people *always* wish to be a sex other than that they were assigned at birth.

Some transsexual people, although by no means all, go through a stage of fetishistic cross-dressing, followed by a stage of dual role cross-dressing with little or no erotic component; followed by actually wishing to be a gender other than the one they were assigned at birth; possibly considering hormonal or surgical means to alter their bodies. If a person believes themselves to be transsexual but has significant sexual excitement associated with the thought of themselves as a gender they were not assigned at birth that may be a concern regarding provisions of hormones or surgery. This is because the sexual arousal may act as a drive for surgery which would then attenuate due to familiarity, or shift as some forms of sexuality can. (See also Chapter 12 on Further Sexualities for some sexualities which *may* shift, but by no means necessarily will). This risks leaving the person in a very uncomfortable position with a body which is no longer arousing or congruent.

SEXUALITY

People who have arousal associated with cross-dressing may also have any of the other sexualities found in this book (for example, they may be LGB, heterosexual, etc.). It is unusual that the wearing of clothing is the only sexuality, and it is often associated with a more fetishistic preference for certain materials or items of clothing (see Chapter 12). This is often the case, for example, with men aroused by hosiery and tight or restricting items. Some people who engage with kink or BDSM wear clothing which is not commonly worn by their birth-assigned gender (see Chapter 6).

COMMON CONCERNS

Broadly speaking there are three categories of people who wear clothing not normally worn by people of their birth-assigned gender and who present to a counsellor, psychologist or other health professional:

- Those for whom this is completely incidental to the reason that they are seeking help or support.
- Those who are experiencing problems related to other people's perceptions of their choice of presentation.
- Those who have some concern about their choice of presentation which they would like help with.

By far the most common group is the first, and indeed it may well be that professionals are not aware of a client's cross-dressing, or it comes up as only incidental to the reason for the contact. In the latter instance it is imperative that the cross-dressing does not cause diagnostic overshadowing (where a professional fails to attend to another issue, like depression, because they are so focused on the cross-dressing). It is also vital that it is not seen as a problem in its own right because cross-dressing is not associated with increased psychopathology or interpersonal difficulties.

For those whose presenting issues do relate to cross-dressing, this is often linked to other people's perceptions. This may be a matter of relationship breakdown or strain due to being 'found out', or concern about being 'mad' or 'abnormal'. Such issues are often far greater for men than for women in most Western countries, as a woman in these cultures who wishes to wear male attire or present in a masculine manner is, to a marked degree, free to do so. She may wear jeans, a shirt and boots and no one will bat an eyelid. Even if she wears a full dinner or morning suit she may be considered somewhat eccentric or "cute" but would not generally meet with opprobrium. Most offices and schools allow women and girls to wear trousers, and even the day-to-day uniforms for the police and armed forces do not differ markedly for men and women, being based on a masculine style of clothing.

Things are rather different for men who wish to wear feminine attire or to behave in a feminine manner. Even minor items such as jewellery or subtle make-up may be remarked upon and the wearing of skirts by men or boys meets with opprobrium which may turn to violence: a boundary which is policed by men and women alike. Thus, while there are women who wear overtly masculine clothing and are masculine in presentation, they are less likely to require assistance from professionals and it is often far easier to simply let the matter pass as a sartorial rather than a social, medical, or otherwise professional, issue. It is useful for professionals to consider their own boundaries around gendered clothing, for themselves and others, for this reason.

Men who present in a 'female' manner may approach professionals for a variety of reasons. They may be at risk of losing housing or children due to relationship breakdown (the second group above), or they may wish for psychological or psychopharmacological assistance to stop. Alternatively, they may be concerned that they are transsexual and consequently wish to have assistance with that (see Chapter 2). It is always important to separate the wearing of feminine clothes – itself a rather innocuous thing done by much of the population on a daily basis – from the cause of any distress. There is no evidence that men who wear female clothes or present in a feminine manner are poor fathers. Indeed, while it is hard to measure these things, from clinical experience they seem to be rather better fathers as they are often a touch more gentle than their peers and their concern that they may be poor fathers because of their presentation means that they try harder.

RELATIONSHIPS AND SEXUALITY

As mentioned, people who cross-dress may be of any sexual identity. One common concern of this group is that they may be gay because they prefer to wear the clothing, and present in the manner, of another gender. While gay people are perhaps a little more likely to do this for reasons of fun or play – at a fancy dress party for example – there is no marked difference between heterosexual, LG or B people in this regard. People who wear clothing for the purposes of sexual excitement are most usually, although by no means exclusively, heterosexual men. For many, heterosexuality seems to be largely independent from their sexual excitement with wearing female clothes.

One cause of difficulty can be with partners. Very often partners, not uncommonly wives or female partners of men (but sometimes 'same-gender' partners and husbands and male partners of women) become concerned when they find out that their partner wishes to wear clothing or present in a manner not normally attributed to their sex. This may be due to concerns about their own sexuality – for example a lesbian partner becoming concerned that her partner is presenting in 'too masculine' a way and that she may therefore be mistaken as heterosexual.

In couples where both are heterosexual, and to some extent within relationships of people with other sexualities, there can be concerns around 'normality' and it can be useful to reassure clients that these practices and identities are very common. It is important for all parties to recognise their own feelings and needs. For example, a wife may project her fears on to children, elderly parents, neighbours, etc., while wishing to appear supportive. Her concerns need to be addressed, possibly though individual psychotherapy, in order for a more comfortable relationship structure to be reached.

In cases where there is an intimate partner involved in any difficulties, for example where they are unhappy with their partner's clothing choices, it is important for the client to recognise that such presentation (assuming it is not too revealing or sexual) is not in and of itself harmful to adults or children. It is therefore appropriate for a mutual negotiation to be carried out rather than the person who cross-dresses making all of the concessions on the basis that they are lucky their partner is 'letting' them do it at all. In clinical practice it is not uncommon to see men who lose their homes (although they continue to pay for them), regular access to their children, and much contact with their wives, all without making any complaint on the assumption that presenting in a female manner is fundamentally wrong. This *internalised transphobia* can be usefully addressed through psychotherapeutic or other interventions, while community groups like Trans Media Watch in the UK continue to address the wider social representations that perpetuate *transphobia*.

Similarly it is important that people who present in a way not societally usual for a person of that birth-assigned gender are compassionate and flexible in their approach: giving time for people to adjust and providing reassurance about any fears in as non-judgemental a way as possible. Psychotherapeutic assistance with this can be useful.

REPARATIVE THERAPY

'Reparative' or 'conversion' therapies have been attempted with people in a misguided effort to 'cure' them of presenting in a way not societally usual for a person of that birth-assigned gender (cross-dressing). This has included electric shocks and emetics as well as psychotherapy. All have been unsuccessful (e.g. Bancroft, 1969) and professionals attempting such things should be mindful of ethical breaches of the relevant professional codes as well as the proven inefficacy. Instead, exploratory and supportive interventions, social as well as psychological, should be considered where they are necessary, although simply cross-dressing should not be regarded as de facto evidence of the necessity of intervention.

PEOPLE WITH LEARNING DISABILITIES AND MENTAL HEALTH PROBLEMS

People with learning disabilities and mental health problems may, of course, wish to present in a way not societally usual for a person of that birth-assigned gender. Many professionals find this distressing and so endeavour to suppress what is a rather harmless activity. Of course, if the behaviour is a part of a person's distress it should be dealt with as appropriate (although not necessarily suppressed), but these groups of people have the right to express their sexuality and/or identity in this way (as with all sexualities) just as other people do. Any moral concerns staff may have should be subsumed to the policy codes of the organisations they belong to and the relevant anti-discrimination laws.

Of particular note is that many people present in a way not societally usual for a person of their birth-assigned gender for reasons of stress relief and comfort. Cutting off this means of self-soothing can have very poor results, especially in inpatient wards. Instead, if needed, education about appropriate, non-sexualised clothing and/or presentation may be undertaken. The complaints of others should be dealt with as with any prejudicial matter through a zero tolerance towards the prejudice, rather than through addressing the subject of the concern. A useful experiment can be to substitute another category (such as race, accent, religion) for the item under consideration and see what your thoughts would be then.

KEY PRACTICES

SEXUAL ENCOUNTERS AND SAFER SEX

Cross-dressing may be associated with sexual encounters with other people. For some, this is a part of the eroticisation of the presentation, whereas for others there may be no eroticisation of the presentation as such, but sexual contact while presenting in such a manner may occur. In both cases it is not uncommon for people to feel that their gender presentation is supported. Thus if a person presents in a male role they may feel that that role is enhanced through penetrating a woman with their phallus, often, sensibly, referred to as their cock or dick. Sometimes people do not practise safer sex as they feel this might in some way lessen their gender presentation: professionals should be au fait with the different types of sexual encounters within this book and elsewhere, and advise on safer sex as necessary. Reassurance about gender presentation may be usefully given in these situations, indeed a person may look *more* masculine when unrolling a condom onto his cock.

Other key practices here concern obtaining the desired presentation. This often involves having a name which is adopted for the alternate gender persona.

FOR PEOPLE ASSIGNED MALE AT BIRTH

People assigned male at birth may use a *gaffe* – a sort of restrictive strap – for their penis in order for it to be hidden while *dressed*[1] in 'female' clothing. Careful shaving may be undertaken with quality foundation used to hide any beard shadow. Sometimes two layers are used, a more orange base layer, followed by a skin colour top layer. Wigs may be employed and hair removed as far as everyday life allows. Some have silicone breast forms similar to those used in breast augmentation surgeries, which may be glued to the chest using medical adhesive or supported in a bra. Dried peas in tights and other inventive methods may also be used. Voice and movement may also be altered so as to be more feminine.

For some, a more *camp* presentation is desired where the intention is to have fun with presentation and sometimes to entertain in a cabaret manner. In this case larger breast forms, highly stylised and elaborate clothing, make-up, etc. may be worn. This mode of presentation may sometimes be referred to as *drag* and the person as a *drag queen*, with the person performing songs or cabaret at bars and clubs.

Some people assigned male at birth may wish to temporarily present, and indeed identify as female, perhaps for an evening or weekend before returning to a male role for work or family. In this case a more prosaic look is adopted, much as with any cisgender woman. Some partners of this group of people are very supportive and often surprise themselves with how unremarkable their time with their partners *en femme* is. From being most concerned about neighbours' reactions they can adapt to shopping, dinner, etc. in a comfortable manner. Indeed, it is often remarked that the partner is more relaxed than usual when dressed.

Some men may wish to adopt a more sexualised presentation, sometimes alone or sometimes with partner(s). Here the sexualised accoutrements of femininity may be adopted including lingerie, heels, etc. Some will do this at home, in their own female clothing, which is sometimes hidden in a *stash* – often in a car, the back of a wardrobe or the attic. Others may dress in a female partner's clothing when they are out. Whether the clothing is their own or their partner's, this can be accompanied by intense excitement at the thought of being discovered associated with intense sexual arousal. After achieving orgasm some men who dress in this way may feel guilt or disgust and may *purge* their own female clothing through putting it in a bin, donating it to a charity shop or burning it. Most often the wish to wear

---

[1] People often state that they were "dressed" to refer to cross-dressing. For example, a man saying "I was dressed when we went out" means that they were wearing female clothing on that occasion, not that they usually venture out naked.

female clothing resurfaces days or weeks later necessitating costly shopping expeditions which can lead to financial difficulties. Some who are too embarrassed to purchase their own clothing may obtain it by theft from washing lines or shops – a criminal matter which should be dealt with appropriately but also considered carefully in the light of the wider psycho-social context, possibly through therapy to address any internalised transphobia and self-esteem issues.

In contrast, some men who wear 'female' clothing for sexual purposes are quite happy with the situation and attend clubs and bars when dressed in sexualised clothing either with partner(s), with the intention of finding a part-ner, or alone. Some people have beautiful bespoke clothing tailored for this purpose. Some people and their partners make cross-dressing a part of their sexuality, with both partners finding it erotic and both or either dressing.

It is worth noting that men who present in a female manner will not usually have been socialised in adolescence as to appropriate attire and presentation in different situations. Most of the information obtained will therefore be from popular culture, which can have very sexualised repre-sentations of women, which, for want of a better alternative, some men will recreate. It is not generally within most professional's purview to com-ment on a client's clothing, but if sufficient rapport allows, and a person has only recently started presenting in public *in role*, some gentle guidance may be appreciated for those without a friendship circle who will provide this. Professionals should be careful however as unsolicited advice may irreparably damage rapport if given injudiciously. It is, of course, for you to determine whether sexualised clothing is acceptable in your office.

FOR PEOPLE ASSIGNED FEMALE AT BIRTH

People assigned female at birth presenting in some form of male role are drawing upon cultural roles which are often less sexualised and thus there is less scope for conflict. Females may wish to *bind* their breasts to present a flat chest and to *pack* such that a bulge is apparent in the front of their trou-sers, either though the simple medium of a pair of rolled up socks in their underpants or through proprietary devices for that purpose. In addition they may effect facial hair through hairpieces or gluing their own hair trimmings on to their faces to form a moustache, beard, etc. (using hair trimmings has the benefit of being an exactly appropriate colour).

For some, a more *camp* presentation is desired – as above with people assigned male at birth – where the intention is to have fun with presenta-tion and sometimes to entertain in a cabaret manner. Again, this mode of presentation may be referred to as *drag* and the person as a *drag king*, with some performing songs or cabaret at bars and clubs in the role of a famous male singer.

Some women wish to be more sexual while in a male presentation, and while male clothing allows for little latitude to do this through presentation itself, a stylish manner can be adopted. The use of sex toys that fit into the vagina by means of a shorter, wider, egg shape that can be gripped by the vaginal muscles attached to a phallus of erect silicone can allow the woman to penetrate a partner in a manner similar to having a penis. This has the added advantage that sensation is felt by both parties, although some people feel uncomfortable being reminded of their vagina in this way (see *manhole* in the Glossary for further complexity). Alternatively, a *strap-on* sex toy may be used which involves a phallus strapped on to the genital region, again such that a partner can be penetrated. Vibrators in the base of the strap-on allow for sensation for the penetrating partner also. These sex toys may also be used by trans men, bisexual women, lesbians, etc.

Eroticisation of 'male' clothing by women is rarer than that of 'female' clothing by men, but does sometimes happen, especially if associated with other sexual contexts such as BDSM or kink. It is extremely rare, however, for women to feel guilt and to hide clothing or to purge as is the case with some men and feminine clothing.

Some people assigned female at birth wear masculine clothing and present in a masculine manner on a day-to-day basis and pass rather unremarked. Some have a more male identity and sometimes a male, or androgynous, name by which they are known. It is unusual for people who present in this way to move from male to female and back for work or family, as is the case for people assigned male at birth above, perhaps due to the greater latitude afforded people assigned female at birth for masculine expression. Some feminist writers have questioned the implicit sexism of this: the acceptance of women in male roles as they've 'traded up'; versus the opprobrium given to males in female roles who have 'traded down' (e.g. Serano, 2007).

PAUSE FOR CONSIDERATION

Take a moment to think about what you consider to be the limits of acceptable day-to-day clothing for your clients and for yourself. Would your grandparents or great grandparents have agreed? Who determined what your thoughts would be about this?

WIDER SOCIETY

Wider societal views about cross-dressing shift markedly over time. While some latitude has developed for women in their presentation, especially in

Western contexts, as a result of feminism, less development has occurred with regard to acceptable presentation for men (although there is more flexibility for urban men who have embraced forms of metrosexuality). These presentation standards are not necessarily to do with the style of clothing itself as the gendering of clothing style is culturally specific. Thus, a man may not be able to wear non-bifurcated garments in many contemporary Western societies as it would be regarded as a (female) skirt, however, it is acceptable to do so in some places – for example, the Scottish kilt – or for some roles, such as ecclesiastical robes. Similarly, many non-Western societies have non-bifurcated garments for males – for example – the sarong or similar garment in many parts of Asia, Africa and the Pacific. Presentation standards also shift over time (see Chapter 4).

As time and place create shifts in the appropriateness of certain types of clothing and presentation it is important to recognise that any difficulties or pathologisation will be culturally situated. The legal situation in the UK and many other places has shifted with the liberalisation and secularisation of wider society. Thus, a man or woman who is not exposing themselves is highly unlikely to be prosecuted for presenting in a way not societally usual for a person of that birth assigned gender as it is not in the public interest. There were, however, historic rules that related to just that – with certain numbers of, or types of, items of 'sex appropriate' apparel being required to avoid prosecution.

MEDICINE AND PSYCHOLOGY

Medicine and psychology have previously regarded cross-dressing as a perversion. While some practitioners, especially from the psychodynamic tradition, still view it as such, most contemporary practitioners recognise that it is an inherently unharmful activity and endeavour instead to treat any distress associated with it. This may be through normalising the behaviour or examining the systemic effects it has within the client's life. Oftentimes simply giving a person the opportunity to explore their feelings can assist with lowering anxiety and distress. As it is so often, the fear associated with the practice can be far more toxic than the practice itself.

GROUP NORMS

As we have seen, people who present in a way not societally usual for a person of that birth-assigned gender are diverse, have different reasons for so doing, and come from a variety of backgrounds and demographics. There are few group norms as such, but within subcultures there are some norms around who is more accepted or rejected. One of the most commonly encountered norms is that relating to 'passing'. Passing is a problematic term used by many trans people to refer to being accepted as a member of the gender they are presenting as. Very often hierarchies are formed in which people who 'pass' best are hierarchised above those people who do not 'pass' so 'well'. Thus, 'passing' is a problematic term as it does not allow for a person whose body does not match their preferred presentation to be considered to be as 'real' as a person whose body fortuitously does match their presentation. Of course one's internal sense of gender need not match their body type, and one's wish for a temporary presentation as a certain gender need not match this either (see also Chapter 2 on hierarchies).

Intersecting with this is a hierarchy relating to age. Often younger people are accepted more than older people, especially within younger groups and in clubs, bars, etc. Trans women may look more like cisgender women when younger, especially if they have not aged into their feminine presentation, which can lead to the hierarchies mentioned. In addition, there can be an expectation of conservatism in older people by younger people which can sit uneasily with a wish to be extrovert on the part of the older person. Not uncommonly younger people may assume that an older trans woman is necessarily wearing female attire for sexual purposes, when this may well not be the case.

Professionals can usefully question this hierarchy in their work, including any explicit or implicit assumptions clients may bring regarding it. Professionals should also be careful not to inadvertently reinforce the hierarchy, for example through considering cisgender to be a 'gold standard' of behaviour and communicating this.

SUMMARY AND CONCLUSIONS

Good practice in this area includes the following:

- Recognise the diversity of experience and requirements of people who cross-dress.
- Do not assume a sexual motivation, although this will be the case for some.
- Be aware that people may present in this manner as part of a transsexual trajectory, or for reasons of comfort, or pleasure, or for some other reason.
- Remember that the presentation in and of itself is not harmful and so should be normalised, while the associated anxieties and concerns should be addressed both with the individual and systemically with family, social groups, etc. as necessary. Any associated pragmatic concerns such as safer sex education, housing, etc. should be addressed on their own merits and not with specific reference to appearance.

- Remember that, as well as men wearing feminine clothing, women wearing masculine clothing may also have concerns around this, as may their wider social group. This can be a hidden issue and so should be considered even when not readily apparent.
- Be aware that the wish to present in a way not societally usual for a person of that birth-assigned gender seldom abates of its own accord, although it can increase and decrease in intensity over time. Consequently, people should be supported in their presentation and identity through professional means where possible.

FURTHER READING

Ekins, R. & King, D. (2006). *The transgender phenomenon.* London: Sage.

Garber, M. (1992). *Vested interests: Cross-dressing and cultural anxiety.* London: Penguin.

Halberstam, J. (2005). *In a queer time and place: Transgender bodies, subcultural lives.* London: New York University Press.

Much of the further reading from Chapters 2 and 5 also addresses the issues covered in this chapter.

ADDITIONAL REFERENCES

Bancroft, J. (1969). Aversion therapy of homosexuality: A pilot study of 10 cases. *British Journal of Psychiatry, 115*, 1417–1431.

Blanchard, R. (1989). The classification and labeling of nonhomosexual gender dysphorias. *Archives of Sexual Behavior, 18*(4), 315–334.

Lawrence, A.A. (2007). Becoming what we love: Autogynephilic transsexualism conceptualised as an expression of romantic love. *Perspectives in Biology and Medicine, 50*, 506–520.

Moser, C. (2009). Autogynephilia in women. *Journal of Homosexuality, 56*(5), 539–547.

Serano, J. (2007). *Whipping girl.* Emeryville: Seal Press.

FURTHER SEXUALITIES

12

This chapter aims to:

- Introduce a range of further sexualities which are not covered elsewhere in this book, or in much of the literature and research in this area.
- Consider the common concerns of those who practise and/or identify with such sexualities and who approach counsellors, psychologists and health professionals.
- Provide an overview of common language, activities and dynamics.
- Explore wider cultural perceptions, and legal and medical perspectives about these sexualities.
- Outline good practice for working with clients in this area.

INTRODUCTION

This chapter explores professional practice with people who have sexualities and identities which are, perhaps, less common than those detailed in the other chapters. It is important to bear in mind however the difficulty in obtaining exact statistics on any marginalised sexual identity or practice, and the continua with more common activities on which many of these practices lie (see below). There is very little published literature on any of these sexualities (outside of a small amount of pathologising literature and a similar amount of more theoretical literature). Consequently, much of the information here is drawn from clinical experience and community-based publications.

There are a wide range of further sexualities in which people, fairly commonly, engage. It is often assumed that sexuality simply refers to the gender of person to whom we are attracted (see Chapters 8, 9 and 10). However, these sexual practices and identities demonstrate that there are a multiplicity of dimensions on which human sexuality can be understood. For example, these relate to the kinds of roles people enjoy taking (see also Chapter 6); the sensations (visual, tactile, etc.) they find pleasurable; the extent to which creativity and imagination come into their sexual encounters, aesthetics and appearance; the level of desire they experience (see also Chapter 7); and the relationship between sex and other aspects such as transgression, power, security, nurturance, etc. Of course, we are unable to cover all of these for reasons of space and consequently we have selected a number of further sexualities which you may reasonably expect to come across in the course of your practice. These include:

- Having a liking for particular materials, such as leather or rubber (sometimes categorised under *fetish*).
- The reading and writing of erotic fiction.
- Enjoying taking on the appearance and/or identity of an animal (often known as *furry*).
- Enjoying being treated as a child or baby (sometimes called *ageplay, adult baby* or *infantilism*).
- Excitement over being seen by, or watching, others being sexual (sometimes classified as 'voyeurism' or 'exhibitionism' in medical and psychological contexts).

For some people these practices and identities do not have a sexual component, but rather are undertaken for reasons of personal comfort, congruence, aesthetic appreciation, etc. As mentioned in relation to BDSM (Chapter 6), such practices and identities can blur the boundaries between what we define as sex versus, for example, leisure, spiritual, creative or playful activities. For example, many people enjoy reading and writing fiction about their favourite television shows or movies (fan fic). Some of this material includes sexual elements (*erotic fan fic* or *slash fiction*[1]). But the dividing line between the two may be unclear, and even erotic fan fiction is not read, or written, entirely for sexual reasons. Readers and authors also enjoy the creative aspects of imagining their favourite characters in various situations in between the events which occur on the show or movie (the *canon*).

Further, many people may have an identity which would fall under the broad rubric of the headings above, but which will not always (or may never be) sexual. For example, somebody may identify as furry and have a lupine identity within that, with all the practices and accoutrements detailed below, but only rarely or never have sexual encounters within this identity. This is similar to a person who may define as heterosexual, for example, independent of when (or even if) they are actually having sex.

---

[1] Slash fiction refers specifically to fiction which imagines romantic and/or sexual relationships between, often 'same gender', characters who do not have such relationships in the original canon (or where these relationships are only hinted at in the subtext). Common examples include Kirk/Spock, Holmes/Watson or Buffy/Willow. The 'slash' refers to the punctuation mark between the names of the characters (cf. Barker, 2002).

PAUSE FOR CONSIDERATION

People often hold strong views on the further sexualities listed above. Take a moment to consider what your current understandings of these practices and identities are, and where those ideas have come from. How might these affect your professional practice with a client who engages in these activities?

COMMON CONCERNS

As professionals, our training is often woefully inadequate in equipping us with the basic information needed to engage with these client groups. Even if we ourselves have engaged with one or more of these practices or identities, we are unlikely to identify with all of them, and as such it may be difficult for us to understand them all, or to bracket our assumptions about them.

The concerns of professionals and clients alike are frequently exacerbated by popular media representations of these sexualities in poor-quality documentaries, police procedural dramas, and so on, which often include them for sensationalist reasons, and do not portray them in the benevolent, even banal, light which best reflects the reality of the situation. Professional training, and client concerns, are often based upon a lack of knowledge (or knowledge gained from such popular sources) rather than any real association between these sexualities and anything untoward. This is similar to the point made in Chapter 6 about representations of BDSM.

OTHERING

One reflection of the problematic ways in which these sexualities are situated was the difficulty we had in devising a name for this chapter. We considered 'other sexualities', with 'other' meaning the same as when one says "Do you have any socks other than the grey ones as I wanted blue?", but we were aware that this may be read as 'other' within the term 'othering', which means to consider a person or group as distinctly different from oneself or the norm. There are similar problems with the word 'alternative'. It is worth bearing in mind how such subtle uses of language can damage rapport, for example if you refer to a client as 'alternative' when they do not use that term themselves.

CATEGORIES OF PRESENTING ISSUES

Broadly speaking there are four categories of people who participate in further sexualities who will present to a counsellor, psychologist or other health professional. In rough order of likelihood of presentation, these are:

- Those who engage in these sexualities but for whom this is completely incidental to the reason that they are seeking help or support.
- Those who are concerned about potential clashes between their sexuality and social norms.
- Those whose sexuality conflicts with their day-to-day life in ways they find problematic.
- Those who experience the sexuality itself as problematic in some way.

As elsewhere, the vast majority of clients will fall into the first of these categories. Indeed, in many cases, the professional will never know about their sexual practices. An example where this might come up in professional practice would be a client who is receiving counselling to deal with bereavement of their mother. In one session they talk of seeing somebody whose face reminded them of their mother, at a rubber ball[2] event which they attended. In this instance the enjoyment of rubber is completely incidental to the presenting issue and should be treated as such. This illustrates the importance of awareness of such sexualities on the part of the professional such that their reaction does not impinge on their practice. The clinical endeavour here is clearly focused on the bereavement rather than following a line of conversation about the sexuality that has been revealed.

Some clients present suggesting that their sexuality is necessarily a problem. In these instances, it is useful to examine the reality of the day-to-day situation in which they find themselves. For example, questions such as "When was the last time a difficulty arose?" (and really asking for a date so as to avoid "Oh it happens a lot", as a response) can be useful in determining whether the client is genuinely experiencing social difficulties, or whether it is their own perception of the sexuality which is being expressed. If the latter it is useful to make this explicit. An example would be somebody who identifies as furry and works in a bar. They like to wear clip-on cat ears and their employer is quite happy with them doing so, as – apparently – are all the customers who have not commented upon this or have only done so in a positive and friendly manner (saying, for example, "Those are cool"). The therapeutic endeavour in such cases is for the client to explore their own feelings.

---

[2] A *rubber ball* is a social gathering for those who share a common interest and enjoyment in the sensation and material of rubber. *Ball* here refers to the ball in ballroom rather than a spherical bouncy object. Obviously there is a play on words involved.

Most people who present with concerns, or who mention such concerns in addition to their presenting issue, will have taken on board the surrounding negative cultural messages about their sexuality. For example, a client may present stating that *of course* the fact that they enjoy consensually watching their wife masturbate is a problem, even though they have not broached the subject with their wife. The therapeutic endeavour is usually most helpfully directed at examining the "of course" here, rather than the voyeurism[3] per se, as their wife may in fact be entirely happy to include this as part of their sexual menu.

This may be the case for the sexualities covered here even more than with LGB or even BDSM sexualities, given the common perception of many of these as even more transgressive. It is therefore especially incumbent upon ethical professionals not to further stigmatise such clients and they may need to judiciously utilise their professional power to ameliorate such stigmatisation (see Chapter 9 on gay affirmative therapy).

Some clients may report that their sexuality conflicts with their day-to-day life in a way which they find problematic, for example a couple where one partner would like, on occasion, to be mothered by her partner and take the role of a little girl, but the partner says that she is very uncomfortable with this and resists attempts to fall into such a dynamic. Similarly, a woman might enjoy writing slash fiction on the internet, but find that her partner is uncomfortable with her engaging in a sexual activity away from their relationship. The therapeutic endeavour in such cases is, once again, exploration of the client's own feelings regarding their sexuality, while acknowledging the realities of their difficulties. That is not to say that the difficulty is necessarily a part of the sexuality, but rather that, for this client at this time, a difficulty has arisen that is associated with it.

If one is working professionally with the *relationship* (in cases like the ones given above) rather than the individual, it is appropriate to follow the kinds of suggestions laid out in Chapters 13 and 14, for all situations where two or more partners have differing interests, values, desires, etc. In these instances, a consideration of a variety of possible ways forward is helpful. For example, the partner who wishes to be more childlike may be able to find occasions when they can express a younger self which their partner is comfortable with through open negotiation, or may find other people (friends or openly non-monogamous partners) with whom to express this self. There may be ways for the partner to engage with the slash fiction (through reading or contributing to the writing by being a beta reader[4]), or

---

[3] This is usually a safe word, but is derived from a medical context and so is worth being cautious with.

[4] Someone who reads through their writing to check for consistencies, typographical errors, etc.

the couple may negotiate sexual activities which they engage in together, and those they keep separate.

On rare occasions, clients may have a presenting issue where the sexuality is clearly creating a problem in and of itself for the client. Again, this is not to say that the sexuality will necessarily be a problem for all clients but that, in this instance, it may be regarded as objectively problematic. In such cases it is important that in endeavouring to accommodate or adapt a person's sexuality we are not endorsing 'reparative' or 'conversion' therapies in any way. As we saw in Chapter 9, all of the relevant professional bodies state incontrovertibly that such therapies are unethical and should not be practised. We propose that, in contrast, the client come to terms with their sexuality and that any adjustment is made on the basis of that. It is important for practitioners to bracket any assumptions about such practices, then to ensure that the client themselves has come to terms with the practice being okay, and – only after this – that the client considers the various options available to them.

The fact that these sexualities are outside of the mainstream, and may even be eschewed within certain 'alternative' spaces means that people can have problems with their (innocuous) sexualities which are *somewhat* irreconcilable with the society in which they live. The people in category 4 above then should not feel that they are to 'blame' – there is no blame to be had, rather that there is a societal root to their distress.

Of course, the situation is somewhat different in the case of any sexualities which have a coercive element to them, because it is vital that clients do not act upon these. Appropriate ways of working in such cases is touched upon in Chapter 6 under Wider Society.

KEY PRACTICES

Many aspects of sexuality can, and do, shift and change over time. While people may identify strongly with one or more of these at a given moment, they may alter or morph into another after some time – often years – has passed. It should be recognised, however, that *any* particular sexuality or identity could be regarded as 'just a phase' (see Chapters 8 and 9) as, of course, many aspects of our identities – independent of sexuality – will also shift and adjust over time. For example, one's identity as a parented child may shift from being dependent in childhood towards a more friendship-based relationship in adulthood, to being a carer with a dependent as the parent becomes older.

In the remainder of this section of the chapter we outline a few of the common practices associated with each of the further sexualities we are focusing on here, although it is important to be mindful of the diversity within each and the multiple meanings they may have.

FETISHES

People who have a particular fetish often focus on specific materials (commonly rubber, leather or denim), or clothing (such as particular types of underwear – stockings, bras – or shoes – high-heels, trainers), or parts of the body (e.g. feet). It should be noted that many people (but not all) are comfortable with the word *fetish* and have reclaimed this from the more medical terminology as a positive identity. However, it is always worth checking what word a particular individual is comfortable with (e.g. some may use interest, preference, kink, etc.).

People with a fetish often engage with it as part of their expression of sexuality. This may involve masturbating alone, with a partner, or others, while in physical contact with the object of the fetish (for example, while wearing a certain pair of jeans), or engaging in other forms of sex (such as penile-vaginal intercourse, oral sex, etc.) while including certain images, clothing, body parts, etc. People may also attend social events wherein people engage with a particular preferred fetish in a public environment but in a less specifically sexual manner. For example, attending a bar or nightclub wearing leather clothing to drink, socialise or dance with like-minded people.

There are few terms directly associated with this, however you may wish to be familiar with the following: *chaps* are a form of leather over-trouser commonly worn by cowboys and cowgirls; *leatherman, leatherdyke, leather-club, leatherdaddy,* etc. are all terms used within the leather fetish community to indicate an element of leather together with another identity. For example, leatherdyke refers to a dyke who is part of the leather community. Leatherdaddy would be a male-identified person who takes a dominant role to a younger adult within the leather community.

EROTIC FICTION

People can be into erotic fiction as readers, writers or both. These days most erotic fiction is exchanged online. Originally it took the form of zines which were mailed out to members of communities. Early slash fiction (in the 1960s and 70s) was generally written by middle-aged heterosexual women (Kustritz, 2003). More recently slash fiction is written by a wider range of ages, genders, sexualities, etc. The best-selling *50 Shades* trilogy, which began as fan fiction, has recently opened up the possibility of publishing erotic fiction in a mainstream arena.

People tend to cluster in *fandoms* relating to specific canons (the television show, book, movie, pop band or whatever which they are interested in). Particularly common fandoms emerge around specific genres (science fiction and fantasy being common) and also fiction which involved strong 'same-gender' relationships which are not consummated (e.g. Bodie/Doyle from *The Professionals*).

There are also some genres which are particularly common within erotic fiction, and slash specifically. These include the *first time* story, about the first realisation or expression of attraction between characters, the *hurt/comfort* story where a character is harmed and then looked after (for example tortured for information and then rescued), the *PWP* (*plot what plot?*) where the action is entirely sexual, and the *Mary Sue* where the author places themselves into the story (often frowned upon by other authors).

People inhabiting online environments, such as message boards or MMORPGs (massively multiplayer online role-playing games) such as *World of Warcraft*, *Second Life*, etc. may well engage in text-based erotic role-playing which – in effect – is a form of interactive fiction. Some erotic fiction authors will take on characters and write together from different character perspectives on an internet chat site or similar. This is not dissimilar to role-playing in BDSM contexts (see Chapter 6).

Often erotic fiction authors use their writing to explore specific aspects of sexuality in which they themselves are interested, and sometimes a particular community will focus on a certain sexuality (e.g. Harry Potter and adult/child relationships, Sherlock Holmes and asexuality). However, as with all sexualities, it is important to remember that people write and read such fiction for a multiplicity of reasons and it has different meanings for different authors/readers at different times (e.g. creativity, relaxation, arousal, etc.).

FURRY

The term furry is an umbrella term referring to a variety of people who identify with an animal or mystical creature (*otherkin*). Some furries wear fur suits which emulate the look of their preferred creature, or are an approximation of an illustration – often anime – of that creature. Some have an identity of a creature but do not wear apparel to approximate that creature. Common furry identities include cats, wolves and foxes. Common otherkin include unicorns, dragons, vampires (*sanguinarians*) and fae (*fairy folk*).

Furries often present their creature identity in online fora, especially via avatars that more closely fit that identity. This has the added benefit that the approximation need not be flawed compared to the person's idea of what it should be. It is for this reason also that many people don't wear suits of their favoured creature, as the approximation is not close enough, and instead wear suits approximating a more secondary identity. Furry fandoms are online, or 'real life' (offline), groups consisting of people who identify as some form of creature. Such fandoms often include a great deal of creativity in art and literature.

Some people attend conventions or social events where they are able to mingle comfortably in their preferred identity while wearing some form of apparel suitable to that identity. This may include all-over body suits, as well as more subtle adjustments such as prosthetic make-up, ears and tails, etc. A subgroup of furries includes *babyfur* who identify as younger versions of their preferred creature, for example a kitten rather than an adult cat. Sexual activity in the furry identity (online or offline) is known as *yiffing*. *Scritching* can be sexual or non-sexual and involves pleasantly scratching another person. Such activities may take place between two or more people.

ADULT BABY/CHILD – AGEPLAY

The term *adult baby* is often shortened to AB, or sometimes, if the person finds wearing a nappy/diaper comforting or enjoyable, AB/DL for *adult baby diaper lover*. In the medical literature it is sometimes referred to as 'paraphilic infantilism', although this is generally not used by clients and should be avoided (*infantilism* alone is sometimes used in communities).

For most people this sexuality involves dressing and/or being treated as a person who is markedly younger than their chronological age, usually as a child or a baby. This may be for sexual reasons and/or for the sense of comfort and security that comes with taking on this role. It may be to do with the giving up of responsibility for a time, or because of the remembered security from that time in a person's life.

For those people for whom ageplay has a sexual element, it is important to recognise that this has nothing to do with paedophilia, as the erotic element is concerned with the person *themselves* being a child or baby, sometimes in the presence of an adult, rather than with any actual children. Indeed, for many people, as with erotic cross-dressing for some (see Chapter 11), it is the paradox which has the erotic element: in the case of AB/DL, that of an *adult* being treated like a child, in cross-dressing that of being treated as the 'other gender'.

Being an adult baby or child may be part of a person's identity that they, and others, cherish. For example, it may give them the opportunity to be more playful and silly than in the general course of their lives, or to wear clothing which they enjoy, but would not otherwise feel comfortable in. As most adults have to live in the world of jobs, taxes, actual children, etc. this identity may only be foregrounded on certain occasions when it is appropriate, however it nonetheless remains valuable. For such people there is often less of an erotic element.

Slightly different are those for whom being an adult baby or child is a shorter or solely playful activity which has an erotic element. In the BDSM community this is sometimes called *ageplay*. Here the usual power differences between adults and children are played out between an adult and an adult child or adult baby. As with all BDSM activities it is important for participants to gain informed consent while still in adult–adult roles, and to be especially aware of any actual childhood traumas which may inadvertently be triggered by ageplay. Partners may set limits on things that they are willing to engage with, for example a partner may be willing to 'parent' an adult baby but not to engage with nappies etc. Terms which may be encountered here include *daddy's little girl (DLG)* in which an older male top treats a younger female bottom as a nurtured child. The term 'sissification' intersects with ageplay as it is where an adult male is consensually 'forced' to don the clothes of, and behave as, a young girl as part of a BDSM scene. The humiliation the adult male feels at being dressed as a young female is the source of the eroticisation. Sissification is frowned upon in some circles due to the necessarily derogative stance towards femininity that it adopts.

All of the accoutrements of childhood may be used by people being adult babies or children. Some people wear adult, but more childish clothes; some use items such as dummies, etc. that are designed for actual children and babies; and there are a wide variety of purpose-made items including clothes, cots, chairs, nappies, etc. in adult sizes.

VOYEUR/EXHIBITIONIST

Voyeurs and exhibitionists enjoy watching people behave in an erotic manner (voyeurs) or being watched behaving in an erotic manner (exhibitionists). These practices rarely constitute an identity in the way that being gay does, for example, but are often part of wider practices which may be part of a person's identity. For example, a person may enjoy being watched by, or watching, strangers having sex and so may become part of the *dogging* scene at local out-of-the-way car parks (see Chapter 14). People may also enjoy *voyeurism* and *exhibitionism* while *swinging* (see Chapter 14). People may attend sex clubs and parties in which they are able to watch, and be watched, having sex. Additionally, they may enjoy watching a partner be sexual alone – or with another partner – in more private locations, such as their bedroom. There are many websites devoted to couples advertising for a person to join them for sex (and vice versa).

Sex is widely considered to be something which should be done in private, even with the lights switched off for additional privacy and so people whose sexuality involves a desire to watch or be watched may feel uncomfortable about this. Provided everyone is consenting there is no reason why these things cannot comfortably be brought into people's sex lives. The aim of a practitioner should, again, be primarily addressed at considering whether any problem lies in the client's concern with societal norms, and – if so – how they wish to resolve the conflict. Open negotiation as to likes and dislikes can be useful, with partners saying what they are comfortable with, might like to try under the right circumstances, and what they cannot countenance. For example, a woman might wish to watch her husband have sex with another man, but her husband might only feel comfortable with this if it was a family friend. These things can only be discovered through sensitive negotiation.

WIDER SOCIETY

People with further sexualities are often treated as pariahs, not only by mainstream society who sensationalise them or consider them too strange to countenance; but also by other sexual and gender minority groups who endeavour to gain social respectability by ostracising them, in effect saying, "At least we're not as weird as *those* guys …". This was a trope used by some heterosexual feminists in the 1960s and 1970s who distanced themselves from lesbian communities, and by some lesbian communities in the 1990s who distanced themselves from trans communities.

In fact, much of what is outlined above is present in one form or another in wider mainstream culture. For example, in common with AB/DL, people often use babytalk and childish words when speaking to adult loved ones "hey babe", "sweety", "you're so cute", etc. In common with fetish identities many people have an erotic response to silk, satin, lace, etc. In common with furry identities, people commonly dress in fur and animal prints, and wear bunny ears/tails. In common with exhibitionism and voyeurism people watch pornography, attend strip clubs and learn to pole dance. They also wear short skirts and low-cut tops to work or the cinema, play football or go to the gym with their tops off, etc. In common with the reading and writing of erotic fiction and fantasy a great many mainstream novels and television programmes, films, etc. contain erotic elements. When engaging with people with further sexualities professionally it can be useful to consider these continua, rather than attending only to differences which are usually a matter of degree rather than kind.

For many of the practices covered, and in contrast to traditional penis-in-vagina sex, the chances of sexually transmitted infections and unwanted pregnancies are either low or non-existent. These are also sexualities that do not necessarily rely on standard definitions of physical attractiveness or on physical ability.

LEGAL ASPECTS

There is little in the way of specific legal or medical engagement with the sexualities covered here, with the exception of voyeurism and exhibitionism. In the case of these the issue is to do with consent. As stated in the introduction we are only engaging with identities and sexualities that are consensual, although, in common with heterosexual 'missionary position', vagina surrounding penis sex, they do, of course, have the potential to be undertaken non-consensually.

The complexity with further sexualities arises due to the social opprobrium associated with them. People may take umbrage with an adult presenting as a baby in a public place or with a person having sex with their partner in a car park. Clients may need to navigate a line between reasonable behaviour, which may nonetheless be transgressive, and behaviour which has the likelihood of upsetting others. This is not to say that all behaviours which are transgressive should not be practised in public. Some people are outraged by the sight of gay people or people from different racial backgrounds kissing or holding hands, for example – this does not mean that these things should not be done in public.

It is worth noting that few of the identities or practices mentioned here are protected under law in the way in which being LGBT is. Consequently, people may feel ostracised to a greater degree and may be at greater risk of exploitation than other groups. Professionals should be mindful of this and should be especially cautious in their notes etc.

MEDICAL ASPECTS

The medical literature has tended to pathologise people with further sexualities, and indeed people with non-heterosexual sexualities more widely. One difficulty is that clinicians often suffer from the clinician illusion (see Introduction), having only come across people with further sexualities in their consulting room (i.e. people who are struggling in some way). When reading about these practices and identities it is therefore worth looking outside of the medical literature, which has a history of pathologising sexual difference, and also engaging with literature produced by the communities themselves.

PAUSE FOR CONSIDERATION

Take some time to perform an internet search for information regarding a sexuality with which you are unfamiliar, perhaps one of those covered in this chapter. Try to engage with sources written both by and for the communities as much as possible, rather than academic or scientific sources which are often written about them. Consider what you have learned that you did not know before; whether you could have gained this information from an academic or scientific source; and how it made you feel to engage with a community source.

RATES AND 'COMORBIDITY'

From what little literature there is regarding people who consensually engage in further sexualities it appears that, taken broadly, the behaviours are not uncommon, although the rates of each of the specific behaviours and identities are rarer. Indeed, there are many internet groups devoted to the topics covered here.

There does not appear to be raised incidences of psychological 'comorbidities' in these groups and indeed some reports suggest that, for example, the average AB/DL is employed and in a relationship (Hickey, 2006). As ever, with people with marginalised identities/practices it is important to recognise that while the practice itself may not be pathological, the conflict with societal norms can induce difficulties such as anxiety and depression. The primary task of the professional should be to engage with the sexuality or identity as a reasonable thing per se, and then discover how it is for the client themselves, with the option of work towards resilience in the face of social opprobrium as a possible option.

GROUP NORMS

Because the practices and identities covered have only really become groups and communities in their own right since the inception of the worldwide web (around 1997) there has not been a great deal of time for community norms to develop and become established. Local groups may establish certain norms and these will certainly differ according to culture, nationality, age, socio-economic status and the like. In general, but by no means always, the more fully engaged one is, the more respected one is within the group – up to a certain point (for example, someone who has had a furry identity for a long time, identifying with a consistent animal, and wearing appropriate clothing, may be more respected than someone who fluctuates more, for whom it is a recent thing). At the other extreme, as with all groups, whether or not sexuality is involved, people who are more obsessive are sometimes frowned upon: this applies equally to hobbies like cross-stitch or fishing (for example, some would frown on intensive surgical procedures in relation to furry identities or living AB 24/7).

People within these groups often recognise the wider societal opprobrium attached to them and endeavour to act in such a way as to cause no further difficulties. While this is useful in, for example, being polite to bar staff where a meeting is held, it can cause problems when people feel pressure to be a 'poster child' for their sexuality (ensuring that they behave perfectly and normatively in every other respect). It can also be problematic when there are difficult intersections of identity and practice. For example, if a person has a mental health issue as well as having an identity detailed above, the added stresses on the group can cause difficulties, especially as these groups are often underresourced and undersupported by wider societal structures, such as advocacy groups, charity funding, etc.

COMMUNITY

For many people finding a community of like-minded people (online or otherwise) can be a life-changing experience. The loss of the sense of isolation can ameliorate the depression and anxiety which is often associated with having an identity which is not reflected in the world around. However, for some, group norms can be restricting and clients should be encouraged to determine how they themselves would best like to engage with their practice or identity. For some clients finding a set of rules where before there were none can be like clinging to a cumbersome life raft – very useful when all out at sea, but sometimes one must learn to swim if one is to make progress.

SUMMARY AND CONCLUSIONS

In summary people with further sexualities will often not bring their sexuality to the attention of professionals, just as others do not. However, some will, and for those a knowledgeable careful approach is needed for ethical practice:

- Recognise that, while at first blush there may seem to be significant differences from other portions of the population, in fact there are a number of commonalities and it is difficult to draw strict distinctions due to the continua on which these practices lie.

- As these client groups often feel alienated, do not further alienate the clients by asking inappropriate questions – it is vital to educate yourself to a basic level about your client's world. If you are aware of what fucking is, you should also be aware of what dogging and yiffing are, if you are seeing a client who is engaged with these practices. Of course, you will need to find out what it means *for them* but they will become further alienated and exhausted – to a grave detriment to the rapport – if they must explain the basic elements of their lives. If you require education you should pay a community representative for continuing professional development and not require it from the client who is paying you.
- If you find that you are unable to bracket you own feelings regarding these client groups, or if you are unwilling or unable to obtain the necessary basic information, then refer the client on to someone with the necessary expertise. It is also important not to refer to people with a forensic interest unless there is a forensic matter at hand. Many people with a forensic interest do deal with people with a wide variety of sexualities, however there is a greater risk of the clinician illusion with these practitioners who may be unused to dealing with people with diverse sexualities who do not have a forensic history and are involved in only consensual sexualities.

Most people with further sexualities will be primarily concerned with the banalities of everyday life – paying bills, looking after their children, ill parents and the such. Taking account of further sexualities without giving them undue prominence unless it is warranted takes a deft professional touch which should be carefully marshalled and constantly evaluated in order that people do not feel further stigmatised, and in order that any unrelated issues the client brings are not lost.

FURTHER READING

Gates, K. (Ed.) (2000). *Deviant desires: Incredibly strange sex.* New York, NY: Juno Books.

In order for there to be literature and resources on a topic, communities must be formed who take on that identity and wish to propagate knowledge about it. For example, there is often information about fetish as part of the BDSM communities, but little distinct from it. AB/DL is starting to develop a community with several websites and a few books becoming available, while furry communities have started websites, but have published no specific books as yet. While there is a good deal of slash fiction available, there are few community resources – beyond the stories themselves – which are readily available to the wider population outside of some conventions and the academic literature. Exhibitionism and voyeurism do not, yet, seem to have an identity as such associated with them. This means that, while there are a variety of channels to express these practices, little has been written *about* their consensual practice. Performing an internet search periodically should update you on these topics as more information becomes available, and we provide some relevant links on the website for this book at sexandgender.org

ONLINE COMMUNITY ETIQUETTE

Minority communities often use the internet as a means of support and for the sharing of information and creation of community. This is partly for ease of access and anonymity reasons, but also because it offers a forum for people to communicate which does not necessarily require the same material and financial resources, skills and time which non-online spaces require. It is incumbent on professionals to engage with online communities and sources of information, while respecting the need for these to be safe places for the community members involved. It is ethical for you to introduce yourself as a professional and to bear in mind that potential and current clients may be behind their online avatars.

ADDITIONAL REFERENCES

Barker, M. (2002). Slashing the Slayer: A thematic analysis of homo-erotic Buffy fan fiction. Presentation to the first annual conference on readings around Buffy the Vampire Slayer, Blood, Text and Fears, University of East Anglia, Norwich, 19–20 October. Available from http://oro.open.ac.uk/23340/2/Barker(1).pdf.

Hickey, E.W. (2006). *Sex crimes and paraphilia*. New Jersey: Pearson Education.

Kustritz, A. (2003). Slashing the romance narrative. *The Journal of American Culture, 26*(3), 371–384.

III

RELATIONSHIP STRUCTURES

MONOGAMY

13

This chapter aims to:

- Consider the, often taken-for-granted, relationship style of monogamy.
- Explore problems that can occur in monogamous relationships, particularly around expectations and where the boundaries of relationships are.
- Explain key monogamous practices such as those around implicit or explicit commitments and contracts, and ways in which these shift over time (for example with new technologies).

INTRODUCTION

This chapter explores *monogamy*: the practice of having one sexual or romantic relationship at a time. It will be useful for you to read this chapter together with the following chapter on *non-monogamy* because the dividing line between these two forms of relationship structures is blurred. Also many of the everyday concerns of people in monogamous and openly non-monogamous relationships are the same (money, household tasks, trust, communication, sex, etc.), and the kinds of conversations and negotiations they have around their relationships are increasingly similar (Frank & DeLamater, 2010).

FORMS OF MONOGAMY

In this chapter we focus on relationships in which the explicit, or taken-for-granted, rule is that there won't be any other sexual or romantic relationships outside a main partnership. Monogamy is a broad umbrella term covering everything from lifelong monogamous partnerships, to forms of *serial monogamy* (having one monogamous relationship after another), to secret non-monogamy where the rule is monogamy but one or both people are actually having additional relationships which they are hiding. The latter can be regarded as a coercive form of relating, as it does not have the consent of all concerned, and therefore is not considered as a legitimate relationship style here (see Introduction). However, we consider how such situations might be dealt with when they come to light given how common they are.

This chapter, and the next, relate both to people who come together to a professional as members of a relationship (e.g. for relationship therapy), and to those who come as individuals (whether they are currently single, in a relationship, or in the process of breaking up). Therefore, we give examples of working with both individuals and with people in relationships.

PAUSE FOR CONSIDERATION

What are your own rules for relationships regarding monogamy? What boundaries would you like to draw around your own, and partners', behaviour (e.g. physical and emotionally close contact with others)? Has this changed at all over your life?

MONOGAMY AS THE NORM

Of course, as with being cisgender (Chapter 4) or having a heterosexual and 'vanilla' (non-kinky) sexual identity (Chapter 10), monogamy is generally seen as the default, or norm, in wider Western culture. People are assumed to be monogamous unless they say otherwise, and it is often taken for granted that everyone shares an understanding of what this means (i.e. not having sexual or romantic relationships with people other than one's partner).

As mentioned in other chapters, being part of the perceived norm means that a person doesn't experience the stress of constantly having to identify or explain themselves to others, or of deciding to remain closeted or to pass as something else. Also, they are not faced with the fear of prejudice or attack on the basis of perceived difference. However, there are other problems which are common to locating oneself within the perceived norm in any way, including:

- Feeling constrained or trapped within this norm if it is not something that completely fits.
- Fearing what will happen if one strays from it in any way because of not having experienced being outside of it, and because it seems apparent how other people who stray are treated.
- Being shocked when situations reveal that there is actually diversity within the norm, when it was assumed to be universal. For example, people in a couple often eventually realise that they have different understandings of what is meant by monogamy, but this comes as a surprise because they assumed that it would be the same (whereas those in non-monogamous relationships would be more likely to have had a conversation early on about how they each understood relationships).

Such problems may be particularly the case for people who fall into all of the perceived 'norm'[1] categories: being cisgendered, heterosexual, non-kinky and sexual as well as being monogamous. If somebody is outside the 'norm' in one category (being trans, LGB, kinky or asexual, for example) the way they have had to question the 'norm' may mean that they are more likely to view other norms, like monogamy, as up for question and negotiation. However, this is not always the case, and some may strive to be as 'normal' as possible in every other way to counteract their perceived difference (as in homonormativity, see Chapter 9).

COMMON CONCERNS

Broadly speaking there are three categories of monogamous people who will present to a counsellor, psychologist or other health professional:

- Those for whom monogamy is incidental to other issues they are dealing with.
- Those for whom monogamy has come up as a specific issue because they have realised that they have different ideas from their partner/s (or from friends, family, and others) about monogamy and related aspects of relationships.
- Those who are having a crisis because one or more people in a relationship feels that the monogamy rules have been broken in some way.

The vast majority of people fall into the first category. Most monogamous people who seek help and support, even from a sexual or relationship specialist, will present with an issue that is not explicitly related to being monogamous. However, it is worth keeping in mind that the way in which they structure their relationships *may* be relevant and worth exploring, and that they may not mention monogamy simply because they take for granted that they should want a monogamous relationship, or that a certain form of monogamy is the only possible way of relating (see Wider Society, below). Therefore coverage of the rules and dynamics at play in the clients' relationship, or the kind of relationships they would like to have, would be one of many topics (like family background, cultural context, spiritual beliefs, etc.) that it may be helpful to cover in assessment and/or to be aware of with any new client.

---

[1] We use perceived norm here because, as we have mentioned elsewhere in the book, some of these things are far more common than is often assumed (e.g. it is more common to have some form of kinky desires or fantasies such as bondage than it is not to have them), and some of them depend on the way terms are defined (e.g. it could be argued that all people are trans to some degree – not sticking exactly to the gender roles that those present at the birth expected for them, and that some form of bisexual attraction is more common than none at all).

MONOGAMY-RELATED PRESENTING ISSUES

There are also situations in which monogamy is more obviously relevant: either when a person realises that their understandings and expectations of monogamy differ from those of a partner (or other people in their life), or when something happens where one or both partners feel that the monogamy rules have been broken.

The realisation that monogamy means different things to different people is becoming increasingly apparent. For example, around a third of young heterosexual couples do not agree on whether or not they have discussed their monogamy agreement, and over half disagree on whether the rules of monogamy have been kept or not (Warren, Harvey & Agnew, 2011). In such situations it would, again, be useful to bring the topic of monogamy out into the open and to explore what it means to each person (if that is appropriate to your professional role): what they feel that they are agreeing to when they promise to be monogamous. Various ways of doing this will be explored later in the chapter. When working with couples directly, it is useful to allow each person to explore their preferences without the influence of the other person's presence before they come together to try to reach agreements.

It may be that a couple agrees on the rules of monogamy for them, but that these differ from their family, friends or others around them. For example, in what has been termed the *new monogamy* or *monogamish* many younger couples agree to have various kinds of attachments outside the relationship as long as these don't threaten the main relationship. This may be difficult to understand for their parents who might well not have considered such flexibility a possibility. Similarly, such versions of monogamy are likely to be more acceptable in certain countries, certain (probably urban) areas, and among people of certain cultural, class and religious backgrounds.

SITUATIONS WHERE MONOGAMY RULES HAVE BEEN BROKEN

Situations where the rules are broken are becoming increasingly common. This may be either because there has been an assumption that rules were shared which actually were not (for example around whether cyber-sex counts as infidelity), or because somebody knowingly has broken the rules. In the latter case, around 55% of married women and 65% of married men report being unfaithful at some point in their marriage (Atwood & Schwartz, 2002).

In such cases it may well be necessary for individuals to have space for dealing with the, often intense, feelings such as loss, betrayal, anger, guilt, and insecurity before it is possible to examine agreements or renegotiate relationship boundaries going forward. Referral to someone who is trained at working with couples (such as a relationship therapist or mediator) is appropriate here. If you work with couples yourself it is certainly worth having separate sessions for some of this work and for finding out what each individual would like to happen from here.

It is particularly important not to assume that either staying together, or breaking up, is going to be the best outcome from the outset, but rather to help each individual, and the couple, to explore the situation rather than rushing to a solution. It is vital to recognise that there are many options in between remaining exactly as they were and never seeing each other again (for example, taking some form of break, deciding not to be sexual partners any more but continuing to live together, opening up the relationship, renewing vows, or ending the relationship amicably). It is important to resist the culturally dominant notion that such situations always involve one 'good guy' and one 'bad guy' (generally the person who breaks the rules and/or instigates the break-up). Rather it is helpful to recognise that relationships are co-constructed and change over time. Given the high current rates of separation, and the fact that others – including children – are often involved, it is important to move towards more open and flexible approaches towards relationship renegotiation, while acknowledging that emotions often run very high at such times.

KEY PRACTICES

Perhaps the most obvious key practice of monogamy is to have some kind of formal, public, ceremony where promises and commitments are made. The traditional marriage vows of various religions do not always explicitly mention monogamy. Indeed in the places and times that many of them originated monogamy probably was not the norm. However, many in minority (Western) culture today assume that marriage/commitment equals monogamy.

RELIGION AND MONOGAMY

It is vital to remember that religions are complex and multiple. It can be helpful to consider all the different forms of the religion that you are most familiar with and remember that the same multiplicity and complexity is true of all the major religions. With religious clients, professionals can usefully explore how they understand the rules around monogamy and fidelity in their religion, being prepared to find out more about that religion themselves, and also being aware that the specific version practised by the client may differ from what they find out.

COMMITMENT CEREMONIES

With any – religious or non-religious – clients who are planning to commit, or have recently committed, in such ceremonies, it is worth exploring what this means to them. What do they each understand, for example, by phrases such as "faithful", "true", "loyal" or "forsaking others" if they are using them? Similarly, it is useful to open up other promises such as "protecting", leading a "healthy lifestyle", "honouring" each other, staying together, and sharing "worldly goods". For example, people often have different ideas about financial independence (having a completely joint account to keeping separate incomes); whether relationships must stay sexual over time; whether it is acceptable to keep any part of their lives private; and by which time they hope to have reached certain relationship goals, if they have them (such as buying a house, having a child, retiring and so on).

COMMITMENT OVER TIME

Although we often focus on one big celebration of commitment, there are also implicit rules of monogamy at different stages of a relationship which could also be usefully brought out into the open. For example, many people have an idea that they are implicitly agreeing to stop seeing other people when they agree to go out on a date, when they get to the third date, when they have sex with someone, when they say "I love you", when they agree to be "partners", or when they get engaged. It is quite possible that two people will have personal rules which differ. Similarly, there may be different rules around whether certain events alter the rules of monogamy (for example, if one person stops being sexual, if their appearance changes, or if they have to be in a long-distance relationship for a while).

It can also be useful to explore the ways in which monogamy, and other forms of commitment, are communicated on a more everyday level. For example, it is important for some people to have forms of continual commitment such as marking anniversaries, saying certain phrases which affirm the relationship (such as "I love you" or "I'm yours"), daily rituals (such as sharing meals, going to bed at the same time, and sleeping together), or public signs that they are together (such as holding hands or calling each other "my partner" or "my spouse"). Again, different things can have different meanings to different people in the relationship. One common example would be a couple where one person likes gifts as declarations of love while the other feels loved and committed to when their partner does practical things which demonstrate that they care. Another example would be whether they take sex, or other forms of physical intimacy, to be declarations of love and intimacy or simply fun shared activities. It can be tremendously difficult to grasp quite how differently a partner can feel about such things, as there is such a common assumption that we will share our views and values in couples. It is useful for the professional to challenge the idea that there is anything wrong with such differences.

ATTRACTIONS OUTSIDE THE RELATIONSHIP

Other key practices worth considering in monogamous relationships are those used to deal with attraction to people outside the relationship when this does happen. Again, these may be explicit but are more likely to be implicit and unspoken. It is useful for the professionals to normalise such attractions given that the popular – but erroneous – belief is that people are naturally and easily monogamous (Brandon, 2011). If couples are aware that attraction to others will happen perhaps it will be more possible to negotiate how they will manage it. Many have lighthearted lists of five or ten people (often celebrities) who each would be allowed to have sex with if the situation presented itself. These could be a useful, and fun, starting point for such conversations. As discussed in Chapter 14, some people's preference is for as much information as possible, whereas some is for as little as possible (and it is possible that each person in a couple will have different preferences). Some find security in hearing about their partner's attractions while some find it in not knowing.

In relationships where secret infidelities are happening it is possible that there is some implicit agreement to this. Many people are aware that their partner has affairs or one-night stands, for example, and choose to consciously ignore it. There are risks to such implicit agreements, of course. It can never be known for sure that a partner really *does* agree to one's other relationships (thus presenting a problem to the notion of consent, see Introduction). Even if they do implicitly agree, one will not know the boundaries of this and what things would not be deemed acceptable or would end the relationship. Finally, the risk of HIV and other STIs his highest in relationships where monogamy is claimed (so partners have unprotected sex as part of demonstrating their trust) but where people are actually having additional secret sexual interactions.

Secret non-monogamy poses a problem for the professional who decides to see members of a couple separately and then together (as previously suggested). It is wise to agree ground rules for this in an initial couple session so that you don't find yourself holding secret information which you have not agreed to. For example, the ground rule might be that all material from individual sessions will be shared in the joint session, or that clients and practitioner agree not to share emotional content jointly, but that factual content (such as someone "breaking the rules") would be shared. Some practitioners are comfortable offering confidentiality to individuals in such situations, but it is certainly worth considering in advance.

WIDER SOCIETY

The issues covered in this – and the next – chapter are playing out in practice with increasing frequency due to the societal situation regarding monogamy. Many people view finding and maintaining a monogamous relationship as *the* most important aspect of their lives, at the same time as they struggle with some of the restrictions that these impose (in terms of other relationships, social life, and potentially different views on having children, or whether work or the relationship is prioritised). This is reflected in mass media which often presents finding 'The One' perfect partner as vital, and suggests that it can lead to a simple 'happily ever after'. The fact that people are living longer means that people often shift and change a great deal over the course of their relationships – in relation to sexual desires, life goals and connections with other people – which can be difficult when people change in different directions.

The following list outlines ways in which wider societal expectations around monogamy may be relevant to issues that clients present.

- Finding and maintaining a monogamous relationship is widely regarded as an essential element of being a happy and successful person, to such an extent that being single or going through a relationship break-up are viewed as failings and worthy of sympathy or derision. Therefore, the desire to find a relationship, and/or problems in past relationships, are key aspects of difficulties that people have. Pressure for a certain kind of monogamous relationship may result in people remaining in relationships which are not good for them, ending relationships which are not perceived as perfect, or finding it difficult to meet people who match their ideal of a partner.
- People struggle with tensions around freedom and togetherness: wanting to be able to make their own choices in life *and* to belong with other people, particularly partners. This can relate to issues of dependence/independence, privacy/ sharing, and individual/relationship goals and values. Often, in couples, people are in at least slightly different places: one stretching for more independence and freedom while the other craves more togetherness and security (although which partner is in which position often changes across time and situation). Making this explicit, and normalising the tension, can be immensely helpful.
- Problems such as anxiety and depression are often located in the dynamics between people rather than in the individual. For example, an anxious/depressed person may feel constrained, trapped and possessed, or insecure, anxious and rejected, by the form of monogamy that is being practised (due to assumptions about the 'right' way of doing it), or the way it has (or has not) been negotiated.

- Many common sexual difficulties are related to expectations around monogamy. For example, people may continue to have painful or unsatisfying sex because they are scared of losing their partner to somebody else. People may feel that they must continue to have 'great sex' throughout their relationship in order to affirm it, which creates the kind of pressure which can make it difficult to relax and tune in to what they really enjoy. When people are considered to be 'sex addicts' it is often because they want different kinds, or amounts, of sex to their partners, and also to be in a monogamous relationship which does not seem to allow for this (see Chapter 10).
- Monogamy is precarious because people are required to say that they are monogamous in order to be socially accepted, but they are also aware that most people are not monogamous in practice. There may be increasing pressures towards various forms of secret non-monogamy, for example in laddy groups who go to lap-dancing clubs for business meetings, or for the reader of romance fiction who is bombarded with representations of passionate love which do not match her own marriage.

MEDICAL AND LEGAL SITUATION

Monogamous relationships are generally presented – even in health and psychology trainings – as synonymous with mental health and 'normal' development. Break-ups and divorce are presented as problems, and infidelities as sinful, wrong and even pathological (in the concept of 'sex addiction'). Legal protections of married, and civilly partnered, couples also support an expectation of monogamous relationships (see Chapter 14).

GROUP NORMS

The societal norm around monogamy, as portrayed in romantic comedies and popular magazines, is taken up by most monogamous individuals. Although they rarely form anything as organised as communities, there are differentiable groups of monogamous people which differ somewhat from one another.

DIFFERENT FORMS OF MONOGAMY

Various forms of *serial monogamy* emerged in the 1990s and 2000s to replace the monogamy-for-life norm for some groups. In the 1990s it became popular for young, middle-class heterosexual women to follow self-help books like *The Rules* which presented a method of serial dating and 'playing hard to get' as the way to find 'Mr Right' and to get him to propose. This was presented on popular TV shows like *Sex and the City*, and is still a staple of women's magazines. In the 2000s, as a kind of backlash to this, the online 'seduction communities' emerged: these taught men how to become 'pick up artists' and become master seducers of women through various techniques (based in body language, evolutionary psychology and neuro-linguistic programming). For this group, the ideal relationship structure was to have many sexual conquests with women before (generally) settling down with one woman.

These examples, along with the *new monogamy* mentioned earlier (where restrictions around relationships outside the couple are looser), demonstrate how ways of doing monogamy can change over time, and also how new technologies impact on relationship structures. For example, the possibilities of accessing pornography 24/7, having cybersex, forming relationships through an avatar on *Second Life* or *World of Warcraft*, or becoming emotionally close to strangers online, present new challenges for couples negotiating their rules of monogamy (often with disagreements over what 'counts' as cheating).

When working with a monogamous client it is useful to discover the implicit rules around monogamy that are present in their particular cultural, class, generation or friendship group, as well as the rules in their individual relationship.

MONOGAMY CONTINUA

One useful way of conceptualising monogamy with clients is on the following continua of emotional and sexual closeness. This can help to open up what is implicit and taken for granted, and to aid conversation about where individuals, their relationship, and their wider group draw their lines.

Table 13.1

Continuum of emotional closeness/love	
Monoamory	Polyamory
One close intimate relationship and no close relationships outside this	*Multiple close relationships*
Continuum of sex/physical contact	
Monosex	Polysex
No sexual or physical contact outside the relationship	*Multiple sexual encounters*

PAUSE FOR CONSIDERATION

Think about where you, yourself, would put your (current, past or ideal) relationship on these continua. Where would your partner/s have put their preference? To make it more concrete you might consider, on the emotional continua, having a close friend other than your partner (perhaps with someone of the same gender as them), being friends with an ex-partner, staying up all night talking with someone you have just met, and having someone in your life who is as – or even more – important to you than your partner. On the sexual continua you might consider fantasising about a celebrity, watching pornography, flirting with a colleague, having cybersex and having a one-night stand.

The continua idea can be useful for other aspects of relationships such as how important it is to have shared interests, how separate or joint finances are, how much privacy people like, or how much time they want to spend together and apart.

With all such negotiations, it is useful to make it clear to clients that there are various possible outcomes. They may end up realising that they actually agree with each other; they may find that they disagree but come to a compromise; or it might be that they are in quite different places. If so, this will probably be a tension which crops up in their relationship from time to time when events trigger it, but they can be aware of this likelihood and respect their differences (i.e. "what works for me doesn't necessarily work for you"), or change the relationship in some way.

SUMMARY AND CONCLUSIONS

In summary, the following are good practice points when working with monogamous clients.

- Reflexively engage with your own assumptions about monogamy (and encourage all staff within a clinic or organisation to do the same).
- Be aware of the diversity of ways in which your monogamous clients might be practising monogamy (rather than assuming that it will be the same for everyone).
- Be prepared to raise the issue of monogamy (recognising how relevant it is to many issues, while not assuming that it will be a key issue for all clients).
- Consider exploring the tension between freedom and togetherness that underlies tensions around monogamy with clients, normalising the fact that people struggle with this.
- Normalise the difficulties inherent in monogamy, rather than reinforcing the myth that it is natural, easy or normal (given the numbers of people who are secretively non-monogamous and the number of non-monogamous cultures).

- Explore what your clients would like themselves, in terms of monogamy agreements, and what the norms of monogamy are in their group.
- Encourage open negotiation and communication around monogamy rather than operating on implicit taken-for-granteds, being open to the full spectrum of possibilities rather than advocating one end of the emotional/sexual continua over the other.

For all of these it would be useful to also be aware of the various styles of non-monogamous relationship structure that are possible, and the large overlap between monogamy and non-monogamy which suggests that the distinction itself is problematic. For example, it is hard to say which category the new monogamy, the seduction communities, secret infidelities, and contracted open relationships fall into. We will consider non-monogamy in more depth in Chapter 14.

FURTHER READING

Conley, T.D., Ziegler, A., Moors, A.C., Matsick, J.L. & Valentine, B. (2013). A critical examination of popular assumptions about the benefits and outcomes of monogamous relationships. *Personality and Social Psychology Review.*

Perel, E. (2007). *Mating in captivity.* London: HarperCollins.

ADDITIONAL REFERENCES

Atwood, J.D. & Schwartz, L. (2002). Cyber-sex: The new affair treatment considerations. *Journal of Couple and Relationship Therapy: Innovations in Clinical and Educational Interventions, 1*(3), 37–66.

Brandon, M. (2011). The challenge of monogamy: Bringing it out of the closet and into the treatment room. *Sexual and Relationship Therapy, 26*(2).

Frank, K. & DeLamater, J. (2010). Deconstructing monogamy: Boundaries, identities, and fluidities across relationships. In M. Barker & D. Langdridge (Eds.), *Understanding Non-Monogamies* (pp. 9–22). New York: Routledge.

Warren, J.T., Harvey, S.M. & Agnew, C.R. (2011). One love: Explicit monogamy agreements among heterosexual young adult couples at increased risk of sexually transmitted infections, *Journal of Sex Research, 48*(1), 1–8.

NON-MONOGAMY

14

This chapter aims to:

- Provide an overview of the common forms of openly non-monogamous relationships that exist.
- Consider how such relationship structures may, and may not, be relevant to clients.
- Summarise common non-monogamous languages, activities and dynamics.
- Explore the role of wider cultural perceptions of such relationships in client experiences.

INTRODUCTION

This chapter explores openly *non-monogamous* relationships: the variety of relationship structures that are not based on *monogamy* but which involve some form of consensual openness to having more than one sexual or romantic relationship.

DIFFERENT FORMS OF OPEN NON-MONOGAMY

We focus on the most common styles of *open non-monogamy* that have emerged in minority (Western) culture in recent years: *swinging*, *open relationships* and *polyamory* (having multiple intimate relationships). However, it is important to remember that, worldwide, forms of *polygamy* (marriages to more than one person) are vastly more common than *monogamy*. For reasons of space it would be impossible to do justice to even some of this vast diversity here so we will not attempt it, suffice it to say that in our increasingly multicultural practices it is important to be mindful of the potential for a wide range of non-monogamous traditions in the backgrounds, and present lives, of clients, as well as monogamous ones.

In addition to this, many individuals across cultures find their way to some form of openly non-monogamous relating which is unique to them, and which they never identify under labels like *polyamory*, *polygamy* or *open relationship*. For example, people may have relationships involving three adults all living together or near to each other, which are accepted by family and neighbours as the way they do things. Rather than imposing specific concepts on clients, it is useful to approach them with a cultural, and general, curiosity to find out how their own relationship structure operates and in what wider cultural context. However, it should not be up to clients to spend large amounts of the time educating professionals about their culture, religion or generational context (see Chapter 1). Professionals should be prepared to do some background research of their own, while also ensuring that they check with clients whether what they have found applies to them (given that there is multiplicity and complexity in all religions, countries, cultures and communities).

MONOGAMY AND NON-MONOGAMY

It will be useful to read this chapter together with the previous one as the dividing lines between monogamy and non-monogamy are less clear than they might at first seem. Many seemingly monogamous relationships are actually secretly non-monogamous at some point. Several recent forms of monogamy have some consensual openness regarding other emotionally close, and even sometimes sexual, relationships (for example, the new monogamy or the seduction communities discussed in Chapter 13). The kinds of conversations and negotiations that occur in monogamous and non-monogamous relationships are increasingly similar.

PAUSE FOR CONSIDERATION

Consider what forms of openly non-monogamous relationships you are currently aware of? What are your opinions and beliefs about such relationships? How might this impact on your practice with openly non-monogamous clients?

Obviously one interesting and challenging aspect of open non-monogamy is that it may involve more than two people. For this reason it is important that those who work with people in relationships refer to what they do as relationship therapy/coaching/mediation/work etc. rather than referring to it as 'couple therapy/work etc.'

COMMON CONCERNS

Broadly speaking there are three categories of openly non-monogamous people who will present to a counsellor, psychologist or other health professional:

- Those for whom non-monogamy is incidental to other issues they are dealing with.
- Those who are experiencing problems because their non-monogamous relationships or beliefs are in conflict with others around them, or wider society.
- Those whose non-monogamous way of relating (or beliefs around this) is involved in the problems they are experiencing.

INCIDENTAL NON-MONOGAMY

As with so many of the genders, sexualities and relationship structures that we have explored in this book, the majority of non-monogamous people coming to a professional will fall into the former of these two categories: their issues have nothing to do with the fact that they are non-monogamous.

However, as with so many of the identities and practices which are currently situated outside 'the norm', professionals may assume that open non-monogamy is inherently problematic and therefore that it must be examined and questioned, for example on the basis of an assumption that the person has a personality or intimacy problem. Around 10% of professionals respond negatively to people's self-disclosures of open non-monogamy and attempt to change a client's relationship structures (Weber, 2002). Obviously this can lead to feelings of alienation and withdrawal from engagement with professionals.

The most important thing a professional can do is to fully educate themselves on the forms of open non-monogamy that are currently in existence. This chapter provides a broad overview, and there are many helpful resources for professionals and others, particularly on polyamorous relationships (see Further Reading). However, if you have not had time to educate yourself, or if you feel that your own biases may get in the way of working affirmatively, refer the client on to somebody more appropriate. There are lists of 'poly-friendly' professionals available online, and many LGBT services include professionals who are familiar with open non-monogamy. If a client does want to talk about issues relating to their relationship structure then it is vital that they have a practitioner who is educated and affirmative in this area.

DIFFICULTIES RELATED TO NON-MONOGAMY

By far the most common problem that people experience around open non-monogamy relates to the difficulties inherent in being non-monogamous in a *mononormative*[1] world. This may take the form, for example, of family, friends or colleagues not accepting their relationships; of prejudice or discrimination on the basis of their non-monogamy (or the stress of keeping this secret); of partners or potential partners having difficulties with them; or of them worrying that there is something 'wrong' with them due to their difference.

In such cases it is essential to normalise open non-monogamy and to work to challenge mononormativity. This might take the form, for example, of pointing out how rare monogamy actually is in practice (therefore non-monogamy could, broadly, be said to be 'normal'); of questioning the importance of being 'normal' anyway; and of demonstrating that all consensual relationship structures are equally valued. The professional might present the view that different relationship structures work for different people at different times, and give examples of different forms, perhaps drawing on the continua presented at the end of Chapter 13, or on the comments of celebrities who have spoken about being openly non-monogamous.

Most problems experienced by openly non-monogamous people also relate to wider mononormativity in the sense that they are about not having a 'rulebook'. People in openly non-monogamous relationships are often inventing their relationship structures from scratch, or working from the limited amount of information and self-help literature that is available but which may not always fit their situation. Therefore, it is likely that people will struggle and experience difficulties as they negotiate their relationships. However, it is worth remembering that the rules of monogamy are also often not a simple fit for people and can be just as complex and contradictory as those of open non-monogamy (see Chapter 13).

KEY PRACTICES

The most common forms of open non-monogamy which clients are likely to be involved with are swinging, open relationships and polyamory. Estimates are that around half of gay men and bisexual people have forms of

---

[1] Like heteronormativity (see Chapters 8, 9 and 10), mononormativity refers to the fact that current Western society assumes monogamy to be the norm and relationships to be monogamous unless otherwise stated.

openly non-monogamous relationships, whereas it is somewhat less common among heterosexual people and lesbians.

SWINGING

Swinging involves couples having sex with other people, either separately or together, often in a social context such as a party or club. It is predominantly a heterosexual practice, with women swingers more often than men identifying as bisexual or 'bi-curious'. Generally, the rules are that only sex, and not love, with people outside the *primary relationships* is acceptable (although friendships may develop between couples over time). Other activities which are somewhat similar to swinging include *dogging* (watching people having sex in cars) and couples seeking singles online (and vice versa) for sex (which is very common but often kept secret from everyone else in their lives).

OPEN RELATIONSHIPS

The most common form of open non-monogamy among gay men is the *open relationship*: a dyadic relationship which is open to partners having sex with others, but not forming love relationships with anyone other than the primary partner. Commonly this takes the form of men in a primary relationship *cruising* for other men (either together or separately) and having brief sexual encounters with them. Sometimes there are longer-term sexual friendships. Many younger gay men view open non-monogamy as something to participate in prior to forming a monogamous, or only somewhat open, primary partnership. However, increasingly there are also gay and bisexual men who practise forms of polyamory.

POLYAMORY

Polyamory (or *poly*) differs from the previous two forms of relationship because it is considered acceptable to love more than one person as well as to be sexual with more than one person. It can therefore be thought of as involving *multiple relationships* rather than one *open* relationship. Polyamory also differs in that many polyamorous people consider polyamory to be an identity that they have. This differs from swingers and people in open relationships who generally view their non-monogamy as something they do (although they may share a view that monogamy is not for them). Common models of polyamory include *primary/secondary relationships* (one or more main relationship/s and other subsidiary ones), multiple equal partners in '*V*' arrangements (where one person has two or more separate partners) or in *triads*, *quads*, tribes or families, where everyone is involved with each other. Poly constellations may be *polyfidelitous* and closed to other relationships outside the unit, or open. Polyamory is the most common model of open non-monogamy for bisexual people, although there are also heterosexual, gay, lesbian and queer polyamorous people.

As well as the distinction between sex and love which is made in all three of these relationship structures (see the continua of physical and emotional closeness at the end of Chapter 13), there are two other key practices common to all three which are worth being aware of: contracts and disclosure.

CONTRACTS

In all three openly non-monogamous relationship structures it is common to have a more or less formalised contract in place that determines that activities are, or are not, acceptable, and where the boundaries and limits on openness lie. The purpose of such contracts is generally to keep the *primary relationship* feeling safe enough and to manage potentially difficult emotions such as jealousy. For example, *soft swinging* is where no penetrative, genital sex takes place outside the primary relationship. Other swingers keep certain sexual activities special to the couple. There may be rituals such as choosing each others' clothing, bathing together before going out, or checking in after having sex with someone else. People in gay open relationships may also keep certain kinds of sex special. Other common negotiated rules include: not having sex in the mutual home, not sleeping over, not seeing other people more than once and viewing the other person as a plaything (Adam, 2006). Some polyamorous people use similar contracts to these with 10–20% restricting behaviours such as spending the night, fluid-bonding, vaginal and anal penetration (Wosick-Correa, 2010), and many keeping certain activities, locations or times special within a specific couple (or *triad*, *quad* or *family*).

However, many people in open and polyamorous relationships (and to some extent swinging) prefer not to impose such specific contracts and boundaries. Some find that contracts make them feel more free to have other relationships while some find more freedom in a flexible model where specific rules are not laid down, but where there is continual negotiation and open communication (Finn, 2010).

Some have coined the terms relationship anarchy and relationshipqueer for a more deliberately non-possessive style of relationship rooted in the idea of mutual freedom, trust and continual negotiation. Such styles are often more explicitly located in politics such as feminism, Marxism and anarchism. People who prefer such models to the more common form of polyamory often talk of breaking down the divisions between love and friendship, and of valuing multiple different kinds of relationship (including the relationship to friends, neighbours, the planet and oneself).

DISCLOSURE

Similar to the spectrum from having a rigid contract to having no contract at all, there is a spectrum in open non-monogamy relating to the amount of disclosure within the relationship about other relationships. All consensually non-monogamous people are open with partners about the fact that they are non-monogamous, however there is a spectrum of preferred disclosure from those who prefer a "don't ask, don't tell" policy about the details of who the other person has seen and what they have done with them, to those who prefer to hear every detail. There are some who only have sex with other people when their partner is present (sometimes referred to as "three way or no way").

As with contracts, disclosure is related to freedom and safety. Some feel freer if they do not have to disclose what they get up to, others feel freer if they can tell their partner everything. Some feel safer not knowing, and others feel safer if they know that they will be told (or be present at) everything.

WIDER SOCIETY

As mentioned in Chapter 13, wider Western society is overwhelmingly mononormative. Despite the fact that many relationships are secretly non-monogamous, monogamy is still presented as the normal, even natural, mode of relating. Lifelong monogamy remains widely viewed as the 'happily ever after' that people should aspire to despite high rates of break-up and separation.

EVERYDAY MONONORMATIVITY

Openly non-monogamous people often have difficulties around this, and will certainly be faced with everyday decisions about whether to challenge mononormative assumptions about their relationships or to leave them unquestioned. There are serious stresses to both being openly non-monogamous (dealing with the comments of others and the pressure to be a *poster child*, see Chapter 9) and to keeping it hidden (worrying that it will come out and feeling unable to express who they are). Prejudice may be gendered in that non-monogamous women can be seen as 'sluts' or just doing it for the benefit of men, whereas non-monogamous men can be viewed as enviable (missing the fact that non-monogamous relationships are not always easy) or as sexual predators.

Common forms of social discrimination can take the form of 'plus one' invitations to social events (for those with multiple partners); water-cooler work conversations about fancying people other than one's partner (where the answer that this is not a problem is not expected, and may be responded to badly); and assumptions that the break-up of a non-monogamous relationship will be less painful than that of a monogamous one, or that it is caused by the non-monogamy (when monogamous break-ups are never blamed on monogamy). Professionals can therefore try to ensure that they take break-ups as seriously whatever the relationship style of their clients, and to avoid assuming that mention of one sexual/romantic partner means that there will not be other ones.

THE LEGAL SITUATION

Many of the concerns of non-monogamous people centre around the lack of legal recognition of their relationships, in a way which is analogous to the situation for LGB people before forms of relationship recognition were put in place (see Chapter 9). As with 'same-gender' relationship recognition, not everyone who is non-monogamous wants legal recognition for more than one partnership. Some do not want state involvement in personal relationships at all. However, given the current situation (with legal recognition of only monogamous relationships) there can be problems such as polyamorous partners not being recognised as family in medical contexts, additional parents in polyamorous families struggling to gain custody following a break-up or death, and problems over property rights when somebody dies. While the law represents the lowest level to which professionals must adhere, this does not mean that professionals cannot have a higher level of recognition of openly non-monogamous relationships in their own policy and practice. Good practice in this area could, for example, involve allowing for more than one next of kin on forms and in situations where partners or family members are involved.

Difficulties can particularly arise when openly non-monogamous people have children. As with old prejudices about 'same-gender' relationships (see Chapter 9) there are widely held assumptions that children will be badly off in non-monogamous households. This is despite the fact that extended families for other reasons are commonplace and have been for much of history. Anecdotally there are many accounts of social services being called in by neighbours purely on the basis of a family including multiple parents, which is an horrific situation for adults and children alike. Evidence suggests that children in such households are not disadvantaged in any way and may benefit from having multiple parents, including the extra emotional and practical resources available, several role models and the emphasis on open communication. Drawbacks include the problems of attachment following a break-up (in common with many monogamous situations) and stigma due to being non-monogamous (Sheff, 2010). The existence of stigma does not mean that people should not parent. As with racism or homophobia, practitioners should leverage their power against *polyphobia* rather than raising questions over openly non-monogamous people parenting.

HEALTH/PSYCHOLOGICAL MODELS

There can be difficulties for practitioners if their training has reinforced a monogamous model of psychological healthiness and well-being. Psychoanalytic and psychodynamic approaches are often rooted in a nuclear family model (one father and one mother in Freud's early theories) and the idea that adult attachments should be formed with one single partner (for example, in the theories of Bowlby and Erickson). Similarly, cognitive-behavioural approaches are grounded in mainstream psychology which often only draws on research and theories of monogamous relationships. Multiple sexual partners are often only considered in such texts in the context of pathological categories (e.g. borderline personality, sex addiction) or transmission of HIV and STIs.

In recent years, there has been a burgeoning of research on openly non-monogamous forms of relating which has found that such relationships can certainly be as satisfying as monogamous ones and last as long, and that the people who form such relationships are no different from monogamous people in terms of mental health, attachment style, personality or risk of STIs.

MEDIA REPRESENTATIONS

Popular representations of non-monogamous relationships have changed somewhat over the years, from non-monogamy only being represented in its secret form (as affairs and infidelities), and generally being regarded as utterly unacceptable, to some recognition of openly non-monogamous forms of relating. These are generally represented as strange or freakish, for example on talk shows and in magazine articles, but increasingly they are presented as a possible solution to crises in relationships (such as the high divorce rate). Most journalistic and documentary presentations now put open non-monogamy across in a fairly positive light, but often end by saying that it would be too complicated or difficult for that journalist or presenter (or by extension any 'normal person') to seriously contemplate. As previously mentioned, some celebrities have also been reported to be openly non-monogamous in recent years, and these – as well as available self-help books – can be useful to mention with clients who are struggling to access models for different possible ways of being openly non-monogamous.

Media coverage means that open non-monogamy is far more available to people than it has been in previous decades. The proliferation of various communities on the internet has also been important in providing possible non-monogamous relationship structures. This is perhaps most notable in relation to polyamory which has many websites, blogs, social networking groups and email lists devoted to it, including those for relationships where one person is monogamous. These may well be useful for professionals to refer clients to (if they are interested in accessing such support and community).

GROUP NORMS

There is diversity even within each of the three major groups we have considered here (swingers, open gay relationships and polyamory) as well as overlap between them. While there may be a sense of the 'right' way of doing each of these types of relationship, actually there are many different ways of approaching them, as we saw when we considered different approaches to contracts and to disclosure. It is useful for professionals to raise awareness of the diversity of ways of being openly non-monogamous with clients who are considering this, rather than either suggesting that there is only one possibility or questioning the whole concept of non-monogamy.

MOTIVATIONS FOR NON-MONOGAMY

If people want to explore their open non-monogamy with a practitioner it can be helpful to explore what it means to them and the motivations behind it (just as for monogamy). People are non-monogamous for a variety of reasons. About half feel that they are naturally non-monogamous, saying that they have felt like this from a young age and were very relieved when they realised they were not alone. Around half see non-monogamy as something they have chosen consciously for themselves, with many different reasons for this. Examples included seeing it as a preferable alternative to *infidelity*; having a hedonistic desire to have sex with multiple people; wanting to be free from constraints; wanting the safety of multiple close people; making a political (feminist and/or anti-capitalist) move away from the monogamous marriage where women work unpaid in the home reproducing the workforce; part of communal and sustainable living; and a spiritual practice. Some feel that non-monogamy is a more integral part of their sexuality than the gender they are attracted to or what they like to do sexually. Others feel that it is something they could be at some times in their lives, or in some relationships, but might not always be (Barker, 2005). It is useful to find out what an individual client's motivations are for being non-monogamous. When working with people in relationships it can be helpful to raise awareness of different possible reasons so that clients can respect that they might not all be coming from the same place (if this is appropriate to your professional role).

NON-MONOGAMOUS LANGUAGE

Due to the mononormative language of relationships which exists in wider society, openly non-monogamous groups have developed their own languages for talking about themselves and their relationships. There are the identity terms like swinger and polyamorous, as opposed to negative words such as 'adulterer'. Also, as with queer (see Chapter 5), pejorative words like 'slut' have been reclaimed as in the self-help book *The Ethical Slut*. This challenges the double standard of sexuality (whereby men who have many sexual partners are highly regarded whilst women are disparaged) by applying the previously feminine negative word 'slut' to all genders positively. Words like ethical, honest, open and consensual are used frequently, presumably to counter the general assumption that monogamy is unethical, dishonest and secretive.

Language has also developed to describe specific relationships. Mainstream language only provides words like 'the other woman' or 'the mistress' which do not fit a situation where people are open and positive about additional partners. The language of primaries and secondaries is one way around this (although not all people like the hierarchical model implied in this). Others have used *metamour* as a word for their partner's other partner.

Additionally, new words have emerged to describe emotions. Conventional understandings of jealousy, in particular, suggest that it is a natural and overwhelming response to *infidelity*, which is the fault of the person who was unfaithful and which justifies extreme reactions (break-up, destruction of property and even violence). Polyamorous people and swingers have challenged such understandings by encouraging a perspective where jealousy is *owned* by the person experiencing it who takes responsibility for communicating what they are feeling and what they want from the situation. Words like *wibble*, *wobble* and *jelly moment* have been used to describe mini-jealousies, in a way which captures the imper-manence of the experience without the connotation of overwhelmingness or the imperative to act on it. Words like *compersion* (US) and *frubble* (UK) have also developed to express the opposite of jealousy: a feeling of joy or pleasure at seeing one's partner happy with another partner (Ritchie & Barker, 2006). Professionals can be well-served by learning such language and employing it judiciously.

RIGIDITY IN NON-MONOGAMY

As can be seen, there is a good deal of playfulness around language in openly non-monogamous communities, such as the word *polysaturation* for having as many partners as one can manage. However, there can also be a tendency, as with any groups outside the perceived social norm, for people to become quite rigid in their view of open non-monogamy to quell the anxiety and uncertainty of being outside the widely accepted rules. There is evidence for this in the occasional spats that break out online between swingers and polyamorists over which is the most appro-priate way of doing non-monogamy, for example.

Such rigidity can lead to people seeking the 'poly grail' (their ideal rela-tionship set-up, such as living in a triad with two equal female partners) rather than being open to the relationships that develop in their lives. It can be assumed that open non-monogamy will solve all the difficulties of intimacy that were experienced in monogamous relationships, and people can dive too quickly into it and/or fail to recognise the limits on time and energy which mean that one can't have infinite numbers of partners. Such situations can lead to experiences of burnout, or anxiety and depression, which can be dealt with by professionals as usual in their practice. It may be worth opening up the different possible ways of being openly non-monogamous, exploring clients' limits and how they might communicate these, and normalising the fact that relationships are challenging (rather than suggesting that non-monogamous relationships are necessarily par-ticularly difficult in comparison to other forms).

Fixed ideas, such as how many dates a week are necessary to sustain a relationship, or what kinds of sex partners are expected to have, may also make it different for relationships to change and to be renegotiated (if a secondary partnership becomes closer, for example). Also, it is com-monly recognised that people can neglect existing partners when they are caught up in *new relationship energy* (NRE). There can be a taboo around jealousy which makes it difficult to admit when people are expe-riencing it. It can become easy to make unhelpful comparisons between partners, and – of course – openly non-monogamous relationships are not immune to people breaking the rules and keeping secrets, just as they often do in monogamy.

It is important to remember, and to explore with clients, the diversity of relationship structures which are possible and equally valid. For example, in cases where one person's preference is for monogamy and another's for polyamory, or where one person is happy to be open to sexual, but not love, relationships, and the other person does not really distinguish sex and love in this way. As with the previous chapter, such negotiations may end in agreement, compromise or recognition that values are different (and either continuing aware of this tension or changing the relationship).

COMMON ISSUES

Topics that non-monogamous people may want to explore include:

- What style of open non-monogamy would suit them. Here professionals can usefully introduce the diversity of forms, and stances towards contracts and communication, that are possible.
- Coming out as openly non-monogamous (e.g. to family, at work). Here professionals might signal websites where clients might ask how others have done this and get support, as well as helping clients to rehearse.
- Negotiating a contract within a relationship, for example around how relationships with new people will be managed, or how the relationship will run without explicit contracts. Here the continua provided in Chapter 13 may be useful, as might encouraging all concerned to write about what they would like before coming together to discuss this.
- Communication and conflict in their relationships. If you are a professional who works with couples it would be useful to open this up to more than two people for polyamorous situations, and the usual communication education can be given and practised.
- Negotiating shared tasks, finances, child-care or living arrangements. Again, working with all involved can be useful in such situations. If working in a more psychotherapeutic way, useful possibilities include negotiating slightly longer sessions than you generally have with monogamous couples and being mindful of the importance of giving equal attention to each person. As with monogamous couples it may be worth drawing out habitual interaction patterns which reinforce the status quo as well as getting them to create a genogram (using their own symbols) of their wider networks so that you can understand the key people in their lives and how they are involved with them.
- Breaking up and renegotiating relationships. Here it can be helpful to emphasise that all relationships change over time, and to encourage clients to think about how they would like the relationship to be now and what changes that might require.

SUMMARY AND CONCLUSIONS

In summary, the following are good practice points when working with non-monogamous clients.

- Reflexively engage with your own assumptions about non-monogamy (and encourage all staff within a clinic or organisation to do the same).
- Be aware of the diversity of ways in which non-monogamous clients might be practising non-monogamy (rather than assuming that it will be the same for everyone).
- Don't assume that non-monogamy will be a key issue for all non-monogamous clients.
- If necessary, help clients access support from other openly non-monogamous people by knowing about online resources and local groups.
- Normalise non-monogamy rather than reinforcing the myth that monogamy is the only natural, normal, acceptable way of relating.
- Explore what clients would like themselves, in terms of non-monogamy agreements, and what the norms of non-monogamy are in their group.
- Encourage open negotiation and communication around non-monogamy rather than operating on implicit taken-for-granteds; be open to the full spectrum of possibilities rather than advocating one end of the emotional/sexual continua over the other.

FURTHER READING

Barker, M. & Langdridge, D. (Eds.) (2010). *Understanding non-monogamies.* New York, NY: Routledge.

Labriola, K. (2010). *Love in abundance: A counselor's advice on open relationships.* California, CA: Greenery Press.

Weitzman, G. (2009–2010). What psychology professionals should know about polyamory. National Coalition for Sexual Freedom. Available from: http://ego.thechicagoschool.edu/s/843/images/editor_documents/What%20therapists%20should%20know%20about%20Polyamory.pdf.

ADDITIONAL REFERENCES

Adam, B.D. (2006) Relationship innovation in male couples. *Sexualities, 9*(1), 5–26.

Barker, M. (2005). This is my partner, and this is my... partner's partner: Constructing a polyamorous identity in a monogamous world. *Journal of Constructivist Psychology, 18*(1), 75–88.

Easton, D. & Hardy, J. (2009). *The Ethical Slut*. California, CA: Greenery Press.

Finn, M. (2010). Conditions of freedom in practices of non-monogamous commitment. In M. Barker & D. Langdridge (Eds.), *Understanding non-monogamies*. (pp. 225–236). New York: Routledge.

Ritchie, A. & Barker, M. (2006). 'There aren't words for what we do or how we feel so we have to make them up': Constructing polyamorous languages in a culture of compulsory monogamy. *Sexualities, 9*(5), 584–601.

Sheff, E. (2010). Strategies in polyamorous parenting. In M. Barker & D. Langdridge (Eds.), *Understanding non-monogamies* (pp. 169–181). New York: Routledge.

Weber, A. (2002). Who are we? And other interesting impressions. *Loving More Magazine, 30*, 4–6.

Wosick-Correa, K. (2010). Agreements, rules, and agentic fidelity in polyamorous relationships. *Psychology & Sexuality, 1*(1), 44–61.

This main glossary is followed by a 'shadow glossary' of less safe terminology (see Introduction).

24/7   Being in a submissive/dominant relationship all of the time. Usually rather prosaic and thoroughly negotiated.

AB/DL (adult baby/diaper lover)   A person who likes to spend part of their time in a much younger role than their chronological age – often as a baby. This may involve apparel and include a nappy/diaper. See also *infantilism* and *ageplay*.

Aftercare   The period after a BDSM scene when the top looks after the bottom, bringing them up from any submissive headspace, often praising them in general and in relation to the scene they have endured. For some this is as/more important than the scene itself.

Agender   Having no gender in terms of presentation, identity, etc.

Ageplay   Spending part of one's time in a much younger role than one's chronological age. May be as a baby or a child. See also *AB/DL* and infantilism.

Anal sex   Having sexual intercourse using the anus – through penetration with a penis, finger, tongue or other body part, a sex toy, etc.

Androgynous   Having a gender identity and/or presentation including both masculinity and femininity.

Androphile   Being attracted to men.

Anilingus   Sexually stimulating a person's anal region using the mouth.

Armchairing   Having some form of sexual contact over an armchair (or less commonly a sofa).

Aromantic   Not wishing to have romantic relationships with others.

Arranged marriage   A marriage in which others, commonly parents, have taken part in suggesting partners. Very different from forced marriage (in which the person getting married is not given any choice as to whether to agree). See also *marriage*.

Asexual (Ace)   A person who does not experience sexual attraction (or occasionally those who do but do not act upon it). Sometimes shortened to *ace*.

Ask etiquette   Simply asking people their preferred mode of address if one is unsure.

Assigned gender   The gender assigned at, or before, birth. May or may not match the child or adult's gender identity.

Babyfur   A person who has an identity of a young animal who may wear apparel appropriate to that identity.

Ball gag   A ball on a strap. The ball is placed in a person's mouth as a gag and the strap secures it in place.

BDSM/kink (bondage and discipline, dominance and submission, and sadomasochism) Some use the umbrella term *kink* to refer to sexual practices and identities which involve the exchange of power, restriction of movement, or intense sensation. Particularly common practices include spanking and being tied up during sex.

Bear An identity term for a heavy set, often hairy, gay man. Younger/smaller men may identify as cubs.

Bigender Identifying as both male and female. Possibly moving between these.

Binary In the context of sex/gender, the idea that there are two, and only two, separate genders – male or female. See also *dichotomy*.

Binding Using bandages or a proprietary binder to flatten breasts and effect the contour of a breast-free chest.

Biphobia Negative attitudes, emotions, behaviours and structures relating to bisexual people and others who are attracted to more than one gender.

Biromantic People who are romantically attracted to more than one gender. When coupled with asexual (biromantic asexual) the term refers to people who seek romantic relationships for various reasons, including companionship, affection and intimacy, but are not sexually attracted to their romantic partners.

Bisexual (bi) Being attracted to more than one gender.

Blow job See *fellatio*.

BME Black and minority ethnic (see also *queer people of colour*).

Boi A combined sexuality/gender term that can be embraced, for example, by younger butch lesbian people, by younger trans men, by submissive butch BDSMers and by more genderqueer people.

Bondage Restraining/restricting someone, e.g. with ropes, chains, cuffs.

Bottom General term for a submissive, a masochist or a gay man who is the recipient of penetration. In a more specific BDSM context, this can mean a person who enjoys being given various physical sensations as opposed to a *submissive* who enjoys being controlled psychologically.

Bromance A close, usually non-sexual, relationship between men.

Butch Being traditionally masculine in presentation. Sometimes used by lesbian women to refer to themselves. Sometimes used to refer to a more butch partner. Not always a safe term.

Camp Being somewhat theatrically effeminate in presentation. Not always a safe term.

CBT Cock and ball torture – strong sensations to the male genitals. Also an acronym for cognitive behavioural therapy. The two should not be confused.

Chaps A form of leather over-trouser commonly worn by cowboys and cowgirls.

Cheating See *non-monogamy*.

Cisgender (Cis) Being content to remain the gender assigned at birth.

Cisgenderism   Assuming that there are two, and only two, genders, and that people remain in the gender that they were assigned at birth, and that those who don't are somehow inferior or abnormal.

Closet   Being closeted or in the closet refers to not being open about one's gender or sexuality.

Cock ring   A ring placed around the penis and sometimes also the testicles to retain an erection.

Collar   Usually made of metal or leather, BDSM collars often denote that a person wearing one is submissive to another.

Coming out   The process of becoming open about your sexuality or gender with yourself, other people close to you and/or publicly.

Compersion   The feeling of warm regard or contentment that a person feels when they see their partner being happy with their other partner. Also called *frubble*.

Condom   A latex or other material sheath that covers a penis or sex toy. Usually used to prevent the transmission of STIs or to prevent pregnancy.

Cosmesis   A method of constructing exterior female genitalia without the creation of a vagina.

Cottaging   Looking for sex in public buildings, commonly toilets.

Coupledom   The common social practice of providing for and expecting people to group in romantic dyads.

Cross-dressing   Wearing the clothing not normally worn by people of that birth-assigned gender. Also sometimes problematically know as *transvestism*.

Cruising   Looking for sex in public areas, commonly parks or nightclubs.

Cunilingus   Sexually stimulating a person's vulva using the mouth.

Cybersex   Having sexual contact with another person via the internet through text, sound and/or images, possibly via an avatar.

D/s   Dominance and submission. Note the uppercase D and lowercase s.

Daddy's little girl (DLG)   A form of relationship within the BDSM community in which an older male top treats a younger female bottom as a nurtured child.

Demisexual   People who only feel sexual when there is a very strong emotional attraction. See also *Grey-A*.

Dental dam   A sheet of pliable material used to prevent STIs in cunnilingus and anilingus.

Dichotomy   In the context of sex/gender, the idea that there are only two separate genders – men and women.

Dildo   A term for a phallic sex toy.

Discipline   Training someone to behave in a certain way through punishment.

Dogging   A practice in which people drive to certain known, usually out of the way, car parks to have sex with their partners while in view of others who have congregated there for that purpose.

Dominant (dom/domme/dominatrix/master/mistress) A person who takes control over others, e.g. giving orders, inflicting pain/sensation.

Drag king A person who usually identifies as a woman presenting a somewhat theatrical masculine role, sometimes for purposes of entertainment.

Drag queen A person who usually identifies as a man presenting a somewhat theatrical feminine role, sometimes for purposes of entertainment.

Dressing A term sometimes used by trans people who have not transitioned fully into a role they were not assigned at birth to refer to wearing clothing not normally worn by people of their birth assigned sex. Never used by those who have transitioned.

DSD (diversity of sexual development) Having some physiology which is not strictly taxonomically male or female and would more commonly be so. People with a DSD often identify as simply male or female. See also *intersex* and *disorder of sex development* (shadow glossary).

DSM (Diagnostic and Statistical Manual) The American Psychiatric Association's taxonomy of psychiatric disorders. Much used and much debated.

Ecosexual Refers to people who link their relationships and/or sexuality directly to ecological concerns.

Electrolysis The removal of hair through inserting a needle into the hair follicle and passing an electric current through the root. The only universally agreed method of permanent hair removal.

Exhibitionism Excitement at being watched by others while in a sexual context. This is usually a safe word, but is derived from a medical context and so is worth being cautious with.

Fellatio A person sucking another person's penis or phallus.

Femininity Presentation and behaviours stereotypically attributed to women such as gentleness, caring and being submissive. Culturally constructed.

Femme Sometimes used to mean simply feminine, also used to denote a feminine partner and a *genderqueer* deliberate parody of femininity.

Fetish A reclaimed term used to refer to having a, sometimes sexual, liking for certain materials such as rubber, leather, etc.

Fisting Inserting a fist (very carefully) into a person's vagina, manhole, anus, etc. Skill and lubrication are required.

Fluid bonding Engaging in penetration without using condoms (see also *barebacking* in the shadow glossary).

Friends-with-benefits Two, or more, people in a friendship, but not a romantic relationship, who also have sex. See also *fuckbuddies*.

Frubble See *compersion*.

Fuckbuddies People who have a friendship and who have sex (fuck) together, but who are not romantically attached. See also *friends-with-benefits*.

Furry A person who has an animal identity and may wear apparel suitable to that identity.

Gaffe   A strap used by people to hide their penis in order to effect the outline of a genital region without a penis.

Gay   Being attracted exclusively to the 'same gender'. Often used with reference to men who are attracted to other men.

Geek   A person with a high degree of technical skill who may be a part of online and/or face-to-face communities.

Gender   A sense of being a woman, a man, another gender, or some combination of these.

Gender confirmation surgery(ies)   The surgical construction of primary and secondary sexual characteristics (see also *genital reconstruction surgery*).

Gender dysphoria   A deep sense of unhappiness with one's birth-assigned gender.

Gender identity   One's internal sense of one's self as a man, a woman or some other gender.

Gender neutral   Feeling that one is neither male nor female. Sometimes confused with *androgynous*, *bi-gender*, etc.

Gender performativity   Gendered expression for purposes of communication, both to others and oneself. This is undertaken by trans and cisgender people as well as many who have different genders.

Gender presentation   One's presentation of gender through clothing, mannerism, etc.

Gender role   The gendered presentation, including clothing, tasks, speech, etc. that one performs (see also *gender performativity*).

Genderfuck   Troubling the gender dichotomy of male or female through presentation, etc. See also *genderqueer*.

Genderless   Having no gender in terms of presentation, identity, etc.

Genderqueer   Identifying and/or presenting in a way which is outside the gender dichotomy of man/woman.

Genital reconstruction surgery (GRS)   The surgical construction of genitalia.

Going down   See *cunilingus*.

Goth   A person who enjoys certain types of gothic music and styles of dress. Often relating to the night and the late seventeenth century.

Grey-A   Being asexual to some extent. See also *demisexual*.

Grrrl   From 'riot grrrl', referring to an alternative, often punk and feminist, form of femininity that rejects aspects of stereotypical femininity.

Gynephile   Being attracted to women.

Headspace   The state of mind somebody goes into during BDSM play (e.g. submissive/dominant headspace).

Heteronormativity   The assumption that heterosexuality is normal and that anything other than heterosexuality is abnormal. Often used to refer to the omnipresence of heterosexual images and representations and the assumption that people will desire the 'other gender' (e.g. in advertising, women's and men's magazines, movies, etc.)

Heterosexism   Discriminating against non-heterosexual people. For example, regarding them as inferior, assuming that they are heterosexual unless told otherwise, or expressing 'tolerance' towards them.

Heterosexual   Being attracted exclusively to 'other gender' people.

HIV (human immunodeficiency virus)   The virus which can lead to acquired immunodeficiency syndrome (AIDS). May be passed through sexual contact.

Homonormativity   A mode of living in which gay, lesbian and some bisexual people adhere to predominant cultural mores. In contemporary Western society these may include consumerism, monogamy, having children, etc.

Homophobia   Negative attitudes, emotions, behaviours and structures relating to people on the basis of their attraction to the 'same gender' and/or identifying as gay or lesbian.

Hook-up culture   An arrangement common in many Western colleges and universities in which younger, often heterosexual, people have casual sexual encounters without the intention to form committed relationships.

Hypervigiliance   People being particularly concerned about what others may be thinking or doing. Sometimes found in trans people concerned about being 'found out' as being trans.

ICD (International Classification of Diseases)   The World Health Organization's taxonomy of diseases. The psychiatric element of this is much used and much debated.

In role   Often used by trans people who have not transitioned fully into a role they were not assigned at birth to refer to presenting in a role other than that of their birth-assigned gender. Never used by those who have transitioned.

Infantilism   Used to refer to people who enjoy being very childlike, but not preverbal. See also *AB/DL* and *ageplay*.

Infidelity   See *non-monogamy*.

Institutionalised homophobia   Recognises that homophobia does not reside in individuals alone, but within homophobic structures, organisations and societies. However, this notion should not be used to excuse individuals from homophobic acts.

Internalised transphobia   See *transphobia*.

Intercrural sex   Stimulating somebody between lubricated thighs.

Intersections   The fact that people's sexuality does not impact on their experience alone, but rather it *intersects* with other aspects of identity such as gender, race, religion, culture, class, age, disability and geography.

Intersex   Having some physiology which is not strictly taxonomically male or female and would more commonly be so. Intersex people may identify as male or female or as some other gender. See also *diversity of sexual development*.

Jelly moment   See *wibble*.

Kinky   General term for BDSM, fetish or non-'vanilla' sexual behaviour or people engaging in this.

Leather   Refers to people who enjoy wearing leather and may attend community events, clubs parties, etc.

Leatherdyke   A dyke who is part of the leather community.

Leatherdaddy   A male identified person who takes a dominant role to a younger adult who is generally also within the leather community.

Lesbian   Refers to women being attracted exclusively to other women.

LGBT   Lesbian, gay, bisexual and trans. Sometimes just LG or LGB, sometimes LGBTQ to include queer. Other additional initials can include a second Q for questioning, I for intersex, and A for asexual.

Line family   A group of three or more people in a consensually non-monogamous relationship who all have two sexual and/or romantic relationships with each other, except for two people who have one (at either end of the line). With only three people involved this is the same as a *V*.

Lower surgery   Term used primarily by trans men to refer to a variety of genital surgeries.

Man with a trans history   A man who was assigned female at birth (see *trans man*).

Manhole   A term used by trans men to refer to what in medical–anatomical terminology would be called their vagina. As the people who have them are men, and vaginas are generally perceived as something that women have, the term manhole is sometimes used.

Marriage   A legal and sometimes religious ceremony which bonds two people (historically a man and a woman, but in an increasing number of countries any two people) together for life, and often involves a celebration and the exchange of some physical token such as a ring in the sight of friends, family, etc. Globally the law is unequal in this regard as only in some countries can two 'same-gender' people marry, and relationships of other kinds are almost never recognised legally.

Mary Sue   A form of slash fiction in which the author places themselves within the plot.

Masculinity   Presentation and behaviours stereotypically attributed to men such as aggression, autonomy and dominance. Culturally constructed.

Metamour   A (consensual) partner of your partner who is not also your partner.

Metoidioplasty   A surgical procedure to create a phallus through the release of the clitoris.

Metrosexual   Usually applied to men being open to different sexual experiences and general modes of expression of sexuality and gender; perhaps while remaining predominately heterosexual. Often used to refer to people in urban areas.

Minority stress   Psychological distress as a result of being in a minority and suffering discrimination and/or abuse. Sometimes confused with the identity or practice itself being psychopathological. A term to be somewhat cautious of as some groups who suffer this are marginalised but are not minorities in the sense of their being a low proportion of them (e.g. kinky people or people who are attracted to more than one gender).

Missionary position   The sexual practice where a woman lies facing up underneath a man who faces down with their heads at the same end.

Mixed gender   Having mixed aspects of both male and female presentation and/or identity.

Monogamy   The practice of having one single, often sexual, highly intimate relationship at a time (includes lifelong monogamy, serial monogamy, secret non-monogamy, and other forms).

Mononormativity   The common social practice of expecting people to have, or want, only one partner.

Monosexual   Being attracted to only one gender (includes heterosexual, lesbian and gay identified people).

MSM   Men who have sex with men. A health research term for this group (who may or may not identify as gay).

MSMW   Men who have sex with men and women. A health research term for this group (who may or may not identify as bisexual).

Multiple relationships   Having many different relationships of different kinds including sexual, friendship, colleagues, kin, etc.

Neo- (vagina, phallus, etc.)   Prefix for a surgically constructed or adapted body part.

Neuter   Having no gender in terms of presentation, identity, etc.

Neutrois   Having no gender in terms of presentation, identity, etc.

New monogamy   Also called monogamish, a form of monogamy that is somewhat open to other sexual/emotional connections.

New relationship energy (NRE)   The feeling of excitement and happiness that comes with finding a new partner before you have to pick up their pants and put the cap back on the toothpaste.

Non-gender   Having no gender in terms of presentation, identity, etc.

Non-monogamy   A term for all relationship styles where people have more than one sexual and/or romantic relationship at a time. This includes secret non-monogamy (often called 'cheating' or 'infidelity') as well as open forms of non-monogamy such as sexually open relationships and polyamory.

Normativity   The act of being in line, or constrained by, what is socially expected in a given culture.

Omnisexual   Being attracted towards people of all genders (see also *pansexual*).

One-night stands   Having sexual intercourse with a person for one night only. May or may not become/remain friends afterwards.

Open relationship   Having a relationship in which the partners are welcome to find additional partners.

Orgy   A party involving a great deal of sex and usually food.

'Other gender'   Refers in this book to relationships with, or attraction to, people of a different gender to the one you have yourself.

Outing   Revealing somebody else's sexuality or gender without their consent.

Pack   Using socks, packing or a proprietary device to effect the contour of a male genital region.

Pangender   Having mixed aspects of both male and female in presentation and/ or identity. Possibly moving between male and female. Possibly identifying outside of male and female.

Pansexual   Being attracted towards people of all genders (see also *omnisexual*).

Pearl necklace   A person ejaculating semen on a person's upper body.

Pegging   A person without a penis anally penetrating a person who has a penis with a phallus (usually a *strap-on dildo*).

Phalloplasty   A surgical procedure to create a penis.

Piggy pile   A group of people having simultaneous sex.

Play   Engaging in sex or BDSM e.g. "I played with her", "Want to play?", or a specific activity e.g. arse play, sensory deprivation play.

Play party   An event in which people have a party, perhaps with food, drink, etc. and engage in BDSM.

Polyamory (poly)   Having simultaneous multiple love/romantic relationships with the knowledge and consent of all concerned.

Polyfidelity   Having more than one partner, but not having an open relationship meaning that no new partners are allowed.

Polygamy   Marriage involving more than two partners.

Polyphobia   Being phobic of people (and the notion of people) who have more than one partner.

Polysaturation   Having so many partners that one is unable to maintain commitments and adequate self-care.

Poster child   A person who feels pressure to be free from all human failings because they are aware that others are evaluating a whole group of people (to whom they belong) on the basis of their actions alone.

Primary relationship   A relationship between two people that is prioritised in some fashion over the consensual relationships either or both of those people may have with other partners.

Purge   When a person who cross-dresses becomes overcome by shame and destroys their collection of 'cross-sex' clothing.

Quad   A group of four people in a consensually non-monogamous relationship. Usually all have sexual and/or romantic relationships with each other.

Queer   A reclaimed term of abuse used by some (e.g. queer activists and queer theorists) to refer to LGBT people in general, or more specifically to those who challenge the binaries of sexuality (that people are either gay or straight) and gender (that people are either men or women).

Queer people of colour (QPOC)   A term for LGBTQ people who are not white. Some prefer the term *BME* LGBTQ people.

Queer politics   A political movement aimed at deconstructing strict hierarchies of power and/or winning rights for a wide diversity of people.

Queer theory   A diverse theoretical movement which questions identity labels, particularly in relation to sexuality and gender, and the implicit power hierarchies attendant in these.

Questioning   People who are unsure of their sexuality.

Relationship anarchy   A deliberately non-possessive style of relationship, a more explicitly political version of polyamory.

Relationshipqueer   See *relationship anarchy*.

Rimming   Licking the anus.

Risk aware consensual kink (RACK)   A term used to differentiate consensual BDSM from coercive practices. Preferred over *safe, sane and consensual (SSC)*.

Rubber ball   An evening gathering of people who enjoy rubber. Often involving food, drink and dancing. Sometimes also involving sexual activities.

Sadomasochism   The consensual exchange of power and/or sensation, pain and/or humiliation. (See also *BDSM/kink*).

Safer sex   Sexual practices which take precautions against harm, most commonly sexually transmitted infections (such as condom use). Note it is safer rather than 'safe' as no precaution is entirely safe.

Safeword   An (often unusual) word that BDSM players can use to end the scene. If speech is not possible some other means of communication is used instead.

'Same gender'   Refers in this book to relationships with, or attraction to, people of the same gender as the one you have yourself. Terms like same-gender attraction and same-gender relationships are inclusive of lesbian, gay *and* bisexual people in such relationships.

Scat play   Sexual activity employing faecal matter.

Scene   As in gay scene, trans scene, etc. Social events and places devoted to a group of people. Also a BDSM encounter/session, sometimes divided into heavier/lighter scenes depending on physical and/or psychological intensity, although what constitutes this differs between people/occasions.

Scritch   The sensation of being lightly consensually scratched by someone.

Secondary relationship   A relationship between two people where one or both has a consensual relationship with another (primary) which generally takes precedence.

Sensate focus   Sensual exploration of one's partner's body often suggested in sex therapy, and beginning away from the genitals.

Sensation play   A term often used to describe play that involves physical stimulation, which may be pleasurable, painful or both.

Serial monogamy   A common form of relating in which people have multiple partners one after the other. Sometimes referred to as dating if short term.

Sex   A term which refers to the physiological make-up of a person as male, female, etc., or to making love/fucking.

Sex reassignment surgery (SRS)   The surgical construction of genitals and/or secondary sexual characteristics (see also *genital reconstruction surgery*).

Sexual fluidity   Seeing sexual identity and desire as something that fluctuates over a lifetime, thus people might be more or less attracted to different genders at different times, or prioritise other aspects of sexuality such as how much sexual desire they have, or the sexual activities and roles they enjoy taking.

Sexual identity   Identity terms which some people use to label their sexuality. In the UK these will most commonly be: lesbian, heterosexual, bisexual and gay. It is important to remember that not all people who are attracted to, or form sexual relationships with, particular genders actually identify in these ways. For example (in another field) while one may have played a computer game one does not necessarily identify as a gamer. Also, there are sexual identities which are not about gender of attraction such as asexual or BDSM/kink.

Sexual scripts   People's usual understanding about how having sexual intercourse will go.

Sexualisation (of culture)   Refers to the idea that (Western) culture has become more sexualised, with images similar to pornographic images used in advertising and music videos, people encouraged to be sexual at younger ages, and a pressure to be sexual in certain ways.

Sexuality   Refers to a complex set of thoughts and emotions as well as physiological responses. May involve seeking pleasure or reproduction.

Singledom   Refers to the state of being single, as *coupledom* refers to the state, or culture, of being in a couple. Some refer to being a *singleton* as a group identity based on the book *Bridget Jones's Diary*.

Slash fiction   Type of fan fiction established on the internet in which two characters from popular media (for example Sherlock Holmes/John Watson) are put into a sexual situation together. The slash refers to the typographical mark separating them.

Sleaze   Things associated with sexuality that have a cheap, tawdry, exploitative or unsavoury nature, and may be enjoyed specifically for this reason.

SoffAs   Significant Others, Friends, Families and Allies.

Soft swinging   Swinging where no genital sex takes place outside the primary relationship.

Squick   Having a strong negative emotional reaction to a practice while acknowledging that it is not wrong or bad in and of itself – as in "I'm sorry I don't want to have sex with the lights off, I have a squick about it".

Stash   A hidden cache of, often feminine, clothing for the purposes of cross-dressing.

Stealth   Presenting in one's preferred gender in such a manner that others are unaware that one is trans. Not always a safe term.

STI   Acronym for sexually transmitted infections.

Straight   Being sexually attracted to people of a different gender than oneself.

Strap-on   A (usually erect) phallus which can be strapped to the groin.

Submissive (sub) (sub/slave)   A person who gives control over to others, e.g. obeying orders, being bound and/or receiving pain/sensations.

Subspace   A place of calm detachment which can be achieved by the *bottom* or *sub* during BDSM.

Swinging   The act of a primary couple who engages in sex with other primary couples.

Switch/switching   A person who can enjoy both sub/dom or top/bottom roles.

Teabagging   Taking a person's testicles in one's mouth.

Tit-wank   The act of masturbating a penis between the breasts.

Top   General term for a dominant or consensual sadist, or a gay man who is the giver of penetration. In a more specific BDSM context this can mean a person who inflicts various physical sensations as opposed to a *dominant* who enjoys being in control psychologically.

Top surgery   Term used primarily by trans men to refer to a variety of chest reconstruction surgeries – usually refers to some form of bilateral mastectomy and associated recontouring.

Toys   Devices designed for BDSM or sex (e.g. riding crops, paddles, nipple clamps, dildos) or used for this purpose (e.g. hairbrush, candle, clothes pegs).

Trans (or trans*)   An umbrella term including people who define as transsexual, transvestite or genderqueer. Changing in some way from the gender that was assigned at birth.

Transfeminine   Being feminine identified but not necessarily being a trans woman.

Transgender   An umbrella term for people who do not present and/or identify as the gender they were assigned at birth either some or all of the time.

Transition   Often used to refer to transition from female to male, or male to female. However people may transition in ways other than across the gender binary and many trans people report that they were never 'male' or 'female' to begin with – see 'MtF' and 'FtM' in the shadow glossary.

Transmasculine   Being masculine identified but not necessarily being a trans man.

Transphobia   Negative attitudes, emotions, behaviours and structures relating to people on the basis of their being trans in some way or otherwise not conforming to conventional gender roles. May also be internalised transphobia wherein a trans person has these attitudes, emotions and/or behaviours.

Transsexual   Term for a person who lives in a gender not assigned at birth. Usually simply man or woman according to the gender of presentation.

Trans man   A person who identifies as a man and lives in a male role but who was assigned female at birth (only used when pertinent – otherwise a man).

Trans woman A person who identifies as a woman and lives in a female role but who was assigned male at birth (only used when pertinent – otherwise a woman).

Triad A group of three people in a consensually non-monogamous relationship who all have sexual and/or romantic relationships with each other.

Trigender Moving between multiple genders.

V A group of three people in a consensually non-monogamous relationship where one person has sexual and/or romantic relationships with the other two, but they do not have such a relationship with each other.

Vaginoplasty The surgical creation of a vagina.

Voyeurism Enjoying watching others engaged in sexual activity when one is not directly engaged oneself. This is usually a safe word, but is derived from a medical context and so is worth being cautious with.

Watersports Sexual activity involving urine. Also sometimes known as golden showers.

Wibble Used within consensually non-monogamous relationships to refer to a feeling of discomfort, fear or jealousy at some aspect of a partner's relationship with another person. Implicitly recognises that the feeling is not necessarily the other person's 'fault'.

Wobble See *wibble*.

Woman with a trans history Someone who identifies as a woman but was assigned male at birth.

WSW Women who have sex with women. A health research term for this group (who may or may not identify as lesbian).

WSWM Women who have sex with women and men. A health research term for this group (who may or may not identify as bisexual).

Yes, no, maybe lists A list of sexual practices which people fill out for a partner to say which they find acceptable.

Yiff The noise made by Arctic foxes mating and coined by some furry communities to refer to sexual contact while in an animal role. May be on- or offline.

SHADOW GLOSSARY

Terms not to use or only to use with extreme caution.

Abnormal/atypical   See normal.

Barebacking   A term for deliberately unprotected intercourse, often used particularly to refer to unprotected anal intercourse within gay communities. Bugchasing is a related slang term for an alleged practice of seeking sex with HIV positive men, but should be used with extreme caution as it is very unclear how common this practice is.

Bent   Derogatory term for people with partners of the same gender as themselves. Should never be used.

Bi-curious   A term sometimes used by people who think they might be bisexual but are not sure. It is also often used in a pejorative sense to describe such people, therefore a safer term is *questioning* (see main glossary). Should never be used.

Bi-sexual   Bisexual is never hyphenated. Doing so causes offence. Should never be used.

Bio-girl or Bio-boy   A term used to differentiate cisgender people from trans people. Derogatory of trans people and incorrectly suggestive that trans does not have a biological base. Should never be used. 'Biological man/woman' is similarly problematic.

Boston marriage   A term said to be used in New England in the late 1900s to describe two women living together financially independent from men. In the present time, as with 'companion', this should be avoided as a euphemistic term for women in a 'same-gender' relationship.

Companion   Term sometimes used by people who are uncomfortable with gay, bisexual and lesbian people to refer to same-gender partners. See also 'friend'. Should never be used.

Couple counselling   Problematic as it excludes people with more than two partners. Sex and relationship counselling is preferred.

Disorder of sex development (DSD)   Some people are happy with this term, others are not. See Chapter 3 for a full discussion of the complexities.

Dyke   A reclaimed term used by and for some lesbian women – not safe for use by professionals without client consent.

Friend   See 'companion'. Should not be used in the context of sexual/romantic relationships.

FtM   Female to Male trans person – sometimes necessarily used for medical reports, but *trans man, man with a trans history*, or simply *man* is preferred. Many trans men were never 'women' in the traditional sense, thus obviating the meaning.

HeShe   Derogatory term for trans or intersex/DSD people. Should never be used.

Homosexual   Being attracted to people of the same gender as oneself. Has been used pejoratively historically. *Gay or lesbian* are preferred.

Hermaphrodite/pseudo-hermaphrodite   Having some physical characteristics commonly attributed to males and females. These are outdated terms which, while still sometimes used, have been replaced with intersex/DSD.

Illegitimacy   Having a child outside of marriage. A dated term which ignores the wide range of relationships children may be successfully raised within.

Lesbian bed death   The cessation of sexual, but not romantic relations in some lesbian couples. The term is used in some parts of lesbian communities, but is problematic as it explicitly links lessening sexual desire with lesbian identities where, of course, sexual desire may wax and wane in all sexualities.

Marriage counselling   Problematic as it excludes people who are unmarried. Sex and relationship counselling is preferred.

MtF   Male to Female trans person – sometimes necessarily used for medical reports, but *trans woman*, *woman with a trans history*, or simply *woman* is preferred. Many trans women were never 'men' in the traditional sense, thus obviating the meaning.

Natural   A problematic means of legitimising an identity or practice as most things humans do (wearing clothes, driving cars, etc.) are not natural, and many things that are commonly found in the natural world (fighting for territory and resources, etc.) are problematic.

Normal   Often an extremely problematic word which should be used with utmost caution if separating out a group of people. Varies widely across time and place. Has connotations of morality, frequency, permanence, etc. often in contradiction to one another. 'Abnormal' is similarly problematic.

Opposite sex/gender   A woman if one is a man, or a man if one is a woman. Should never be used because these terms suggest there are only two genders, where many cultures and groups of people see more than two. *Other gender* is preferred.

Passing   A negative term for allowing people to assume that you are part of the normative group when you are not (e.g. a gay or bisexual person could 'pass' as heterosexual). Also used as a problematic term for trans people to suggest that a person 'passes' as a cisgendered person of their stated gender. Should never be used.

Paraphilia   A medical term used to refer to sexual practices and identities which may be transgressive and/or coercive. Problematic because it includes practices and identities which are consensual and sometimes quite common (such as consensual BDSM). Implicitly makes a moral judgement. (See also 'perversion'.)

Perversion   An older term used to refer to sexual practices and identities which may be transgressive and/or coercive. Problematic because it includes practices and identities which are consensual and sometimes quite common (such as consensual BDSM). Implicitly makes a moral judgement. (See also 'paraphilia'.) Should never be used.

Polymorphous perversity   A theory that all people are born non-heterosexual and sexually attracted to many things.

Queen   A reclaimed term used by and for some gay men – not safe for use by professionals without client consent. Some gay men also use racist terminology to refer to people who are particularly attracted to someone from a certain culture (e.g. rice queen – East Asian, chocolate queen – black). This should never be used and should be challenged.

Queer   A reclaimed term of abuse used by some (e.g. queer activists and queer theorists) to refer to LGBT people in general, or more specifically to those who challenge the binaries of sexuality (that people are either gay or straight) and gender (that people are either men or women).

Real woman or real man   A term used to differentiate cisgender people from trans people and others. Derogatory of trans people and others, and incorrectly suggestive that trans and other people cannot really be female or male. Should never be used.

Safe, sane and consensual (SSC)   An older term used to differentiate consensual BDSM from coercive practices. Problematic as it contains the terms 'safe', when few things in life are totally safe, and 'sane' which suggests a difficult dichotomy between 'sane' and 'mad'. *Risk aware consensual kink (RACK)* is preferred.

Sexual orientation   Problematic term because it tends to imply 'orientation' to a particular gender (or genders) as the defining feature of a person's sexuality, which it isn't necessarily (e.g. it may be more about roles taken, practices engaged in, or specific fantasies or desires). Use *sexuality* or *sexual identity.*

She-male   Offensive term derived from pornography often used to refer to people who have a penis and breasts. Should never be used.

Sissification   This is where an adult male is consensually 'forced' to don the clothes of, and behave as, a girl as part of a BDSM scene. The humiliation the adult male feels at being dressed as a female, indeed a young female, is the source of the eroticisation. Sissification is frowned upon in some circles due to the necessarily derogative stance towards femininity that it adopts and so should be used with caution.

Them   There may be some in the town in which you live.

Those people   There may even be some in the room.

Tranny   Short for transvestite. Sometimes a reclaimed term – more often derogatory.

Transvestite   This is a medical term, partially reclaimed for some people who wear clothing not normally worn by people of their birth-assigned sex, whether for reasons of sexuality, comfort or for some other reason.

Twink   Slang term, mostly in gay communities, for a much younger partner.

Vanilla   A term sometimes used to describe non-BDSM, non-kinky sex. Should not be used.

INDEX